H. P. (Henry Paine) Stokes

An Attempt to Determine the Chronological Order of Shakespeare's

Plays

H. P. (Henry Paine) Stokes

An Attempt to Determine the Chronological Order of Shakespeare's Plays

ISBN/EAN: 9783337055738

Printed in Europe, USA, Canada, Australia, Japan

Cover: Foto ©Thomas Meinert / pixelio.de

More available books at **www.hansebooks.com**

AN ATTEMPT TO DETERMINE THE

CHRONOLOGICAL ORDER

OF

SHAKESPEARE'S PLAYS.

THE HARNESS ESSAY, 1877.

BY THE

REV. HENRY PAINE STOKES, B.A.,

CORPUS CHRISTI COLLEGE, CAMBRIDGE.

London:

MACMILLAN AND CO.

1878.

CONTENTS:

PREFACE.

PERHAPS there is no intellectual treat so great or so instructive as that of watching the development of an author's mind, and seeing "knowledge grow from more to more." If this be so with regard to authors in general, how especially is it true, when we are considering the works of him, who towers head and shoulders above all writers of all times and all countries! The following little work is an attempt to gather together from external and internal sources, such facts and such data as may enable us to ascertain, inductively and systematically, the Chronological Order of Shakespeare's Plays.

Ben Jonson issued careful editions of his dramas, with courtly prefaces and elaborate notes; but Shakespeare differed from his contemporary in this point as in others.

Now this difference, though it may increase our respect for Shakespeare's independence and regard for theatrical rights, is yet attended with this disadvantage to the student of his works—that it leaves the determination of their chronological order, as far as external evidence goes, to the facts supplied by contemporary printers, and the hints thrown out by contemporary writers. The half-century which followed the year of Shakespeare's death, was perhaps the least likely of all periods in our national history to preserve such hints and traditions. The great events which then stirred men's hearts, left no time for the consideration of the drama and the arts; it was only in his earliest publication that Milton could speak so enthusiastically of " my Shakespeare." Nor does the Restoration period help us much; perhaps, indeed, we ought not to expect anything from such a time, or from such men as it produced; perhaps too long an interval had already elapsed; but, however that may be, we certainly owe little to the feeble traditions of Langbaine and Ravenscroft, the patronizing guesses of Pope and Dryden, or the impertinent tinkerings of Davenant and Tate.

The eighteenth century was more fortunate; the learned investigations of Malone and some of his

contemporaries formed a great step forward in the
solution of the problem to which this work is devoted.
Nor is the present century behindhand in the study;
German professors and students have worked at it
with characteristic thoroughness and devotion, while in
England there has been an equal display of learning
and enthusiasm; witness Ulrici, Gervinus, and a host of
others abroad,—Halliwell-Phillips, Collier, and many
another here. Mention must be made lastly of the
elaborate, investigations and the ingenious—the too ingenious—theories of Mr. Fleay, and of the new lines
of thought which have been suggested, and the new im-
petus to Shakespeare-study which has been caused
by the New Shakspere Society, under its energetic
director, Mr. Furnivall.

The writer has to thank Professor Ingram, Messrs.
Fleay, Furnivall, and other gentlemen for their kind
permission to use tables drawn up by them.

It may be added that the (Cambridge University
Triennial) Harness Prize for the year 1877, was awarded
to this work by the examiners, Messrs. Aldis Wright and
Lumby.

METHOD EMPLOYED.

IN conducting the following inquiry into the Chronological Order of Shakespeare's Plays, various methods have been employed, and different kinds of evidence have been used. It may perhaps be well to distinguish here these methods and evidences.

I.—EXTERNAL.

1. Mention of Shakespeare's plays in other works.

2. Quotations from them in other works.

3. Ridicule, or parody, of them in other works.

4. Imitation in other works.

5. Mention in private diaries, MSS. &c.

6. Mention in the Records of the Master of the Revels.

7. Mention in the private theatrical records.

8. Notices of the theatres and actors of the time.

9. Entries at Stationers' Hall.

10. (Contemporary) publication of his works in quartos, &c.

11. Entries, and publication, of works with similar titles.

12. Dates of works, &c. from which Shakespeare borrowed his plots, &c.

13. Ascertained facts in Shakespeare's life.

14. Traditionary statements as to the production of his plays.

II.—INTERNAL.

i.—*Quasi-external.*

1. Allusions to passing events.

2. Quotations from, or references to, other works.

3. Explanatory remarks in Prologues, Choruses, and Epilogues.[1]

4. Allusions to his own life.

ii.—*Style.*

1. Use of prose and verse.

2. Classical allusions.[1]

> [*a.* The number of them.
>
> *b.* The quality of them.]

---

[1] The writer had intended adding Appendices on these points, and indeed has referred to such in the body of the work; but the number of Appendices already given, and want of time, prevent him from carrying out the intention. The references to *Prologues, Choruses,* and *Epilogues,* in the Index, may however be consulted, whilst a specimen of "the classical allusion test" may be seen in the Section on *Troilus and Cressida.*

3. Use of words and phrases.

> [a. ἄπαξ λεγόμενα, which must be " weighed," rather than counted.
>
> b. Ordinary words with extraordinary meanings.
>
> c. Old English words, &c.
>
> d. Peculiar phrases and constructions.]

4. Pronunciation of names.

5. Use of the sacred names, of oaths, &c. [Note 3 Jac. I. c. 21.][1]

6. Puns and conceits, drawn out, &c.

7. Kind of similes, &c.

8. Thoughts "drawn out," or "packed."

9. Passages worked up (afterwards).

iii.—Versification.

1. Rhyme [a. Rhymed heroics. b. Doggerel. c. Alternates. d. Sonnet, or modified sonnet. e. Use of couplets. f. Irregularities.]

2. End pause [i.e. " stopped " or " unstopped " lines.]

3. A development of this, as to the ending of speeches.

4. Weak endings.

> [a. " Weak endings."
>
> b. " Light endings."]

[1] See pages 63, 93, 105, 116, 123.

5. Redundant syllable [also called "feminine ending," "double ending," &c.]

6. Alexandrine lines.

> [*a*. "Well marked."
>
> *b*. "Lightly marked."]

7. Pauses, or beats.

> [*a*. At end of line (*vide supra*).
>
> *b*. "Central pause."
>
> *c*. Beats variously distributed.]

8. Short lines.

iv.—*Mental Tests.*

1. Development of plot, or plots.

2. Development of character.

3. Use of certain characters [notice the clowns, the women.]

4. Æsthetic considerations of other kinds.

5. Moral purpose, &c.

CHRONOLOGICAL ORDER

OF

SHAKESPEARE'S PLAYS.

N.B.—[R] means subsequently revised. See pp. 172, 173.

SHAKESPEARE'S PLAYS.

TITUS ANDRONICUS.

(Her) "Tongue is now a stringless instrument."—*Richard II.*

"On horrors' head, horrors accumulate."—*Othello.*

"When sorrows come, they come not single spies,
But in battalions."—*Hamlet.*

In treating a play of so doubtful a character as this, it will perhaps be better to give the external evidence relating to it before proceeding to state any opinion as to Shakespeare's connection with it.

Ben Jonson, in the Induction to *Bartholomew Fair*, 1614, says: "He that will swear, *Jeronimo* or *Andronicus* are the best plays yet, shall pass unexcepted at here, as a man whose judgment shows it is constant, and hath stood still these five-and-twenty or thirty years." This would place the production of *Andronicus* between 1584 and 1589, if we take the statement literally.

[Cf. the reference to "old Hieronimo, as it was first acted"—"a dozen years since" in the Induction to the same author's *Cynthia's Revels*, 1600.]

. / B

Henslowe's Diary, under date April 11th, 1592, speaks of a play called *Tittus and Vespacia*, as acted "by Lord Strange's men" [whom Prof. Ward unaccountably identifies with the Lord Admiral's Company].

From the same source, we learn that a *Tittus and Ondronicus* was produced as a new play, January 23rd, 1594.

Shortly afterwards, 6 Feb., 1593 [4], there is the following entry on the *Stationers' Register:*—

"John Danter] a booke entitled a noble Roman Historye of *Tyttus Andronicus.* Entered also by him, by warrant from Mr. Woodcock, the ballad thereof."

1594. In this year also, according to Langbaine (1691), *Titus Andronicus* was first printed; but no copy of the quarto is extant.

1594. We also learn from Henslowe, that a play called *Andronicous* was acted on June 5th, 1594, at the Rose Theatre.

1594. In the play entitled *A Knacke to Knowe a Knave, printed* in this year, there is an allusion to *Titus Andronicus.*

1598. Meres, in his *Palladis Tamia*, mentions the play as one of Shakespeare's tragedies.

1600. A quarto edition appeared, bearing the following title :—

"The most lamentable Romaine Tragedie of *Titus Andronicus.* As it hath been sundry times playde by the Right Honourable the Earle of Pembroke, the Earle of Darbie, the Earle of Sussex, and the Lord Chamberlaine theyr Servants. At London, printed by J. R[oberts] for Edward White, and are to bee solde, &c. 1600."

1602, April 19th. We have the following entry[1] on the *Stationers' Register:*—

---

[1] I have quoted this entry in full, because I do not think it supplies ground for Mr. Fleay's statement (*N. S. S. Trans.* 1874, vol. i. p. 47) that *among Millington's copyrights* sold to Pavier was a *Titus Andronicus.* The entries seem quite distinct; and we know that Millington had the copyright of the two

"Tho. Pavier] by Assignt. from Tho. Millington salvo jure cujuscumq. The 1st and 2nd pts. of *Henry the VI.:* ii. books.

"Tho. Pavier] *Titus and Andronicus,* entered by warrant under Mr. Setons hand."

1611. In this year, White brought out another quarto, entitled :—

" The most lamentable tragedie of *Titus Andronicus.* As yt hath sundry times been plaide by the King's Majesties Servants. Printed for Edward White, 1611."

1623. In the folio which was brought out in this year, *Titus Andronicus* was included among "the Tragedies," which were given in the following order : *Troilus and Cressida* [pages unnumbered, (see p. 99)], *Coriolanus, Titus Andronicus, Romeo and Juliet, Timon of Athens* (see p. 132), *Julius Cæsar,* &c.

1624. On the 14th Dec., Pavier again entered the play as *Titus Andronnicus.*

1626. Aug. 4th, " Mr. Pavier's rights in Shakespeare's plays," including *Tytus and Andronicus,* were transferred to Brewster and Birde ; and in

1630. Birde assigned them to Richard Cotes.

It should be added, as Dr. Latham says (*Two Dissertations on the Hamlet, &c.*), that, as early as 1600, a tragedy on this subject was acted in Germany by English players. It has been thought, by Cohn and others, that this must be the play mentioned by Henslowe on April 11th, 1592, as *Tittus and Vespacia,* for Vespasian (afterwards Emperor) is a character in the German play.

That Shakespeare had some connection with a play upon the subject seems to be placed beyond doubt by the mention by Meres, and by the insertion in the First Folio ; but, if the play as given in that edition be the one which is connected

plays mentioned in the first entry (see *Register,* under March 12th, 1593), while we do not know that he had the copyright of any other play attributed to Shakespeare; the *Henry V.,* which he had a share in bringing out in 1600, appears to have been the property of Creede the printer (see May 14th, 1594); and was probably transferred to Pavier on August 14th, 1600.

with our poet's name [as indeed seems probable from a consideration of several passages in it (see Mr. H. B. Wheatley,
N. S. S. Trans., 1874, vol. i., pp. 126—129)], then the classical
allusions, the peculiar words, &c., compel us to adopt
Ravenscroft's tradition that it is an old play revised by
Shakespeare. In what year this revision took place it is very
difficult to say; of course, it must have been before 1598,
when Meres mentions it, and therefore before the Pembroke
and other companies were merged into the Lord Chamberlain's Company, at which time Mr. Fleay thinks several old
plays (*Titus Andronicus* being one) passed into the hand of
the corps to which Shakespeare belonged. The adaptation
was probably early in his dramatic career, though Jonson's
reference in the Induction to *Bartholomew Fair* must surely
be to the old play.

Another point, which seems to follow from a consideration
of the above data, is the existence of at least two dramas
upon the subject; Mr. Halliwell-Phillipps thinks that Shakespeare's play (which may have been the one entered by
Danter in 1594) has probably been lost.

Prof. Ward (*Eng. Dram. Lit.*, vol. i., p. 367), having
quoted Kurz to the effect that "the play is in a manner
earlier than *Henry VI.;* and that while it contains no
reminiscences from *Tamerlane*, it contains one from the
Spanish Tragedy," comes to the conclusion "that this play,
if Shakspeare's, was written by 1589, and produced by that
year; and that it is probably the third of the three plays
mentioned by Henslowe, under the date of June 3rd, 1594."

Mr. Fleay (*Shakespeare Manual*, p. 44) says: "Our
present play is not Shakespeare's; it is built on the Marlowe
blank-verse system, which Shakespeare in his early work
opposed: and did not belong to his Company till 1600." It
may be added that a writer in one of the last numbers of the
North British Review was of opinion "that *Titus Andronicus*
was an ironical censure on Marlowe's style."

HENRY VI.

"I do think, a king ! I would not so !"—Tempest.

It will perhaps avoid repetition if the three parts of *Henry VI.* be treated together ; and clearness may be gained by giving, at the beginning, a list of the chronological facts upon which any argument about them must be founded. Let it be noted, by way of explanation, that Part I. did not appear in print till 1623; that Part II. is founded on the play entitled *The First Part of the Contention,* &c.; and Part III. is similarly due to *The True Tragedie of Richard Duke of Yorke.*

1592. Henslowe's Diary informs us that in this year at the newly-opened Rose Theatre, Lord Strange's Company acted a play called *Henry the VI.* On the same information, we know that this play was frequently performed afterwards.

1592. In the same year, appeared Greene's *Groatsworth of Wit,* &c., in which there is the following well-known reference to Shakespeare : "Yes, trust them not ; for there is an upstart Crow, beautified with our feathers, that with his *Tyger's heart wrapt in a Player's hide,* supposes he is as well able to bumbast out a blanke verse as the best of you ; and being an absolute *Johannes fac totum,* is in his owne conceit the only Shake-scene in a countrie."

1592. In the same year also, Thomas Nashe, in his *Pierce Penniless,* &c., dwelling upon "the plays borrowed out of our English chronicles," says : "How would it have joyed brave Talbot, the terror of the French, to think that after he had been two hundred years in his tomb he should triumph again on the stage, and have his bones embalmed with the tears of ten thousand spectators (at least at several times) who, in the tragedian ، that represents his person, behold him fresh bleeding."

1592. Yet, once more, in this year probably Marlowe produced his *Edward II.* (containing many passages identical with others in *The Contention* and *The True Tragedie*). This play was not printed till 1598.

1593. H. Chettle (*Kind Harts Dreame*) apologised for the abusive passage[1] in Greene's book, which he had edited the year before.

1593. March 12th; Tho. Millington entered on the *Stationers' Register* "a booke intituled the firste parte of the contention of the twoo famous Houses of York and Lancaster," &c. ; and in

1594. A 12mo. edition, bearing this title, appeared ; "printed by T. Creede for T. Millington."

1595. There appeared an octavo, entitled "*The true tragedie of Richard Duke of Yorke, and the Death of good*

---

[1] How keenly Shakespeare resented this abusive passage may be seen by the following circumstances. Chettle says: Greene's letter "is offensively by one or two of them taken; and because on the dead they cannot be avenged, they wilfully forge in their conceits a living author; and after tossing it to and fro, no remedy, but it must light on me;" he then offers a most ample apology to one of those offended (undoubtedly Shakespeare). But that Shakespeare did not forget the insult may perhaps be inferred from his use of the word *beautified*, which Greene had used in the old saying about the crow and the feathers: the only undoubted cases, in which he employs the word, are in *Hamlet* (written some few years afterwards) ii. 2, where we are told that beautified is "an ill phrase, a vile phrase; 'beautified' is a vile phrase ;" and in the nearly contemporary *Two Gentlemen of Verona* and *Romeo and Juliet*, where also the use seems satirical. The passages referred to are: *Romeo and Juliet*, i. 4, 87, 88, where Lady Capulet in some almost doggerel verse says:—

"This precious book of love, this unbound lover,
To beautify him, only wants a cover; "

and *Two Gentlemen of Verona*, iv. 1, 55—58, when Valentine's services are accepted by the men, whom he meets in the forest:—

"—Partly seeing you are *beautified*,
With goodly shape and *by your own report*
A *linguist* and a man of such perfection
As we do *in our quality* much want."

Surely Shakespeare, in these lines, has drawn his own picture, sportively adopting the remarks that were being made about him, for notice that just at this same time, Chettle repeats the obnoxious word at the beginning of his preface (1593); Shakespeare, brings out his *Venus and Adonis* with a learned motto (1593); and Chettle says of him "myself have seen his demeanour no less civill, than he exelent in the qualitie he professes" (1593).

King Henry the Sixt, with the whole Contention betweene the two Houses Lancaster and Yorke, as it was sundrie times acted by the Right Honourable the Earle of Pembrooke his Servants;" the publisher was the same Millington mentioned above.

1598. Meres, in his list of Shakespeare's plays (which includes *Richard II., Richard III., Henry IV., King John,* and even *Titus Andronicus*), does not mention *Henry VI.*

1599. Shakespeare concluded his epilogue to his *Henry V.* with these lines :—

> " Henry the Sixth, in infant bands crowned King
>   Of France and England, did this King succeed ;
> ᵢ Whose state so many had the managing,
>   That they lost France and made his England bleed :
> Which oft our stage hath shown : and, for their sake,
>   In your fair minds let this acceptance take."

1600. Millington brought out a second edition of *The True Tragedie,* &c., and of *The Contention.*

1602. There is the following entry on the *Stationers' Register,* for April 19th :—

" Tho. Pavier] by Assignt. from Tho. Millington salvo jure cujuscumq. The 1st and 2nd pts. of *Henry the VI. :* ii. books."

1619. There appeared " *The Whole Contention between the two Famous Houses of Lancaster and Yorke,* &c. Divided into two Parts ; and newly corrected and enlarged. Written by William Shakespeare, Gent. Printed by T. P."

The initials are doubtless those of the Thomas Pavier above mentioned.

1623. On Nov. 8th, Blount and Jaggard entered among other "copies" of Shakespeare's works "not formerly entered to other men :" "the Thirde Parte of *Henry the Sixt.*"

1623. In the folio edition, which these and other publishers brought out under the care of Heminge and Condell, the three parts are printed and arranged as we have them now.

1626. Pavier transferred his "rights in Shakespeare's plays or any of them," to Brewster and Birde ; and in

1630, on the 8th of November, Bird assigned them (with "consent of a full court") to Ric. Cotes ; among the plays thus transferred we have *Yorke and Lancaster*.

PART I.

From the above data, the following opinions are deduced :—

The epilogue of *Henry V.* tells us three things : (1) that all the three parts of *Henry VI.* are alluded to (for that the 1st part is referred to follows from the lines "whose state so many had the managing that they lost France ;" and, that the other two parts are remembered we know, among other reasons, from the plural in "for their sake") ; (2) that these parts had been produced some time before 1599 ("which oft our stage hath shown"); and (3) that Shakespeare himself had had a share at least in their production ("and, *for their sake*, In your fair minds let this acceptance take").

That Shakespeare was not the sole author of Part I. is almost certain, as well from the style and the allusions (see p. 121), as from the facts that Meres does not refer to it (1598) and that no edition of it appeared until the First Folio came out (1623).

It may be here remarked, and the remark should be compared with a similar one upon *King John*, that the play follows Holinshed's *Chronicles ;* but not with that particularity which we have in Shakespeare's later historical plays. It should be noticed too, as one of the marks, that 1 *Henry VI.* and 2 and 3 *Henry VI.* are not of the same origin, that in the two latter plays Hall is consulted rather than Holinshed.

It seems, again, extremely probable that the quotation above taken from Nash (1592), refers either to this part, or to the older play upon which it was founded. The words applied to Talbot, "the terror of the French," are found in i. 4, 42. "Here," said they, "is *the terror of the French;*" see also ii. 3, 24; iv. 2, 16; and iv. 7, 78; and the word "triumph" recalls the end of the sad scene of Act iii., and La Pucelle's words, "Let frantic Talbot *triumph* for a while;" whilst the remark about "the spectators beholding him fresh bleeding" vividly reminds us of the beginning of Act iv. Sc. 7.

If the reference be to Shakespeare's play, we thus have a revision, in 1592, of the older play; it may be, too, that this is "the *Henry the VI.*" produced (according to Henslowe) in that year by Lord Strange's Company, which Shakespeare was probably originally a member of, and which was merged into the Lord Chamberlain's Company in 1594, as Mr. Halliwell-Phillipps has lately shown.

This part is called "the Thirde Parte of *Henry the Sixt*" in the entry on the *Stationers' Register* in 1623; for it was not till its present arrangement was adopted in the first folio, that the alteration was made; this statement, which is confirmed by T. Pavier's artful entry on the 19th of April, 1602, may be taken as another proof of the separate origins of this part and of the other two. Another proof of this is the fact that the name of Talbot, which is always in our ears or before our eyes in Part I., is never even mentioned in either of the others.

Mr. Fleay says: "Certainly before 1592, when acted by Lord Strange's men at the Rose. The Chamberlain's Company had it before 1599. See Epilogue to *Henry V.*"—[*Shakespeare Manual*, p. 31.]

Mr. R. Simpson [*New Shakspere's Society's Transactions*, 1874, vol. ii., pp. 421, 422] says that Suffolk is Leicester; he supports his identification by quoting a passage from Morgan's *Leicester's Commonwealth*, where Elizabeth is

Henry VI. and Leicester is Suffolk. "This," he says, "would not necessarily require the date of *Henry VI.* to be before 1588, when Leicester died; for Nash's apologue of the Bear at the end of *Pierce Penniless* (1592) similarly refers to the dead statesman."

PARTS II. AND III.

Various theories have been advanced with respect to the authorship of these and of the two quartos to which they are related :—

(1) Malone argued that Marlowe, Greene, and perhaps others, wrote the two quartos (*The Contention* and *The True Tragedie*), and that Shakespeare shaped them into the folio form ; Collier, Gervinus, Ingleby, and others, adopt this view.

(2) Halliwell-Phillipps, the Cambridge editors, and others think Shakespeare had a share in the quartos.

(3) Mr. Grant White (supported by Mr. Rives's *Harness Essay*, 1874) carries this last hypothesis further ; he holds that Shakespeare wrote *The Whole Contention* with Marlowe and Greene, and that his own portion, with additions, forms the folio edition.

(4) Johnson, Steevens, C. Knight, Ulrici, Delius, and the German writers generally, contend that Shakespeare wrote both the quartos and the folio ; and,

(5) Lately, Mr. Fleay (*Macmillan's Magazine*, Nov. 1875) believes "the whole of 2 and 3 *Henry VI.* to be by Peele and Marlowe ;" he adds, however, "of course Shakespeare revised (though he did not write) these plays about 1601."

The German view (4) may pretty safely be passed by ; and the *final* result which Mr. Grant White (3) arrives at, can surely not be accepted. Mr. Fleay (5) seems to forget the plural in the words "for *their sake*" in the epilogue of *Henry V.;* again, Mr. Grant White may be left to deal with

Malone's assertion (1) that there is no Shakespearian work
in the quartos.

The view, numbered (2) above, being accepted, to what
date or dates must Shakespeare's work be assigned?

Now, first, the *Groatsworth* quotation seems pretty convincingly to show

(1) That Greene himself had had some share in *The
Contention;*

(2) That Marlowe had likewise a share in it; [and

(3) This appears, too, certainly proved by the numerous
Marlowe lines in it];

(4) Whilst it also implies that *Shakespeare had been at
work upon it,* before Greene's death in 1592;

(5) At the same time, the way in which Greene speaks,
seems to prove that he and Shakespeare *could not have
worked together.*[1]

On the other hand, it is not at all improbable that
Marlowe and Shakespeare may have co-operated; for we
may note how they are alluded to together in the *Chettle
Apology,* how tenderly Marlowe is referred to in *As You
Like It,* and how he is spoken of (see Massey) in the
Sonnets.

The following conjecture then is hazarded : that two plays
by Marlowe and Greene had, with the former's consent and
perhaps co-operation, been touched by Shakespeare ; that
these are the quartos, *The Contention* and *The True Tragedy;*
that the Lord Pembroke's Company claimed the right of
acting these ; whilst the Chamberlain's men also brought
out the plays, Shakespeare still further revising them for
his Company; the plays thus elaborated forming 2 and 3
Henry VI. as given in the folio edition.

In support of these suppositions, and of the date (before
1592) thus agreed upon, it should be remembered that

---

[1] The improbability of any co-operation between Greene and Shakespeare will
be seen by consulting the note on p. 6; and by remembering the allusion to
Greene in *Midsummer Night's Dream* (see p. 50).

Pavier, from the first entry he made (Ap. 19, 1602), evidently attributed the quartos to Shakespeare, and that they had therefore, doubtless, been so assigned before; while a consideration of the relations which 2 and 3 *Henry VI.* bear to *Richard III.* will show that they preceded and prepared for that play (which we shall see reason to date 1593 or 1594).

TWO GENTLEMEN OF VERONA.

"Who found a bird's nest, and told his comrade, and he stole it."
Much Ado About Nothing.

This play was not entered on the *Stationers' Register*, nor was it printed, till 1623; and the only allusion to it of any kind previous to that date is in the *Palladis Tamia*, where Meres places it first among the six comedies which he mentions. In endeavouring, therefore, to fix the date of its composition, we are driven back upon historical or literary comparisons, and upon a general consideration of the style and versification; and, while it is generally admitted that it must rank among the early works of our author, we think it will prove to belong to his very first period.

The chief source of the play is the *Story of the Shepherdess Filismena* in Montemayor's *Diana;* Yonge's translation of this, not published till 1598, existed in MS. in 1582—3; while another translation appeared in 1595—6; and a play called the *History of Felix and Philomena* was acted at Greenwich in 1584. (See Mr. Halliwell-Phillipps's last work.) But Shakespeare is also supposed to have borrowed incidents or expressions from Bandello's *Apollonius and Sylla*, and from Sir Philip Sidney's *Arcadia*, 1590. Tieck thinks that the tragedy, *Julius and Hippolyta* (acted by English comedians in Germany at the beginning of the seventeenth century), suggests some common origin for that play and our comedy; Prof. Ward adds that a similar conclusion may be drawn from the resemblances, which Klein has pointed out between Parabosco's *Il Viluppo* and Shakespeare's comedy. Indeed, Mr. Halliwell-Phillipps at one time thought that the latter is an expansion of an older play.

Malone pointed out two passages which he thought were suggested by contemporary historical events; but to what particular circumstances they allude has been much disputed.

The lines, i. 3, 8, 9 :—

> "Some to the wars, to try their fortune there ;
> Some to discover islands far away,"

have been referred to Essex, 1591; to Lancaster, 1594; to Hawkins, 1594; to Gilbert, 1594; to Raleigh, 1595; and to others.

The line, ii. 1, 20, "Like one that hath the pestilence," has been illustrated by the pestilence of 1593, and again by that of 1583.

The following corresponding passages have been pointed out :—

(1) Two references to the story of *Hero and Leander* (see i. 1, 21, 22, and iii. 1, 119, 120) have been supposed to refer to Marlowe's poem. Marlowe died in 1593, and the poem was not published till 1598, though the work may have been in circulation in MS. for some time; or the allusion may merely be to the well-known story.[1]

(2) Chalmers, in arguing for the date 1595, laid great stress on what he calls "the obvious allusions to Spenser's *Sonnets* (1595), in the following lines, in iii. 2, 68—72 :—

[1] It should be noticed, however, that Shakespeare, in the first of the passages referred to, alludes to "a *love-book*." Proteus says : " Upon some *book* I love I'll pray for thee " (i. 1, 20), and the quotation from Marlowe in *As You Like It* should be remembered. Mr. Fleay in his statements about Shakespeare's allusions to *Hero and Leander* (none prior to 1596 or 1593), surely forgets Act v. Sc. 1, ll. 200, 201, of *Midsummer Night's Dream* (which he assigns to 1592).

"*Pro.*   You must lay lime to tangle her desires
            By wailful sonnets, whose composed rhymes
            Should be full-fraught with serviceable vows.
"*Duke.* Ay !
            Much is the force of heaven-bred poesy."

(3) Steevens pointed out that Shakespeare in preparing for his *King John* may have found the following passage in the old play of that name (1591) :—

"As sometimes Phaeton,
"Mistrusting silly Merops for his sire."

And upon it he may have founded a passage in the present comedy :—

"Why, Phaeton (for thou art Merops' son),
Wilt thou aspire to guide the heavenly car,
And with thy daring folly burn the world?"
                                        (iii. 1, 153—155.)

(4) Prof. Ward has noted that the pun about "the unkindest *tied* that ever man *tied*" (i. 3, 42) occurs also in Lyly's *Endymion*, 1591. [I have not had an opportunity of seeing whether Shakespeare's extension of it does, too.]

(5) Passages in *The Sonnets* (Shakespeare's) may be compared with lines in this comedy; *e.g.* sonnet lxx. and i. 1, 45—50; sonnet xcv. and the same; sonnet cxxvii. and iv. 4, 161, &c.

Commentators have differed as to the year to which this play should be assigned; Malone (in his earlier edition), Chalmers, Drake, and (lately in a paper of great ability) Mr. Fleay date it 1595; (Mr. Fleay, however, assigning the first two acts to 1593); Malone (in his last edition), Gervinus, and others 1591; while Collier, Grant, White, and Delius would place it even earlier. In the *Transactions* of the New Shakspere Society, Messrs. Furnivall and Hales very strongly oppose the late date, which Mr. Fleay has been led to adopt chiefly through the "rhyme test" and "the double-ending test." The following reasons, together with some of the allusions mentioned above, seem to support the adoption of the date 1591, or perhaps it would be better to say, 1590—1592 :—

The poor and slight plot; the weak characterisation (indeed Dr. Johnson went so far as to say that there was "no diversity of character ;" but this cannot be conceded) ; the simplicity of style generally adopted (Pope said : "the style of this comedy is less figurative, and more natural and unaffected, than the greater part of this author's, *though* supposed to be one of the first he wrote ; "—the answer to the last part of the remark is obvious) ; the pairs of characters (though Gervinus tells us that "the one-sidedness of each character finds its complement as a corrective") ; the sketches of incident or character, which were afterwards expanded (as Mr. Bowden long ago remarked) ; occasional doggerel,[1] alternate verses and sonnets (although, as Fleay and Hertzberg have pointed out, a rigid application of "the rhyme-test" would place the play later in Shakespeare's list) ; two or three careless mistakes, and several improbabilities, which culminate in the "abrupt denouëment " (Blackstone).

A comparison with other plays will maintain the assumption made above ; Mr. Hales, in the *N. S. S. Trans.* 1874, vol. i. pp. 22—26, has given reasons for placing the *Two Gentlemen of Verona* before *Romeo and Juliet*, and considerably before *The Merchant of Venice.* Mr. Furnivall has pointed out links which join it to *The Comedy of Errors* and to *Love's Labour's Lost*[2] ; and, as before remarked, many hints in this comedy are developed in later plays.

Professor Ingram has supported the contemporaneity of

---

[1] Gervinus (i. 217) says: "The single long doggerel verses in the burlesque parts; the repeated alliterations, many lyrical passages in the sonnet style of tender but undramatic poetry, place the piece in the poet's earliest period."

[2] As a confirmation of this, I may note the occurrence of the quibble about "sheep" and "ship" in *Love's Labour's Lost*, in the *Two Gentlemen of Verona*, and in the *Comedy of Errors*; and the following lines in our comedy (i. 1, 29—33) may be pointed out as supporting the statement:—

"To be in *love*, what scorn is bought with groans ...
If happy *won*, perhaps a hapless gain,
If *lost* why then a grievous *labour's won*."

this play, the *Comedy of Errors*, and *Love's Labour's Lost*, by the application of two or three tests ; for instance, he points out that in *The Two Gentlemen of Verona* 236 speeches end with the end of a line ; and he gives the following statistics, as to the "weak" and "light" endings :—

	No. of light endings.	No. of weak endings.
Love's Labour's Lost. . .	3	0
Comedy of Errors . . .	0	0
Two Gentlemen of Verona.	0	0

THE COMEDY OF ERRORS.

"'Tis as like you as cherry is to cherry."—*Henry VIII.*

There are several indications that the subject of this comedy had been dramatised before the appearance of Shakespeare's play ; even so far back as 1563, an interlude named *Jack Juggler* makes it probable that the *Menæchmi* of Plautus (the original source of our comedy) was, in part at least, known upon the English stage. A play called *The Historie of Error* was acted by the St. Paul's children at Hampton Court, on New Year's Night, 1576—7 ; and it was repeated on Twelfth Night, 1582—3, at Windsor (the record, however, calling it *The History of Ferrar* by a misprint). Collier, Fleay, and others think Shakespeare may have founded his comedy upon this play.

Again, we learn, from *The Gesta Grayorum*, that "*A Comedy of Errors*, like to Plautus his *Menechmus*, was played by the players " at Gray's Inn one night in December, 1694. Malone, "from its having been represented *by the players* and not by the gentlemen of the inn, thought it probable that this was Shakespeare's piece."

At this period, too, Plautus's *Menæchmi* was translated

into English by W[illiam] W[arner], whose work, although
not entered till June, 1594, nor printed till the following
year, had yet (we are informed by the printer's advertise-
ment to the reader) been, for some time before, handed
about in MS. among the translator's friends; of whom
Shakespeare may have been one, though there is no evidence
to connect the two plays in any way.

That Shakespeare worked upon some older play seems
extremely probable, as well from the facts that the subject,
as proved above, had previously been dramatised, and
that Shakespeare so often availed himself of old material as a foundation, as from the long doggerel verses which
occur in the play, and from the occurrence, in the Folio
Edition, of the epithets " Sereptus" (Surreptus) and " Erotes "
(Erraticus); these terms, as Malone points out, are not
found in Warner's translation, "there the brothers are
called Menæchmus Sosicles, and Menæchmus the tra-
veller."

Shakespeare's work, whether original or adapted, is certainly very early; the style and versification (*vide infra*)
show this convincingly. But there is nothing to fix the
precise year of the composition, although one undoubted,
and one or two probable, historical references have been
pointed out; for instance, in Act 2, Sc. 2, in the description
of the kitchen wench, the lines, 125—127,

" *Ant. S.* Where *France?*
" *Dro. S.* In her forehead; armed and reverted, making
war against her *hair*,"

have been supposed to refer to the civil war, about the
succession of Henry IV., which lasted from August, 1589,
to July, 1593. The limit thus given accords well with the
date suggested by the style; whilst it should be added
that Chalmers attempted to fix the time to 1591, by
dwelling upon the fact that in that year the English were
particularly interested in the French struggle owing to the

help which Elizabeth then afforded Henry of Navarre. [It should be noticed, however, that another critic (see *North British Review*, April, 1870) thinks that events in French history, of a somewhat earlier date, are alluded to. Henry of Navarre became *heir* on the death of the Duke of Anjou in 1584, and was so till he became king on the murder of Henry III. Aug. 2nd, 1589. The Declaration of the League was made in April, 1585, and was soon afterwards commenced. In 1587 the League lost the battle of Contras ; but Henry III. and Henry of Navarre were reconciled, at Plesses-les-Tours, in April, 1589. If the word "heir" is to be taken literally, the date of the *Comedy of Errors* would lie between April, 1515, and April, 1589.] The same writer sees in the mention of Spain and the Indies in the same scene (ii. 2) allusions which would be more appropriate to the first half of the decade (1580—1590) with which we are dealing ; but surely the statement of *Spain* sending *whole armadoes of caracks* would be very telling after 1588.

Once more, this critic thinks the imprisonment of foreigners, as authoritative reprisals (upon which the pathetic part of this play turns), may refer to the reprisals against Rome and Spain, who had imprisoned Englishmen ; see a statute of Elizabeth's in 1585. But Mr. Chalmers would refer them to the dealings between England and the Hans Towns in 1591.

With regard to the contemptuous allusions to Scotland, in the same scene (ii. 2), it may be noted, that "in April 1595 the English agent in Edinburgh wrote to Burghley, how ill King James took it that the comedians in London should scorn the king and people of Scotland in their play." (Cf. Mr. Simpson's paper on the political use of the stage, in *N. S. S. Trans.* 1874, vol. ii. p. 374.)

Meres, in 1598, mentions the play second in his list of Shakespeare's plays ; and it seems to be alluded to in two of Dekker's plays, in the *Satiro-Mastix*, printed in 1602, and in the *News from Hell*, published in 1605. But these allusions are too late to help us in ascertaining the year of its production. Collier says before 1590; Chalmers, Drake, Delius, and Hertzberg say 1591; while Malone (last edition) and Fleay assign it to 1592. Chalmers's historical parallels are not generally to be relied upon, but in this case his date (1591) may perhaps be accepted, if we consider the reputation which Shakespeare had undoubtedly obtained as a dramatist, when [Spenser alluded to him in 1591] Greene in 1592, and Chettle in 1593, and if we note *the peculiarly early style of the play* itself.

As instances of this early style, we may mention: the prologue-like speech of Ægeon in the opening scene and other chorus-like lines (cf. the soliloquy of the courtezan at the end of iv. 3); certain *forced* descriptions (*e.g.* Dromio's account of the kitchen wench); the quibbles upon words; the repetitive answers; the allusions to the title of the comedy; the observance of "the unities"; and yet the comparative inferiority of the play, which may perhaps be due to the *improbability* of the plot, rendered, as it is, doubly so, by the introduction of the second pair of twins; this, however, Coleridge extenuates, by reminding us that we are dealing with a *farce* rather than with a *comedy*.

Again, we must notice the absence of prose, and the abundance of rhyme; and that of a peculiar kind, for besides couplets and alternate rhymes, we have numerous instances of doggerel, "long hobbling verses," as Blackstone calls them. These are perhaps (see above) remnants of an older play; they certainly remind us of the old rhymesters (before Marlowe), of whose verses Swinburne says: "they jingled their thin bells at the tedious end of fourteen weary syllables" (*Fortnightly*, May, 1875). Mr. Fleay remarks that the play "is more like *Midsummer Night's Dream* than any other in the fantastic tangle of events on which the plot is founded; the opening scenes also are very similar in their motives" (*Shakespeare Manual*, p. 25); and Professor

Dowden points out that the line (ii. 2, 201), "If thou art *changed* to aught, 'tis *to an ass*," strikingly reminds us of the nearly contemporary comedy, *Midsummer Night's Dream.* I have before pointed out the occurrence of the quibble about "ship" and "sheep" in Act iv. Sc. 1, l. 93 of this play, in ii. 1, 219 of *Love's Labour's Lost,* and in i. 1, 72 of the *Two Gentlemen of Verona,* as a remarkable link between three nearly contemporary plays.

ROMEO AND JULIET.

" The course of true love never did run smooth. "
Midsummer Night's Dream.

" No grave upon the earth shall clip in it
A pair so famous. "—*Antony and Cleopatra.*

Malone, very acutely, pointed out a date at which this play must have been acted ; the Company, to which Shakespeare belonged, was under the patronage of Lôrd Hundson, who was Lord Chamberlain when he died on July 22nd, 1596. The Company thereupon ceased to be styled "the Lord Chamberlaine's men," and were simply called after the name of the succeeding Lord Hundson ; but when his lordship was appointed Lord Chamberlain on the 17th April, 1597, the Company once more resumed the more honourable designation. Now the quarto, which was issued in 1597, simply styles them Lord Hundson's men, thus showing that the tragedy must have been "plaid publiquely" between July 1596 and April 1597. But was the play then *first* produced ? Was it not rather, as Malone himself hints, produced, in some form or other, at an earlier date ?

The following considerations suggest that it may have been sketched as early as 1591 at least : the 1599 edition is said to be "newly corrected, augmented, and amended," and thus we see that the play did undergo at least one revision ;

an allusion to Romeo, as a popular character of Shakespeare's, by Weever in an epigram, written probably before 1595, shows positively that the play cannot first have appeared in 1596;[1] and the well-known allusion to the earthquake of 1580 seems, in spite of what has been said to the contrary, to point to the date of 1591; the garrulous old nurse says distinctly enough (i. 3, 23) :—

"'Tis since the earthquake now eleven years ;"

but we are told she was confused, and that her allusions to Juliet's age show that she had made a miscalculation ; at the risk, however, of seeming to miss "the humour of the passage," it must be pointed out that some dozen lines further on (i. 3, 35) the nurse again emphatically repeats her statement :—

"And since that time it is eleven years."

This repetition, which has apparently been lost sight of, seems to fix the production of the play in 1591.

Moreover, Shakespeare must also certainly have produced (though it may be in an elementary form) before [Spenser alludes to him in 1591], Greene in 1592, and especially Chettle in 1593, more works than are generally attributed to him at that period ; and what story is he more likely to have dwelt upon, in the freshness of his young-manhood, than that of the youthful pair, of whose love and deaths the 1587 edition of Brooke's poem had so lately reminded the literary world? "I know," says Lessing, "but one tragedy which love itself helped to elaborate ; and that tragedy is *Romeo and Juliet*."

Brooke, in his preface to the poem above alluded to, says he had seen "the same argument lately set foorth on stage ;"

---

[1] This date, however, has been supported by an entry, under date Aug. 15th, 1596, "cf a new ballad of *Romeo and Juliett*," which has by some been supposed to refer to our play. The entry was made by Edw. White.

and though there is no evidence other than this of an old play upon the subject, nor any evidence to connect Shakespeare with such older drama, yet analogy would suggest that he may have improved some previous tragedy. Brooke's poem appeared first in the year 1562 ; the story was also told in Paynter's *Palace of Pleasure* (1567), the original source, however, being one of Bandello's novels.

The following parallel passages have been pointed out ; some were perhaps Shakespeare's own, others he may have borrowed either originally or at one of the revisions :—

Marlowe's *Jew of Malta* (1588—1590),

> " But stay : what star shines yonder in the east ?
> The loadstar of my life," &c.

With this Dyce compared the well-known passage in *Romeo and Juliet* (ii. 2) ;

Marlowe's *Edward II.* (1592),

> " Gallop apace, bright Phœbus, through the skie,   ⌡
> And duskie night in rusty iron car ;
> Between you both, shorten the time, I pray,
> That I may see that most desired day ; "

With which Malone (2nd Appendix, p. 53) compared iii. 2, 1—5.

Prof. Ward (*ut supra*, p. 194) feels "sure that the nurse in *Romeo and Juliet* has her original in Marlowe's [and Nash's] *Dido;*" but compare the nurse in Brooke's poem.

Malone compares certain passages in the fifth act with lines in Daniel's *Complainte of Rosamonde;* but, as in the similar comparison between passages from this author in *Richard II.*, the question, which was the original, is open. Daniel's book was entered on the *Register* in February 1592 ; in both cases, if the dates here given are correct, Daniel must have been the borrower.

The same may be said (see *Midsummer Night's Dream*) of the following passages :—

"The glorious parts of fair Lucilia,
 Take them and join them in the heavenly spheres,
 And fix them there as an eternal light,
 For lovers to adore and wonder at."
                    Dr. Dodipoll, before 1596.

"Take him and cut him into little stars,
 And he will make the face of heaven so fine,
 That all the world shall be in love with night,
 And pay no worship to the garish sun."
                    Romeo and Juliet, iii. 2, 22—25.

Some lines in this play have also been compared with others in our author's sonnets, which were doubtless written long before they were published ; some, we know, were seen by Meres and others before 1598.

In the third act, says Malone, "the first and second cause" are mentioned ; that passage, therefore, was probably written after the publication of Saviolo's *Book on Honour* and *Honourable Quarrels* (1594) ; compare the corresponding insertion in the revision of *Love's Labour's Lost.*

Some historical allusions have also been supposed to exist ; besides the passage about the earthquake which was alluded to at the beginning of this section, and which was first pointed out by Tyrrwhit ; the reference in v. 2, 8—11 to the sealing up of plague-stricken houses, drawn out as it is, may perhaps be due to the pestilence of 1593 ; Chalmers referred ii. 2, 82—84, to the voyages of Drake and Hawkins in 1594-5, or of Raleigh, in 1595 ; Prof. Ward seems almost to approve of Mr. Massey's characteristic discovery, "in the nurse's difficulty about the first letter in Romeo's name (ii. 4), of a reference to (Henry) *Wri*othesley, Earl of Southampton, to the prevention of whose marriage with Elizabeth Vernon he supposes the action of the play to allude."

That some part, at least, of the play should be assigned to a very early date seems to be proved by the peculiar[1] sonnet-

---

[1] Gervinus points out that Shakespeare in this play uses three species of lyrical poetry : the sonnet, the epithalamium or nuptial song (cf. Halpin), and the dawn-song.

like¹ verse found in many parts of the tragedy, by the frequent rhyme (note especially the numerous alternates), by the alliteration, by the glowing poetry, lyrical rather than dramatic, by the quibbling between the gentlemen and between their attendants, and by the peculiar quality of the classical allusions.

LOVE'S LABOUR'S LOST.

" This keen encounter of our wits."—*Richard III.*

" Witty, courteous, liberal, full of spirit."—3 *Henry VI.*

Perhaps the earliest extrinsic notice of this play is contained in the following lines from a poem, entitled *Alba, or the Month's Mind of a Melancholy Lover*, by R. T[ofte], Gentleman, published by Cuthbert Burby in 1598 :—

> "*Love's Labour Lost* I once did see, a play
> Y-cleped so, &c.
> Each actor plaid in cunning wise his part,
> But chiefly those entrapt in Cupid's snare," &c.

The same publisher (Cuthbert Burby) in the same year (1598) affords us two other pieces of evidence ; one the celebrated *Palladis Tamia*, in which Meres mentions *Love's Labour's Lost*, and the other a quarto edition of the play itself, with the title-page : " A pleasant conceited comedie called *Loves Labours Lost*. As it was presented before her Highnes this last Christmas. Newly corrected and augmented by W. Shakespeare. Imprinted by W. W[aterson], for Cuthbert Burbie, 1598."

No entry² of this upon the *Stationers' Register* has been

---

¹ It may be added that the sonnet-like prologues to the first and second acts are another sign of early work, and that the fact that these prologues are given only to these two acts might seem to favour the idea of those who think these acts were written (or revised) before the remaining three.

² The subsequent history of the copyright may be very distinctly traced. On Jan. 22nd, 1606—7, "by direction of a court and with consent of Mr Burby under his hand wrytinge " *Love's Labour Loste* and two other " copies " were

discovered, nor is there any trace of the earlier *edition* which is perhaps implied by the title-page of the quarto. The work, which Shakespeare revised in 1597, had probably been written some years before; this is evident from the style and from certain internal allusions, which will be referred to below, as well as from the lapse of time implied in Tofte's lines quoted above, "*Love's Labour Lost I once did see.*"[1]

The plot of this comedy has not been traced to any other work; but various passages have been pointed out, the idea or the expression of which Shakespeare may have borrowed. Coleridge says (*Literary Remains*, vol. ii., p. 107): "the mere style of narration seems imitated,[2] with its defects and its beauties, from Sir Philip Sidney," whose *Arcadia* was brought out in 1590—1591. And almost the same words might be used in regard to its relation to Lyly's celebrated work; Mr. Rushton (*Shakespeare's Euphuism*) has pointed out a number of parallel expressions. ,

The origin of two or three different passages may be here given. The opening lines (i. 1, 8—10):—

> "Therefore, brave conquerors—for so you are
> That war against your own affections
> And the huge army of the world's desires," &c.

bear a striking resemblance to the following passage from the old *Historie of Hamblett:* "For that the greatest victorie that a man can obtaine is to make himself victorious and lord over his owne affections, and that restraineth the unbridled desires of his concupiscence."

assigned to Mr. Linge; who in the same year transferred them to John Smythick. The last-mentioned publisher joined in the bringing out of the First Folio in 1623, and in 1631 he brought out another quarto (Q₂) of the comedy referred to.

[1] Another mention of this as an old play is contained in the following extract from a MS. letter by Sir Walter Cope to "the Lorde Vycount Cranbourne at the Courte," 1604: "Burbage ys come, and sayes *ther ys no newe playe that the quene hath not seene*, but they have Revyved AN OLDE ONE, cawled *Love's Labore Lost*, which for wytt and mirthe he sayes will please her excedingly." (3rd Report of the Royal Commission of Historical MSS. quoted in Ingleby's *Centurie of Prayse*).

[2] Cf. with parallel expressions in the *Arcadia* the following passages in *Love's Labour Lost*, v. 1. 2—c (pointed out by Chalmers); v. 2, 11, 12 (Douce); &c.

Speaking of iii. 1, 137—139, 171—173, &c. : "Gardon, O sweet gardon! better than remuneration; 'levenpence farthing better: most sweet gardon! I will do it, sir, in print;" Dr. Farmer says : "Shakespeare was certainly indebted to the *Serving-man's Comfort* for his present vein of jocularity;" and Douce adds that that work "supplied our author with several hints."

The quotation from the 1st Eclogue of *Mantuanus*, in iv. 2, 95, 96, "Fauste precor gelida," &c., may perhaps be remembered in Gabriel Harvey's Third Letter, 1592, where we read "he tost his imagination a thousand waies, and I beleeue, searched euery corner of his Grammer Schoole witte (for his margine is as deepelie learned, as *Fauste precor gelida*)," &c.

Malone thinks that the Eclogues of *Mantuanus* were used as a school-book in Shakespeare's time.

The Italian lines ("Venetia, Venetia, chi non ti vede," &c.) which follow this Latin quotation, are found in the *Second Fruits* (1591) of *Florio*.

An attempt has been made by Tieck, Massey, and others, to identify Holofernes with this Florio, who was an Italian professor and author of considerable reputation in London in Shakespeare's time. Shakespeare may have come in contact with him through their mutual acquaintance with Lord Southampton, and may have been angered (Mr. Massey thinks) by Florio's remark about "plays that are neither right comedys nor right tragedys, but representations of Historys without decorum;" but as Gervinus, Delius, Simrock, Ward, and others point out, there is no evidence to support the supposition [nor the similar attempt to connect Armado[1] (who, in iv. 1, 100, is called "a phantasime, a Monarcho") with a celebrity of the period named Monarcho], and Armado and Holofernes "are two favourites or carica- tures of the Italian comedy : the *Pedant*, that is the school-

---

[1] Dr. Brinsley Nicholson remarks that the scorn to which this bragging Spaniard is held up, would be very telling at a time when English relations with Spain were so very unfriendly.

master and grammarian, and the military *Braggart*, the *Thraso* of the Latin, the *Capitan Spavento* of the Italian stage" (Gervinus, *Eng. Trans.*, vol. i., p. 165). It should be added that the words *Braggart* and *Pedant* are occasionally substituted for the above characters respectively in the folio edition.

The "dancing horse," alluded to i. 2, 57, was probably Bankes's horse, which is mentioned in Tarleton's *Jests*, and therefore must have been exhibited in or before 1589; though it is noticed several years later.

The allusions to the Muscovites, or Russians, point to a period when Russia was attracting attention in England; and such a period (according to Hackluyt) were the years 1590—1591.

There are several indications of the revision alluded to on the title-page of the 1598 quarto; for instance, the alterations in Biron's speech in Act iv., Sc. 3; and the following two references to other works were (as Malone says) doubtless introduced at that revision: v. 2, 579, "your lion . . . will be given to Ajax;" this conceit of *Ajax* and *Ajakes* occurs in *The Metamorphosis of Ajax* by Sir J. Harrington, printed in 1596.

"The *first* and *second cause* will not serve my turn: the *passado* he respects not, the *duello* he regards not," &c.; i. 2, 184—186: Shakespeare (as in *As You Like It*) doubtless availed himself of Saviolo's treatise *Of Honour and Honourable Quarrels*, published in 1595.

In fixing the year, in which *Love's Labour's Lost* first appeared, we must be guided by the allusions mentioned above and by the general style; and we shall not be far wrong, especially when we remember the date of the publication of the *Arcadia*, in assigning as the date 1591—2; this is supported by Tofte's expression before quoted:—

"Love's Labour Lost *I once did see*,"

which certainly carries the memory back for some few years;

by the general state of Elizabethan society at the period referred to ; by a comparison of contemporary plays ; and by the general style and versification of this comedy. Upon this last point, a few observations may be added.

Among marks of an early style, we may mention : the introduction of well-known old characters (besides *The Nine Worthies*, we have what Biron (v. 2, 545, 546) calls : "the pedant, the braggart, the hedge priest, the fool and the boy," and it is to be noted that in the folio we sometimes find written for Armado "the braggart," for Holofernes "the pedant," for Nathaniel "the curate," for Costard "the clowne," and for Moth "the page"); the observance of "the unities ;" the abundance of rhyme, the doggerel, the sonnets [1] (occasionally used for speeches) ; the alliteration "affecting the letter" as Holofernes calls it (iv. 2) ; the quibbles, antitheses, repartees, "the sparkles of wit, like a blaze of fireworks" (Schlegel) ; the proverbial expressions ; the peculiar and pedantic grammatical constructions ; the words used in their native forms : the display of learning ; [2] the bombast ; [3] the pairs of characters ; the disguising and changing of persons ; the mistakes, such as the change of letters ; the chorus-like, alternate answers ; the strained dialogue, "depth of characterisation is subordinate to elegance and sprightliness of dialogue" (Staunton), "it is a play of conversation and situation" (Furnivall); the want of reality about it all, Tofte felt this when it first came out, for he says :—

> "Each actor plaid in cunning wise his part,
> Yet all was fained, 'twas not from the hart," &c.

Even the occasion is unnatural, that a princess should be an ambassadress seems so incongruous ; now and then too we

---

[1] Some of the sonnets which appear in this play were repeated by Jaggard in *The Passionate Pilgrim*, 1599 ; and others may be compared with some of the collection of Shakespeare's *Sonnets*.

[2] The classical allusions are comparatively abundant, but are evidently "affected."

[3] Still it should be remembered, as even Shenstone could point out (*Essays*, &c. ed, 1800, p. 99), that this bombast is intentional, and fits "the persons he chuses to utter it."

come across harsh lines (*e.g.* ii. 1, 25 ; 45 ; &c.) ; notice too the extraordinarily long speech of Biron's in iv. 3 ; lastly, it may be observed, that while the ending is peculiar (the song dialogue), even the title is fantastic.[1]

RICHARD III.

" This bold, bad man."—*Henry VIII.*

In John Weever's *Epigrammes*, printed in 1599, but written (see Drake) in 1595, one (the 22nd) addressed *Ad Gulielmum Shakespeare*, speaks of Romeo and Richard as well-known characters. This may be taken to prove that *Richard III.* was produced in 1594, if not (as Malone and Collier say) in 1593.

It may probably have been suggested to Shakespeare by the production (in 1593, or 1594, by the Queen's Company) of an "enterlude," entitled *The True Tragedie of Richard III.;* the connection with the plays on Henry VI. is discussed in the section on those dramas (see pp. 6, &c.). It may be well here to name two or three plays on the period which this production treats of :—

(1) *Richardus Tertius* was acted in Cambridge in 1583 (see Chalmers) [cf. an allusion to this in Nash's *Have with You to Saffron Walden*, 1596].

(2) Churchyard's *Challenge*, including *The Tragedie of Shore's Wife*, 1593.

(3) *True Tragedie of Richard III.* (*ut supra*), 1593 or 1594.

(4) *Richard Crookback*, by Ben Jonson, in 1602 ; and others later.

Shakespeare's tragedy was entered on the *Stationers'*

[1] Fur·her, the title is paired with that of another play, *Love's Labour Wonne* (see Meres). Compare the use of these titles in *Two Gentlemen of Verona*, i. 1, 29—33.

Register on October 20th, 1597 ; and an anonymous quarto edition was printed in the same year "as lately acted" [Mr. Collier notes, that it was evidently brought out in great haste, there being two mistakes on the title-page] ; this was succeeded in the following year by another quarto edition bearing the author's name. This has been thought by some to show that *"Richard III.* was produced very shortly before its publication in 1597 ;" but the date given above is proved to be more correct, as well by the mention in Weever and other considerations urged above, as by the fact that the drama was always a popular one, and doubtless frequently acted ; by the numerous editions of the play in Shakespeare's life-time (cf. Q_3, 1602, "Newly augmented," &c. ; Q_4, 1605, &c.) ; and by the following supposed allusions :—

> " He capers nimbly in a lady's chamber
>   To the lascivious pleasing of a lute.
>   But I, that am not shaped for sportive tricks,
>   Nor made to court an amorous looking-glass," &c.
>   i. 1, 12—17.

Mr. J. G. Matthews (letter to the *Academy*, Dec. 12th, 1874) compares one of Marlowe's songs : *Fair Wench !* &c., &c. :—

> " I am not fashioned for these amorous times,
>   To court thy beauty with lascivious rhymes,
>   I cannot dally, caper, dance, and sing," &c.

We may also compare, with the same extract, the following passage from *The Mirrour of Magistrates*, 1594 :—

> " God Mars laid by his lance, and took his lute,
>   And turned his rugged frowns to smiling looks."

Mr. Fleay (*Shakespeare Manual*, pp. 20, 21), speaking of Locrine, 1595, says :—
" The wooing of Eshild, Act iv. Sc. 1, seems to be imtated from *Richard III.* i. 2 ;

and   'Methinks I see both armies in the field,'

echoes 'I think there be six Richmonds in the field.'"

<blockquote>
"Now do I play the touch,
To try if thou be current gold indeed."—iv. 2, 8, 9.
</blockquote>

Compare the following passage in *A Warning for Fair Women*, 1589 :—

<blockquote>
"*Now* is the hour come
To put your love unto *the touch, to try*
If it *be current*, or base counterfeit."
</blockquote>

Speaking of the play, from which this last extract is made, Mr. Collier says : "its resemblance to Shakespeare's plays is not merely verbal ; the speeches of Anne Sandus, the repentant wife, are Shakespearian in a much better sense. But for the extreme rarity of this tragedy, it might ere now have been attributed to Shakespeare" [quoted by J. Rees, in *Shakespeare and the Bible* (Claxton and Co., Philadelphia, 1876)].

Mr. Halliwell-Phillipps points out that Marstone's *Fawne* (printed 1606 "as *divers times* presented ") contains a curious reference to our drama, viz. :

<blockquote>
"A foole, a foole, my coxcomb for a foole."
</blockquote>

The same eminent Shakespearian scholar thinks that the turbulent character of this play, as we now have it, is due to an older one ; and Mr. Fleay has "no doubt that it was originally written by G. Peele, left unfinished by him, completed and partly corrected by Shakespeare as we have it in the quartos, and that Shakespeare afterwards altered it into the shape in which it was printed in the folio." (*Shakespeare Manual*, p. 30 ; and *Macmillan's Magazine*, Nov. 1875). For the difference between the quarto and folio editions see also the *Transactions of the New Shakspere Society*, 1875—76, vol. i., where are remarks by Messrs. Spedding, Pickersgill, Delius, and Aldis Wright.

The date assumed for this play, namely, 1593 or 1594, may be supported by the following considerations :—

There are many signs of comparatively early work ; for instance, the prologue-like speech with which the play opens ; the scenes (στιχομυθίαι) where the triology of the common lamentation of the women (ii. 2 and iv. 1) alternates like a chorus, dramatic truth being sacrificed to the lyric or epic form, and to conceits in the style of the pastoral Italian poetry (see Gervinus, *ut supra*, p. 259); the overstraining of many of the characters ; and the analysis of motive sometimes exhibited. [Compare *Guesses at Truth*, pp. 418—421, where Augustus Hare argues that the fact that Richard III. boldly acknowledges his deliberate wickedness, instead of endeavouring to palliate or excuse it like Edmund or Iago, shows that Shakespeare wrote our drama in his youth ; "we may discern," he says, "the contrast between the youth and the mature manhood of the mightiest intellect that ever lived upon earth; a contrast almost equally observable in the difference between *the metre* and *the diction* of the plays" in which these characters above-mentioned occur.]

And yet there is a perceptible improvement upon the works which preceded it ; the play has more dramatic unity than the three historical plays which it succeeds, historical truth is more regarded, the style and versification (see below) are later, and some of the characters are more marked ; while as to the marvellous creation, after whom the piece is named, each succeeding generation, since the time when Burbage entranced the theatre-goers of Elizabeth's days, has testified its admiration for him, whom Goldsmith calls "the maddening monarch."

Prof. Ward quotes from Oechelhäuser (*Essay über Richard III.* in *Jahrbuch*, vol. iii., 1868) the felicitous expression that this play marks "the significant boundary-stone which separates the works of Shakspere's youth from the immortal works of the period of his fuller splendour."

As to the various metrical tests, this play shows that they

cannot be relied upon without modifying them by other evidence; for the "double-ending test" (even if we make allowance for the great length of the play) places the play at a date relatively too late; the "rhyme test," too, does not give quite satisfactory results.

[Note, that the lines i. 2, 228, 229

"Was ever woman in this humour woo'd?
Was ever woman in this humour won?"

recur, with variations, in *Titus Andronicus*, ii. 1, 82, 83,

"She is a woman, therefore may be woo'd,
She is a woman, therefore may be won;"

and in 1 *Henry VI.*, v. 3, 77, 78,

"She's beautiful, and therefore to be woo'd,
She is a woman, therefore to be won."]

THE TAMING OF THE SHREW.

" Was ever woman in this humour woo'd?
Was ever woman in this humour won?"
Richard III.

" If thou canst love a fellow of this temper, Kate . . ."
Henry V.

This play must, of course, be considered in connection with the play entitled *The Taming of a Shrew;* and it may at once be stated that few persons will be found (especially after Mr. Fleay's paper in the New Shakspere Society's *Transactions*, vol. i.) to think that Shakespeare wrote the whole of the comedy as it appeared in the folio edition, and fewer still to attribute to him, as Pope did, the whole of the quarto edition; while we cannot for a minute suppose that any will support the view, which the late Mr. Hickson advanced (in the first vol. of *Notes and Queries*, pp. 194, 227,

345), that the *Taming of a Shrew* was written after, and in
imitation of, Shakespeare's play.

The recorded facts as to the quarto play must be carefully
borne in mind ; they are as follows : (cp. Appendix, p. 183).
It was entered at Stationers' Hall in 1594, in which year
also a quarto edition ["as it was sundry times acted by
the Earle of Pembrook his servants "] appeared ; two years
afterwards (1596) another was brought out ; and, it may be
added, as Malone pointed out, that there is a contemporary
allusion to the work [or to its relative] in Sir J. Harrington's
Metamorphosis of Ajax, 1596, where mention is made of
The Booke of Taming a Shrew.   The next notice is on the
22nd of Jan. 1607, when Burby the publisher transferred to
N. Ling his right to this play and to *Romeo and Juliet* and
Love's Labour's Lost ; shortly afterwards, Ling brought out
the third quarto of the *Taming of a Shrew* (1607) ; and in
the same year he transferred his copyrights to John Smythick.
This publisher, though he brought out editions of two of the
dramas he had acquired, took no steps with regard to the
others, until in 1623 he was induced to join in the publication
of the first folio edition of Shakespeare's works.   One more
fact must be added (and that a remarkable one) ; in 1631,
Smethwicke brought out a quarto edition, which was not a
reproduction of Ling's publication, but a copy of the folio
play.

One of the first questions which presents itself after a
careful perusal of these facts is this : how came Burby, Ling,
and Smethwicke, in 1607, to think that *The Taming of a
Shrew* was Shakespeare's ?   That they thought so is evident
from the entry of 22 Jan. 1606—7.   Nay, we will go a step
further back, and assuming that Burby acquired the copyright at about the same time that he became possessed of
Love's Labour's Lost and *Romeo and Juliet*, say in 1597,
let the question be altered to this : How came Burby, in
1597 or thereabouts, to think *The Taming of a Shrew*
Shakespeare's ?

The only answer that presents itself to me is the following : that Burby, when he acquired the copyright [the date is not known ; but that Burby was no literary pirate is certain], was informed that it was Shakespeare's. [That Shakespeare's name is not given in the quarto, which Ling published, by right of Burby's assignment, does not invalidate this answer ; for, first, we may notice that Burby, when he brought out his *Romeo and Juliet* in 1599, did not give the author's name (although he had done so, in the previous year, in the case of *Love's Labour's Lost*) ; and, secondly, it will be maintained below that at this time Shakespeare had produced a copy of the work in which he had a larger share.] Now Ling's edition was a reproduction of the quartos of 1594 and 1596 ; so that, if the answer above given be correct, we arrive at this conclusion : that, *as far back as May, 1594,* The Taming of a Shrew *was believed to be Shakespeare's in some sense.*

Now nobody, except Pope, has ever attributed the whole of this edition to Shakespeare, so that we must suppose that *he had edited an older play ;* and this supposition is favoured by the several hints we have that he had already made his name as an author or an editor.

But we are told in the quarto of 1594, that the play had been "sundry times acted by the Earle of Pembrook his servants ;" now this was not the company to which Shakespeare was then attached, so that we infer (seeing that he would not be likely to forfeit his right to the work) that *rival theatres were in possession of the subject ;* and the inference is supported by the fact that one other company at least, (Lord Nottingham's), ran a series of plays upon a similar line [viz., Dekker's *Patient Grissel,* 1597, in which he was assisted by Haughton and Chettle ; and *Medicine for a Curst Wife,* which he brought out alone soon afterwards ; indeed the last-named play has (but on insufficient grounds) been conceived to be Dekker's edition of *The Taming of a Shrew*].

To return, however, to Shakespeare and his connection with the play ; as we have inferred, he perhaps first revised it before 1594 ; but that he subsequently on several occasions retouched it is extremely probable. For instance, an early retouching is suggested by the existence of doggerel and paronomasia not found in the quarto [though these may be explained by an hypothesis mentioned below] ; while a later revision is shown by the style and versification of various parts. This reproduction at various intervals is confirmed by the analogous treatment of other plays, by the theatre-rivalry above alluded to, by the printing and reprinting of *The Taming of a Shrew*, and (may we not add, when we remember Smethwicke's action in 1631 ?) by the jealous withholding of the Globe MS. This MS., by the bye, as edited in the folio edition, throws out one or two hints which strikingly favour the comparatively early origin of our play ; we there find, like flies in amber, the following oversights : in the Induction, Sc. i., the character who speaks line 88, is called *Sinklo* instead of "a player" as in corresponding passages ; in Act i. Sc. 1, the stage direction between lines 47 and 48 reads *Pantalowne*, instead of "Gremio ;" and again in Act iii. Sc. 1, the servant, who enters, is called "a messenger" and named *Nicke*. Now, Sinklo is known to have acted at an early date, and is not known to have appeared at a late date, and his name appears instead of "a keeper" in 3 *Henry VI.* and instead of "a beadle" in 2 *Henry IV.*, both which plays are early ; we may therefore take this as a proof of the proposition stated above. This is confirmed, too, by the word "Pantelowne,"[1] the mention of which at once carries the mind back to the old plays. With regard to the other name, "Nicke," which probably stands for Nicholas Tooley, one of the actors in Shakespeare's company, while it must be owned that such records

---

[1] Mr. A. J. Ellis (*N. S. S. Trans.* vol. i. p. 119) might have referred to this. when he rightly said : "this play is an outrageous farce, and that must be fully borne in mind."

as we have of him are rather late than early, still the part, which is here assigned to him, is about as unimportant a one as we can think of, and (especially if we remember that he died in 1623) there is no proof that he did not at an early period join the company, while we must bear in mind that positive evidence always outweighs negative inferences.

It has been objected, that Meres does not mention the play as Shakespeare's; it may be answered, with Dr. Brinsley Nicholson (*N. S. S. Trans.* vol. i. p. 123), that that writer "affects a pedantic parallelism of numbers," and with Delius, that Shakespeare was certainly only the part-author of the work in question. [If it should ever be further objected that Meres names *King John*, a play which Shakespeare had likewise modelled on a previous work, it may be answered that the mention and the omission would favour, on the one hand, such a relation to the old *King John* as is generally allowed, and on the other hand, such a peculiar connection with the old *Taming of a Shrew* as is here contended for.]

Craik and Hertzberg, indeed, endeavour to avoid the Meres objection by identifying our play with *Love's Labour Won;* but their theory need not be accepted, when we find that Craik's chief argument is drawn from one of Mr. Collier's MS. corrections, and that the German Professor's reasons have been answered by his countryman, Dr. Karl Elze.

Two more reasons for the supposition that there was an early revision may be added: viz., that the nearer we get to the 1587 edition of Gascoyne's *Supposes*, which Shakespeare follows closely in some points, the more natural would such an adoption be; and again, that it is much more likely that he would revise an old play early in his literary career than that he should do so later on.

The chronology of this play has given rise to so much discussion that it may be well to allude briefly to the opinions which have been advanced by other writers. *Dr. Farmer*

pointed out that different authors were evidently connected
with the work, and, alluding to Ling's quarto, gave it as his
opinion that *The Taming of a Shrew* was probably "republished by the remains of the [Pembroke] company in 1607,
when Shakespeare's copy appeared at the Black-Friars or
the Globe " (*Essay on the Learning, &c.*) ; *Malone*, whose
account of the publishers of the quartos of this play is most
inaccurate, gave as the date of our author's share first 1606,
and afterwards 1596 ; *Chalmers* compared iv. 2, 81—87, with
the Proclamations of the Emperor Rudolph and of Queen
Elizabeth about merchants trading in their respective dominions. On account of this " remarkable passage which (he
said) the commentators have overlooked, as they did not
know the contemporary history," he dated the comedy in
1598, adding that it must have been revised in 1606 ; *Dr.
Drake*, after asking why Chalmers did not apply his historical
solution to a similar passage in *The Comedy of Errors*, gives
his adherence to Malone's chronology, which, however, he
sets down as 1594 ; a similar date, we may add, was adopted
by *Mr. Knight;* to continue in *Mr. Furnivall's* words,
[inserting dates, however] " Farmer [1607] nearly a hundred
years ago said that ' Shakespeare wrote only the Petruchio'
scenes in *The Taming of the Shrew. Mr. Collier* [1601—3]
hesitatingly adopted this view. *Mr. Grant White* [1601—3]
develop it, and I [1596—7] (and Mr. Fleay [1601—2] afterwards) turned it into figures, &c." (*N. S. S. Trans.* vol. i. ;
and Preface to Gervinus). Mr. Fleay, whose knowledge of
the versification, as well as of the stage history, of Shakespeare's time, gives his opinion great weight, has lately
enlarged his hypothesis in a most elaborate way (see *Macmillan's Magazine*, Nov. 1875, and the *Shakespeare Manual*,
1876).[1]

Before concluding this section, we must notice the following

---

[1] Mr. Tennyson, whose love for Shakespeare, from his Cambridge-under-
graduate days onwards, is well-known, said to Mr. Furnivall of a speech of this
character's that it "has such a rollicking Rabelaisian comic swing about it, that
I cannot but suspect it to be genuine Shakspere."

points which have been thought to aid in settling the date of this play.

1. The line (iv. 1, 221) "This is the way to kill a wife with kindness," has, it may be, an allusion to Heywood's play *A Woman Killed with Kindness*, 1602. But the expression may have been a proverbial one, or it may have been a later insertion [and this, I think, would add point to the remark].

2. Hazlitt (*Character of Shakespeare's Plays*, ed. 1838, p. 286) says : " This is almost the only one of Shakespeare's comedies which has a regular plot and downright moral ; " and Mr. Fleay "would rather omit the 'almost,' and add that no work of Shakespeare's is so narrow in feeling, so restricted in purpose, so unpleasing in general tone." But it should be remembered that we are dealing with a "rollicking Rabelaisian" farce, that was extremely popular from before the period when Shakespeare improved it, till the time when royal oppression and archiepiscopal ritual naturally produced a reaction of democratic rigidity and puritanical coldness.

3. As to Fletcher's "attempt to outvie Shakespeare on his own ground " (Professor Ward) in his *Woman's Prize, or the Tamer Tamed* (cir. 1619), we may balance Fleay's opinion that it is an attempt to "ridicule," with Nicholson's statement that it is a "sequel."

4. It has been thought our play must be subsequent to *Hamlet*, because the name Baptista, there used of a woman, is here correctly applied to a man.

5. Mr. Halliwell-Phillipps compares the story of the Drunkard with a part of Sir R. Buckley's *Discourse on the Felicitie of Man* (1598) ; Simrock with a tale in Goulart's *Trésor d'Histoires, &c.* (1697) ; Ward with a passage in Burton's *Anatomy of Melancholy*. The story is, of course, old ; Percy has a ballad on it, the date of which is not known.

KING JOHN.

" Britain is
A world by itself ; and we will nothing pay
For wearing our own noses."—*Cymbeline.*

This drama has for its source an older play, entitled *The Troublesome Raigne of King John,* &c. ; this was published anonymously in the year 1591 ; whilst, in the year 1611, it appeared with the initials W. Sh. ; which in a later edition (1622) were expanded into W. Shakespeare.

It is remarkable, that *King John* is the only one of the poet's uncontested works which is not entered in the books of the Stationers' Company ; it first appeared in the folio of 1623.

We must therefore (remembering that it is mentioned in Meres' list, 1598) fall back upon internal evidence, and this (*vide infrà*) seems pretty conclusively to group it with *Richard II.* and *Richard III.;* as Prof. Ward (*Eng. Dram. Lit.,* vol. i. p. 368) says, "the play evidently belongs to the same period of Shakspere's productivity as *Richard II.,* and may be dated about the same time ; probably before the body of those in which he mainly followed Holinshed."

A later date, however, is frequently assigned. Malone placed it 1596, on the following grounds :—

(1) Shakespeare's only son, Hamnet, died in August, 1596. Constance's pathetic lamentations on the loss of her boy may owe their bitterness to the poet's own grief.

(2) Chatillon's speech about the English Fleet, in ii. 1, may refer to the grand fleet sent against Spain in 1596. [I may add that the word "Spain" concludes the line next but one before those quoted by Malone, and Shakespeare may have "gone off" at the word.]

(3) As Dr. Johnson had pointed out, the lines, iii. 1, 176—179,

> " And meritorious shall that hand be called,
>   Canonized and worshipped as a saint,
>   That takes away by any secret course
>   Thy hateful life ; "

might seem to refer either (*a*) to the Bull published against Queen Elizabeth [in 1596], or (*b*) to the canonization of Garnet, Faux, and their accomplices.   This latter supposition is, as Malone remarks, negatived as well by the late date (1605) it would require, as by the fact that the passage in question is founded on a similar one in the old play.

(4) Certain passages are paralleled in contemporary plays : *e.g.*

(i.) A line 'is quoted from *The Spanish Tragedy* (1590), [published 1594].

(ii.) *Solyman and Perseda* (entd. at Stationers' Hall, 1592) is alluded to in Act i.

(iii.) Marston's *Insatiate Countess* (printed in 1603) takes nearly verbatim from *King John* (iii. 1, 23) the following line :—

> " Like a proud river peering o'er his bounds."

(iv.) One of the Bastard's speeches, in Act ii., seems to have been formed on one in the old play on *Captain Stukely*. (Malone dates this about 1590, Dyce 1596.)

(5) Malone, comparing notices in Lyly in 1592, and in Jonson in 1598, leaves open the mark of time suggested by a fashion alluded to in Arthur's statement,

> " When I was in France
>   Young gentlemen would be as sad as night
>   Only for wantonness."—iv. 1, 14—16.

Chalmers, however, prefers the date 1598, because of references which he finds to events in the year 1597 ; Drake approves the supposition.   He mentions : the offers made by the Pope's Nuntio to Henry IV. of France against Queen Elizabeth, 1597 ; the siege of Amiens in 1597, as compared with the siege of Angiers in King John ; the unpopularity of the Archduke Albert at the same period, as compared with Falconbridge's contempt for the Duke of Austria in the play; and the dangerous dissensions between the English leaders at Calais in 1597.

The line quoted above, iii. 1, 23, "Like a proud river peering o'er his bounds," and the lines, in v. 4, 53, &c., "and like a bated and retired river, leave," &c. have, with other passages in this play, been referred to the rains and floods which produced the great dearth of 1594—5. [Cf. Furnivall's forewords to *Stafford's Examinations*, &c., *New Sh. Soc.*, series vi., no. 3.]

The late Mr. R. Simpson [*New Sh. Soc. Trans.*, 1874, vol. ii., pp. 397—406] among many far-fetched political allusions to the events of Elizabeth's reign, has the following :—

"The scenes between John and Hubert are considered by Warburton and Malone [Boswell, 327] to be a covert attempt to flatter Elizabeth by throwing on Secretary Davison the blame of the Queen of Scots' death. They did not notice that if Hubert is Davison, John is Elizabeth. She cannot be flattered in the second of these scenes unless she is touched by the murderous suggestions of the first. In truth, both fit her completely [Act iii., Sc. 3, l. 19 to the end; Act iv., Sc. 2, l. 208 to the end], and it is only wonderful that allusions so plain should have been tolerated."

Perhaps too much has been said already of these political and other allusions, but it may be observed, in concluding these remarks, that several of them support the earlier date above adopted [1593 or 1594], and it may be added that the nearer we get to the year of the Spanish Armada, and the few years that followed with their expeditions to Spain, the more pointed would be any covert allusions in such passages as the following :—

(*a*) That already quoted from ii. 1, 66—75; remembering (as before remarked) the mention of the word *Spain* in line 64.

(*b*) "So, by a roaring tempest of a flood
A whole armado of convicted sail
Is scattered and disjoined from fellowship."

iii. 4, 1—3.

(*c*) Speaking of the Pope, England's sovereign says :

"Tell him this tale ; and from the mouth of England
Add thus much more, that no Italian priest
Shall tithe or toll in our dominions ;
But as we, under heaven, are supreme head,
So under Him that great supremacy,
Where we do reign, we will alone uphold," &c.

iii. 1, 152, &c.

The application of the different metrical tests supports, as
well the early date assumed for this play as the grouping of
it with *Richard II.* and *Richard III.;* in addition to the
"feminine-ending test" and the "weak-ending test," the
absence of prose in these three plays should be noted ;
while it may be added that there is a remarkable absence of
"classical allusions" in the three plays.

The early date of the piece may be seen, too, from the
occasional plays-upon-words and conceits in unsuitable
places ; from the antithetical answers ; from the lengthy
speeches (for example, the Bastard's soliloquies); and from
a certain want of connection throughout. Mr. Furnivall
thus expresses the last remark : the drama is "a panorama
of fine scenes almost unconnected, save by Falconbridge."
Schlegel says, that *John* is the prologue to the historical
series, as *Henry VIII.* is their epilogue.

But if, says Dr. Drake, "*King John,* as a whole, be not
entitled to class among the very first-rate compositions of
our author, it can yet exhibit some scenes of superlative
beauty and effect, and two characters supported with un-
failing energy and consistency," Falconbridge and Lady
Constance. "As for the character of John, which from its
meanness and imbecility, seems not well calculated for
dramatic representation, Shakespeare has contrived, towards

the close of the drama, to excite in his behalf some degree of interest and commiseration, especially in the dying scene of the fallen monarch."

The play should be compared, too, with the two parts of the old *King John*, in order to observe Shakespeare's discrimination and artistic taste ; the side of the reign which he has not dramatised should be also noticed, and it will be seen that "for the purpose of securing a dramatic unity, the chronological succession of events, as they occurred in the real history of the times, is constantly disregarded."

RICHARD II.

*" Thou dost look
Like Patience gazing on kings' graves."—Pericles.*

There seem to have been several plays on incidents in the reign of this monarch ;

(1) The play acted at the Globe, in 1601, at the desire of Sir Gilly Merick and other partisans of Essex ; that this could not have been Shakespeare's *Richard II.*, we may judge from the title (as given by the *State Trials* record) and from the drift of his drama as contrasted with the object of the conspirators. [For Mr. Hales's opinion, see *Henry IV., N. S. S. Trans.*]

(2) Another play, called *Richard II.*, was seen by Dr. Forman, at the Globe, in 1611. He states that it began with the rebellion of Wat Tyler ; so that this, too, was not Shakespeare's.

(3) A play, anterior to Shakespeare's, entitled " *The Tragedy of Richard II.*, concluding with the murder of the Duke of Gloster at Calais," has been lately printed from an old MS.

Shakespeare's play was entered on the *Stationers' Register* on August 29th, 1597 ; in the same year a quarto edition appeared; in the succeeding year another quarto appeared; in 1608, came out a third edition, "with new additions of the Parliament Scene." These additions had probably been suppressed from fear of offending the Queen; this appears from an examination of the context, and from the fact which the 1608 quarto states, that it was produced "as acted by the Lord Chamberlain's Servants," implying most probably that it was printed from the old MS.

This point seems, too, to suggest an early date for this play; for considering the historical facts adduced by Malone and others, as to the Pope's Bull in 1597 inciting the subjects of Elizabeth to depose her, and as to the treatment of Hayward shortly afterwards, it may be asked if it is likely that Shakespeare would have written the play at that period?

It is more likely that Shakespeare, having brought out *Richard III.* to complete the *Henry VI.* series of plays, was led by the great success of his work, to write *Richard II.* as an introduction to the Lancastrian plays. We have dated *Richard III.* in 1593 or 1594, and *Richard II.* may be placed in 1594; it is evidently, as has been remarked before, closely allied to *King John* in style, while it is equally certainly much earlier than *Henry IV.*

Shakespeare, in preparing for the play, used Holinshed's *Chronicles* [2nd edition, 1586—7 (see Messrs. Clarke and Wright: Clarendon Press *Richard II.*)], referring now and then to Hall.

Charles Knight and Grant White think Shakespeare borrowed certain passages from Daniel's *Civil Wars* [2nd edition, 1595, in which the part referring to the fate of Richard II. was added]; but Delius, Clark and Wright, and Ward, think the coincidences too indecisive; and if the above-assumed date be correct, the borrowing, if there be any, must be on Daniel's part.

Chalmers argued for a later date (1596) by comparing the description of the rebellion in Act i., with the outbreak in that country in Elizabeth's time in 1594—6.

Chalmers also pointed out that, in Act v. Sc. 3, l. 1—24, in the description of the Prince and his loose companions, there are " sketches, in which we may perceive the workings of the poet's mind, which had drawn an outline that was to be filled up and finished in several subsequent dramatical histories."

The late Mr. R. Simpson (*ut supra*, pp. 407—409) dwells upon the grievances of 1592 and 1593, " a time of fear and discontent." " At a time when the country was full of secret and open murmurs against a fiscal oppression and mis-management which specially pressed upon the poet himself, he produced *Richard II.*, and put into it such passages as these :—

> " ' The King is not himself, but basely led
> By flatterers ; and what they will inform
> Merely in hate 'gainst any of us all,
> That will the King severely prosecute
> 'Gainst us, our lives, our children and our heirs.'

> " ' The commons hath he pill'd with grievous taxes
> And lost their hearts : the nobles hath he fin'd
> For ancient quarrels, and quite lost their hearts ;
> And daily new exactions are devised—
> As blanks, benevolences, and I know not what ;
> But what, o' God's name, doth become of this ? '

" Benevolences were never heard of in Richard's day, and Shakspere would not have used the word unless he meant to refer to times for which he and his audience cared more."

Charles Lamb says :—" The reluctant pangs of abdicating royalty in *Edward II.* [Marlowe, 1592] furnished hints which Shakespeare scarcely improved in his *Richard II.;*" but Fleay says that Shakespeare's play stands to Marlowe's in the relation that *Richard III.* bears to *Henry VI.*

Mr. Fleay, chiefly relying upon the "rhyme-test," classes *Richard II.* in his first period, dating it two years before *Richard III.* and *John;* he adds—" Shakespeare in it seems not to move with the same freedom that he does in later plays, and the whole work has an artificial air." Mr.

Swinburne, too, appears to consider *Richard II.* the earliest of Shakespeare's historical plays.

Mr. Fleay, however, admits that the presence of Alexandrines in *Richard II.* is a sign of the second period, and that the absence of prose in the three plays (*Richard II.*, *Richard III.*, and *John*) is an indication that they may be grouped together. To this, add the remarkable absence of "classical allusions" in this set, which I before pointed out (see p. 43).

In this play, as signs of early work, we may notice frequent rhymes (rhyming couplets, alternate rhymes, and alliteration); a certain want of characterisation ; indeed, Hartley Coleridge goes so far as to say that "except *Richard II.*, the characters are nobodies ;" the unpleasing effect produced, as the same writer observes, from the want of a striking female character ; and a looseness in the arrangement of the play (compare, for instance, the violation of dramatic rules in the connection between the first and second acts. But, as Messrs. Clark and Wright observe, "minor blemishes do not invalidate [S. T.] Coleridge's statement that *Richard II.* is the most admirable of the purely historical plays."

MIDSUMMER NIGHT'S DREAM.

" My tricksy spirit."—*Tempest.*

" If thou art changed to aught, 'tis to an ass."
                                          Comedy of Errors.

There is very little directly external evidence with regard to the date of this play ; Meres mentioned it in 1598 ; Thomas Fisher entered it on the *Stationers' Register* in Oct., 1600, and soon afterwards brought out a quarto edition ; in the same year, too (1600), Roberts the printer issued another quarto, which, strange to say (but see Appendix, p. 181), was used in the publication of the first folio. The quartos state that this comedy had "been sundry times publickely acted, by the Right Honourable the Lord Chamberlaine his Servants."

It has frequently been suggested that a *Midsummer Night's Dream* was composed to grace some marriage festivities; and the supposition has been supported by referring to its lyrical and almost operatic tone, to its masque-like form, and to Oberon's song at the conclusion. But this suggestion may perhaps be answered by noting the difficulty that has been experienced in finding any nuptial event to tally with the supposed date of its composition, by the unlikelihood of so unique an undertaking on Shakespeare's part being unrecorded, by the inappropriateness of such phrases as Bottom's statement in iii. 1, 146—8, "yet to say truth, reason and love keep little company together nowadays," and by the promise in Puck's epilogue that "we will make amends ere long."

It may be well, however, to mention the marriage-occasions to which different writers have assigned it. Tieck and Ulrici think it was composed for the nuptials of Lord Southampton; but the mention by Meres would seem to negative this; unless we suppose with Mr. Gerald Massey that it was written some time before, "when it may have been thought the Queen's consent could be obtained." He suggests 1595; and adds that it may have been performed in January, 1598, before Southampton's departure for Paris, and again at the entertainment in Essex House on February 14th. But this secret marriage can scarcely have been accompanied by such festivities as this would imply.

Elze, Kurz, and Dowden, however, think the play was written to do honour to the marriage of the Earl of Essex with the Lady Frances, the daughter of Walsingham and widow of Sidney; as that event took place in the early spring of 1590, this theory would throw the date back to 1589.

The following passages in the comedy have been referred to contemporary events :—

Titania's description of the disastrous state of the weather (ii. 1, 88—117) is certainly very much drawn out; and when taken with other passages in the play, would seem to point to some recent catastrophes. Now the chief dearth in Shakespeare's time was in 1594—5;[1] and to this the lines probably refer; though it ought to be added Mr. Halliwell-Phillipps has quoted Dr. Simon Forman and Stowe for similar weather in 1591; while Dyce says the inference is "ridiculous, for 'cold Quince's joke,' that 'some of your *French Crowns* have *no hair* at all' (i. 1, 99, 100), has undoubted reference to the paternal anxieties of Henry the Fourth, and could scarcely have been uttered before 1594 or 1595."

Mr. Chalmers, with his usual historical ingenuity, referred the play to 1598, because Parliament, in 1597, passed a Bill "to prevent marriages without bans," and to stay "the stealing away of children without parents' consent;" and because in the same year, "the price of corn rose enormously," producing a famine.

As to the well-known lines, v. 1, 52—56,

> "'The thrice-three Muses mourning for the death
> Of Learning, late deceased in beggary!'
> This is some satire, keen and critical,
> Not sorting with a nuptial ceremony;"

the following opinions have been advanced :—

(1) Mr. Dyce (again) says it would be "ridiculous" to refer to any particular person; while some find an allusion to

(2) The death of Spenser, on January 16th, 1599. This is, of course, impossible, unless we suppose, with Mr. Halliwell-Phillips, that it is a later insertion. Elze thinks it may have been inserted as a compliment to Essex, who

---

[1] Compare Titania's remark "as in revenge" (ii. 1, 89), with Stow's last words in his description of the storms, pestilence and dearth of 1594-5. "such was our sins deserving it." (See Mr. Furnivall's *Forewords* to Stafford's *Examination*, &c. N. S. S. 1876, for extracts from Stowe.)

had sent relief to Spenser on his death-bed. [But notice the word " satire."]

(3) The poem, by Spenser,[1] called the *Tears of the Muses* (on the neglect, &c., of learning), 1591, has been thought by others to be alluded to. Another supposition is that we have a reference to

(4) The death of Greene, who died in the autumn of 1592. Prof. Ward says "the term 'ridiculous' is not too strong to characterise the reference to Greene, upon whose memory Shakspere in that case would certainly have been resolved to heap coals of fire." I venture to incur the ridicule, for how can a "*satire, keen and critical,*" be used to "heap coals of fire"? and we know that Greene was regarded by Gabriel Harvey and others (including Shakespeare himself) with anything but a forgiving spirit. Surely the reference to the death

" Of *Learning,* late *deceased in beggary,*"

must allude to Robert Greene, "utriusque Academiæ in Artibus Magister" (as he styles himself on some of his title-pages), parson (miserabile dictu), doctor, author,[2] who died in misery and want in a London attic.

Perhaps the most celebrated attempt at allegorical explanation ever made is Mr. Halpin's exceedingly ingenious application, to Leicester's (Kenilworth) intrigues with the Queen and with the Countess of Essex, of the lines ii. 1, 155—168. [See Halpin's *Oberon's Vision*, &c.]

There is undoubtedly some reference to the proceedings at Kenilworth in 1575 ; but the solution referred to is too "exact ;" and, as Prof. Ward well remarks, "it is precisely

---

[1] This reference may be supported by the Spenserian phrase, "the thrice-three muses," and by the alliteration in the lines,

> "This is some satire, keen and critical,
> Not sorting with a nuptial ceremony."

[2] Of the numerous works which he wrote, we shall have to mention in this Section his *James IV.* and his *Friar Bacon.*

where exact personal allegory begins, that true poetic allegory leaves off."

Mr. Halpin's conjectures quite throw into the shade the old explanation by Warburton, and the more recent theory of Massey; the same writer maintains that our play must have been written before 1588, because Leicester died in that year; he conjectures, too, that the expression "Dian's bud" may have been borrowed from the graceful compliment which Greene paid Queen Eiizabeth (under the title of *Diana's Rose*) in his *Friar Bacon* (1591).

To the same author (Greene) Shakespeare was probably indebted for his idea of Oberon and the fairy-court, which is doubtless due to the *Scottish History of James IV.* (cir. 1590); though it should be mentioned that the names Oberon and Titania occur in a dramatic entertainment exhibited before Elizabeth in 1591. [See Malone, Variorum ed., vol. ii. p. 337.]

Ben Jonson may have remembered Shakespeare's work both in his *Lust's Dominion*, 1600, and in his masque *Oberon*, 1611, as well as in his later *Love's Welcome at Bolsover*. Chalmers, who contended for a late date (1598), thought that the allusions to *The Fairy Queen* would be pointed by the appearance of Spenser's second book, bearing that title, in 1596; while Kurz, who argues for an early date (before 1590), thinks that Shakespeare's work must have preceded the first volume, for how, after Spenser had identified the Fairy Queen and the English Sovereign, would Shakespeare ever have dared to link her majesty with Bottom "the clowne!"

The *Pyramus and Thisbe*, which Dr. Gale published in 1597, was doubtless posterior to Shakespeare's interlude, as Malone suggested, and not anterior as Chalmers contended. The same may be said of the following passage in *Doctor Dodipoll*, published in 1600, but alluded to in 1596:—

> "'Twas I that led you thro' the painted meads,
> Where the light *fairies* danced upon the *flowers*,
> *Hanging in every leaf an orient pearl.*"

Compare with this :—

"And *hang a pearl* in every cowslip's ear,"

And

"And that same dew, which sometimes on the buds
Was wont to swell, like round and *orient pearls*,
Stood now within the pretty *flowerets* eyes
Like tears," &c.—*M. N. D.*, iv. 1, 58—61.

Comparisons have been made between passages in this
comedy, and passages in the *Venus and Adonis* and in the
Sonnets, as well as in Lyly's *Euphues*. Attention has also
been drawn to the *Maid's Metamorphosis*, also ascribed
to Lyly, and probably to be dated 1600.

Mr. Skeat, in his *Shakespeare's Plutarch*, speaking of the
various editions of North's translation (viz. 1579, 1595, 1603,
1612, &c.), says : "Shakespeare must certainly have known
the work before 1603, because there is a clear allusion to it
in *Midsummer Night's Dream*, ii. 1, 75—80 ; with which we
may compare the *Life of Theseus*, containing the names
of Perigonna, Arglos, Ariadne, Antispa, and Hippolyta."
Other names (*e.g.* Demetrius and Lysander) in this comedy
also occur in North's *Plutarch*.   Mr. Skeat continues :
"Whether this play was written earlier than 1595, I leave to
the investigation of the reader."

The present investigation seems to point to that very year,
and may not the reissue of North's work in this year, after
it had been so long out of print, have directed Shakespeare's
attention to what so soon became his chief storehouse for
material to work upon ?

That this play was written comparatively early in Shakespeare's literary career is evident from the general tone of
the work, and has scarcely ever been disputed ; the play
within the play (the anti-mask, as Elze calls it) smacks of
his youthful days ["doubtless (says Froude) Shakespeare had
seen many a Bottom [1] in the old Warwickshire hamlets,

---

[1] Bottom is sometimes called " the clowne" in the 1st Folio.

many a Sir Nathaniel playing *Alissander* and finding himself
a little o'erparted; he had been with Snug the joiner, Quince
the carpenter, and Flute the bellows-mender, when a boy,
we will not question, and acted with them, and written their
parts for them"]; the glowing pastoral descriptions prove
the same [he must have (says Ruskin) "his kingcups and
clover—pansies—the Avon's flow—and the undulating hills
and woods of Warwickshire"]; the "feminine-ending test"
also shows its early date; and so does the "rhyme-test,"
though considering the musical, lyrical caste of the comedy,
we must not press this too much.   There is a want of
characterisation among the higher persons of the play, but
we must not therefore throw the date too far back, for
remember Bottom! "O sweet bully Bottom! he hath simply
the best wit of any handicraft man in Athens.   Yea, and the
best person too; and he is the very *paramour* for a sweet
voice."   The construction is slight, some of the actions are
unnatural, the play is very little charged with moral significance, even Gervinus can find "no underlying motive," but
we will not therefore say of any part of it, as Hippolyta did,
"This is the silliest stuff that ever I heard;" rather will we
join in Theseus's answer (how full of Shakespeare's wisdom
it is!), "The best in this kind are but shadows; and the
worst are no worse, if imagination amend them."   But we
need no such help to appreciate this comedy's beauties;
only Shakespeare himself, in his diffidence, need apologise :

> "Gentles, do not reprehend ;
> If you pardon, we will mend ; . . .
> We will make amends ere long."

And this reminds us how the play is contemporary with
Romeo and Juliet (see the last line of the prologue, and
note the general tone of that play).   If, then, this comedy
be dated about 1595, we shall meet the allusions mentioned
above, and the views just stated, while we accord with
Hallam's judgment, that "while it should be placed among

the early plays, yet its superiority to *Love's Labour's Lost*,
The Comedy of Errors, the *Gentlemen of Verona*, and other
early plays, affords a presumption that it was written after
them."

1 HENRY IV.

" But one part wisdom,
And even three parts coward."—Hamlet.

We have the following entry on the *Stationers' Register*
for 25 Feb., 1597—8 : "Andrew Wiffe] A booke intitled the
Historye of Henry the iiiith, with his battaile at Shrewsburye
against Henry Hottspurre of the Northe with the conceipted
Mirth of Sir John Falstaffe." A quarto similarly styled
appeared in 1598 ; and in the following year (1599) a second
quarto came out. [It has been argued that the above entry
and the first edition succeeded the production of Part ii. ;
were this established, the date of Part i. would probably have
to be thrown back some little while ; but the argument will
be considered under the remarks on Part ii.]

From the above entry, and from reasons stated below,
1 *Henry IV.* will here be assigned to the year 1597 ; and, it
may be added, *to the end of that year*, for the date of the
entry seems to suggest that it was a Christmas play [this is
rendered the more probable, if we consider the enthusiasm
with which Falstaff must have been received], and, again,
the second part of *Henry IV.* was produced (*vide infrà*) in
1598 ; now, Dr. Johnson does not perhaps put it too strongly
when he says "these two plays are two, only because they
are too long to be one ;" the second part must have rapidly
succeeded the first.

Henry IV., in both its parts, is founded partly upon
Holinshed, and partly upon an old play called *The Famous
Victories of Henry the Fifth*, which was acted before 1588,
and of which editions appeared in 1594 and 1597.

The first and second parts of a play, named after Sir John Oldcastle, were entered at Stationers' Hall, on August 11th, 1600; and the same year there appeared an edition of the work ascribed to Shakespeare; this play, which had probably been produced a year or two before, refers in two or three places to Shakespeare's Falstaff; and it has been thought by some that that celebrated character had been at first named after Sir John Oldcastle; the point will be discussed under part ii.; all that need be noticed here is that 1 *Henry IV.* preceded 1 *Sir J. Oldcastle.*

A writer in one of the last numbers of the *North British Review* (April, 1870) contended for an early date (1590) for this play, on the following insufficient grounds :—

(1) Nash, in 1592, make Piers Penniless refer to Hotspur.

(2) Some of "the quotations which make up Pistol's fustian farrago" are taken from, or are parodies on, Marlowe, Peele, &c.; "these allusions would be more racy in 1590 than in 1598."

(3) The reviewer speaks of two stages of euphuism, and says that the euphuism of Falstaff is of the first stage of Lyly's influence.

Again, in favour of the date 1596, Chalmers urged the following reasons :—

(1) The passage

"So shaken as we are, so wan with care,
Find we a time for *frighted peace to pant;*
And breathe shortwinded accents of *new broils,*
To be *commenced in strands afar remote,*"

"plainly alludes" to the expedition against Spain in 1596.

(2) Falstaff, when commencing a robbery for "recreation sake," remarks that "the poor abuses of the time want countenance;" this Chalmers refers to certain abuses recorded by Camden under 1596, and alluded to in a proclamation issued in the same year.

(3) Alluding to the death of Robin the ostler, we have, in

Act ii. Sc. 1, the expression "the poor fellow never joyed *since the price of oats rose.*" Again this is referred to 1596 on the strength of a *Proclamation for the Dearth of Corn*, &c.

(4) In Hotspur's statement about Glendower having held him "at least nine hours" [which Gervinus so strangely takes literally] "in reckoning up the several *devils' names*," Chalmers sees a stroke at Lodge's *Devils Incarnate*, 1596.

If, however, these allusions have any weight, they would not be very inappropriate to the following year, 1597, to which the play has been above assigned. It may be noted that this date is supported by the following strange point; in v. 4, 40, 41, we read :

> " . . . The spirits
> Of [valiant] Shirley, Stafford, Blunt, are in my arms ; "

where the word "valiant" was perhaps inserted by the actor as a compliment to the celebrated Shirleys, who were knighted by the Queen in 1597.

The line " That I did pluck allegiance from men's mouths " (iii. 2, 52) is perhaps an echo of the line "And pull obedience from thy subjects' hearts," in [Marlowe's] *Lust's Dominion* (1593 ?).

The following early allusions to Falstaff may be pointed out ; Ben Jonson ends his *Every Man Out of His Humour* with the remark "you may in time make lean Macilente as fat as Sir John Falstaff;" and Sir Tobie Matthews, in a letter printed in 1660, but apparently written at the beginning of the century, says : "For I must tell you I never dealt so freely with you in any ; and (as that excellent author Sir John Falstaff says) what for your business, news, device, foolery, and liberty, ' I never dealt better since I was a man ' " (see 1 *Henry IV.* ii. 4, 188).

2 HENRY IV.

" It is meet
That noble minds keep ever with their likes."—*Julius Cæsar.*

It has been said that "the second, as well as the first part of *Henry IV.* was written previously to the date of the entry of the first in February, 1598. This is proved by the fact that this entry makes mention of the conceipted Mirth of Sir John Falstaffe," while in one passage of the quarto edition of the second part, "Old," *i.e.* Oldcastle, is by mistake left standing as the prefix to one of Falstaff's speeches. Moreover, there is an allusion to Justice Silence in Ben Jonson's *Every Man Out of His Humour* (1599). [Prof. Ward, *Eng. Dram. Lit.*, vol i., p. 396, and other writers.]

It has been before remarked that Shakespeare perhaps *at first* gave to his celebrated comic character the name of Oldcastle, borrowing it from the old play on Henry V. ; this is supported by the tradition mentioned by Rowe and others ; by the pun in Part i., Act i., Sc. 2, where Prince Henry calls Falstaff "my *old* lad of the *castle ;*" by the statement, in Part ii., Act iii., Sc. 2, that Falstaff had been in his boyhood "page to Thomas Mowbray, Duke of Norfolk," which the historical Oldcastle was ; by the abbreviation "Old." above referred to ; and by the allusion in the prologue of the play *Sir John Oldcastle.*

But I cannot help thinking that the following remarks refute the inference as to date of 2 *Henry IV.* made in the above quotation :—

(1) The mention of Falstaff as "the fat knight, hight Oldcastle," by Nat. Field in 1618, and two similar allusions in 1604, would suggest (as Mr. Halliweli-Phillipps has remarked) that some of the theatres long retained the name ; this would, of course, weaken the inference from the abbreviation "Old."

(2) The entry in the *Register* on February 25th, 1598 [see it quoted *in extenso* on p. 186], speaks of *The Historye of Henry the iiiith*, &c. ; it does *not* say " Part i.," which I think it would have done had Part ii. been in existence then ; compare the entries under dates March 12th, 1593 ; 11th August, 1600 ; August 23rd, 1600, &c.

(3) A consideration of the words of the entry, and the fact that they reappear on the title-page of the first quarto of 1 *Henry IV.*, show that they were intended to apply to Part i. only, and hence imply that Part ii. had not yet been produced.

(4) Meres, writing [" early," says Mr. Halliwell-Phillips] in 1598, does not seem to know of two parts ; and

(5) When the second edition of the first part was called for in 1599 (the second part having then appeared), it is called *Henry IV., Part i.*, "newly augmented by Wm. Shakespeare ; " while

(6) As to the allusion to Justice Silence in *Every Man Out of His Humour* (v. 2) (1599) ; the reference surely rather favours the date 1598—1599.[1]

The second part of *Henry IV.* was entered at the Stationers' Hall on the 23rd of August, 1600, by Andrew Wise and William Aspley, and a quarto edition was brought out by these publishers in the same year ; on the title-page it is said to have been " sundry times publikely'acted."

Kemp, the comedian, is thought to have appeared as Justice Shallow, and is also supposed to have left the Lord Chamberlain's Company about the end of 1598 [see Appendix, p. 197] ; if this be so, we have a confirmation of the above date. Speaking of Justice Shallow, we may notice that Dekker, in his *Satiromastix* (1602), refers to " these spangle

---

[1] It may be noticed with regard to this allusion that the quotation of it has given rise to a series of most curious literary mistakes. Dr. Drake long ago pointed out that Malone says there is an allusion to Justice *Shallow* in *Every Man Out of His Humour*, and Chalmers tells us there is a reference to Justice Silence in *Every Man* in His *Humour*. Mr. Fleay (*Shakespeare Manual*, p. 36) now tries a double variation, and informs us that Justice *Shallow* is alluded to in *Every Man* in His *Humour*.

babies, these true heirs of Master Justice Shallow;" and
may quote the following from the late Mr. R. Simpson's
paper in the *New Shakspere Society's Transactions*, 1874,
vol. ii., p. 414 : "One of the Percies, Sir Charles, was settled
at Dumbleton in Gloucestershire, in the neighbourhood of
Stratford, and in a letter of 1609 speaks familiarly of himself
as Justice Shallow. This man, who refers to these very
plays, may have furnished some of the matter of *Henry IV.*"

In the same gentleman's edition of *A Larum for London*
(which he dates 1598 or 1599), the expression "we'll mourn
in sack" (p. 44) may be compared with the repenting *in sack*
of the young prince [not of Falstaff, as Mr. Simpson puts it]
(2 *Henry IV.* i., 2, 222).

In the lines, iv. 4, 118—120,

> "The incessant care and labour of his mind
> Hath wrought the muse that should confine it in
> So thin that life looks through and will break out ;"

there seems to be a remembrance of Daniel's *Civil Warres*
(1595), b. iii., st. 116,

> "Wearing the wall so thin, that now the mind
> Might well look through, and his frailty find."

This is given by Malone [Variorum Edn., vol. ii., p. 358 ;
he was apparently in a careless mood, for having a line or
two before written "Justice Shallow" for "Justice Silence,"
he here writes "the last act" for "the fourth act"].

In the lines, v. 2, 56—59,

> "Brothers, you mix your sadness with some fear.
> This is the English, not the Turkish court ;
> Not Amurath an Amurath succeeds,
> But Harry, Harry ;"

it is highly probable (as Mr. Malone remarked) that Shakespeare had in contemplation the cruelty practised by the
Turkish emperor, Mahomet, who after the death of his
father, Amurath the Third, in February, 1596, invited his

unsuspecting brothers to a feast, and caused them all to be strangled.

We may compare the allusion, in Act iii., Sc. 2, to "a Cotswold man," with the mention of Cotsall in the nearly contemporary play, the *Merry Wives of Windsor* (i. 1, 92).

It would be a matter of great interest to trace to their origin many of the phrases put into the mouth of Pistol; truly "the swaggering rascal" (ii. 4, 76) was "a snapper-up of unconsidered trifles" (*Winter's Tale*); truly he had been at many "a great feast of ·languages, and stolen the scraps" (*Love's Labour's Lost*). The following are a few of his borrowed expressions, taken from Act ii. Sc. 4 :—

(1) Lines 170 and 189 : "Have we not Hiren here?" may be a line from Peele's *Turkish Mahomet, or Hyren (Irene) the Fair Greek.*

(2) Lines 178, 179 :

> "And hollow pampered jades of Asia,
> Which cannot go but thirty miles a day ; "

are a mangled version of two lines in Marlowe's *Tamberlaine* (1590).

(3) Line 193 : "Feed, and be fat, my fair Calipolis," occurs twice in Peele's *Battle of Alcazar* (1594).

(4) Line 195 : "Si fortune me tormente, sperato me contento," appeared in a book entitled *Wits, Fits, and Fancies*, entered on the *Stationers' Register* in 1595.

(5) Line 211 : "Death rock me asleep," occurs in an old song attributed to Anne Boleyn.

(6) Line 211 : "Abridge my doleful days" is found in the *Gorgeous Gallery of Gallant Inventions* (1578).

Another of Pistol's expressions : "'Tis 'semper idem' . . . 'tis all in every part," may be paralleled by the following sentence in Sir John Davis's *Nosce Teipsum* (1599) : "Some say she's all in all, and all in every part." [Query: who were they from whom Pistol and Davis borrowed the phrase?]

MERCHANT OF VENICE.

There is pretty conclusive evidence that the subject of this comedy had been previously dramatised. Stephen Gosson, in his *School of Abuse*, 1579, speaks of a play entitled *The Jew*, as "showne at the Bull," and "representing the greedinesse of worldly chusers, and bloody mindes of usurers;" this description almost certainly points out the two plots upon which Shakespeare afterwards worked. Again, from Henslowe's *Diary* we learn that a new play, entitled *The Venesyon Comodey*, was produced on August 25th, 1594; whether this was Shakespeare's play is a question still *sub judice;* in support of the supposition it may be stated that the Lord Chamberlain's Company seem to have been connected with Henslowe at this very time, that Roberts when he entered the play in 1598 called it "a booke of *The Merchaunt of Venyce*, or otherwise called *The Jewe Venyse*" (so that, as Prof. Ward remarks, the comedy might well be known by the local appellation), that Roberts when he brought his quarto edition in 1600, omits, apparently with a fraudulent intention, the mention of the Company by whom the play was acted, and that in this year (1598) on consecutive days there were entered, on the *Stationers' Register*, the *Ballad of Gernutus* (see below) and Marlowe's *Jew of Malta*, the last-mentioned fact doubtless implying a revival of that tragedy, which was perhaps run (by Lord Pembroke's Company?) in opposition to the *Venesyon Comodey*.

On the other hand, it has been urged that "Shakespeare's plays were not at any time acted at the Rose" (see Mr. Fleay, *Shakespeare Manual*, p. 34), and that "the dramatists of that time were fond of laying their scenes in Italy, so that the identification is very uncertain" (see the Clarendon Press Edition, p. xxi. ; which, however, a little lower down, speaks of "its first production in 1594 ").

Again, internal evidence has been called to the aid of the early date ; attention has been drawn to the rhyme, the doggerel, and the classical allusions, as well as to the "fooling" of Launcelot as compared with that of Launce ; but may it not be answered, that the 5-measure *rhyme* is very little more than what we find in *Measure for Measure*, in *Hamlet*, in *Othello*, in *Lear* (while we might almost have expected that the casket-scenes would be entirely in rhyme—especially if they are founded upon an older play), that the short-lined *rhyme* is necessary for the mottoes, &c., that the *doggerel*, if Shakespeare's at all, is reduced almost to a minimum, that the *classical allusions*, if taken by quantity, would place it among the very earliest of his plays (which is absurd), but, if taken by quality, would place it just in that period to which it will be here assigned (1597—8), and that, as to the comparison of Launcelot with Launce, the opinion that they are contemporaries is not universal, and at any rate, Shakespeare has not here given us "twins," there is no Speed to match Launcelot.   Lastly, we may refer to the universally admitted "power of composition, and beauty of style ; " to the marvellous way in which the plots are blended, to the admirable mixture of comedy and tragedy, to the beautiful "æsthetic" and "moral"[1] termination by which the "musical interlude"[2] of the fifth act affords relaxation after the tension of the fourth.

These considerations, taken with the external or nearly external evidence which will be immediately referred to, lead to the conclusion that the play was composed by Shakespeare but a short time before the allusions which are made to it in the year 1598.

Messrs. Clarke and Wright indeed "think that the play

---

[1] Gervinus.   [2] Schlegel.

was in great part rewritten between the time of its first production in 1594 and its publication in 1600." They point
out "slight discrepancies" which may be due to the revision;
"particularly that in Act i., Sc. 2, where only four strangers
are mentioned as about to take their leave, after six have
been described in detail." To this it may be answered that
the editors have produced no evidence of "its first production
in 1594," rather they have just above thought it "very uncertain;" that the careless revision which they attribute to
Shakespeare is not very complimentary to him, and (as to
the particular discrepancy upon which they dwell) that they
are almost rendering themselves liable to be classed with
Mr. Swinburne's "finger-counters" and ": finger-casters."

If a subsequent revision be thought to be suggested by the
undoubted alterations made in i. 2, 84 [where for "the Scottish
Lord" (Q₁), the first folio reads "the *other* Lord," to avoid
giving offence to the new monarch], and in i. 2, 99 [where for
"I pray God grant" (Q₁), F₁ reads "I wish," an alteration to
meet 3 Jac. I., c. 21], it may be replied that such changes
were probably made in all the plays which were revived at
that period.

Beside obtaining his plots from *Il Pecorone* by Giovanni,
and from the *Gesta Romanorum*, Shakespeare has been
thought to owe hints or passages to the following :—

Marlowe's *Jew of Malta* (1588—1590); opinions differ as
to the degree in which our author is indebted to his great
predecessor; Hallam speaks of only "a few hints," and these
Dyce calls unimportant, while Karl Elze says : "the prototype
of Shylock clearly lies in Marlowe's Barabas ; without which
The Merchant of Venice would in all probability never have
been written," and Prof. Ward points out a number of
parallel passages in the two dramas.

Alexander Silvayn's *Orator*, translated from the French
by Anthony Munday in 1596 (or 1598), contains a declaration "of a Jew who would for his debt have a pound of
flesh of a Christian," and may have suggested some parts

of the Trial Scene, and particularly one of Shylock's speeches.

Dr. Farmer pointed this out, and he also conjectured that the name Shylock may be due to a pamphlet, called *Caleb Shillocke His Prophecie, or the Jewes Prediction* (date uncertain).

The *Ballad of Gernutus*, mentioned above, perhaps supplied one or two hints (*e.g.* the whetting of the knife) ; Simrock, Al. Schmidt, Delius, Elze,[1] and other German commentators, however, who claim an early date for *The Merchant of Venice*, think that the play preceded the ballad.

Speaking of iv. 1, 196, the Clarendon Press editors say : "A similar sentiment is quoted by Blackeway from the petition of the Convocation to Queen Elizabeth in 1580, and Malone quotes parallel passages from Harrington's *Orlando Furioso*, and from the play of *Edward III*. It is possible that Shakespeare in writing this passage intended to compliment Elizabeth, whose rule (whatever be the judgment of recent historians) was certainly held by her subjects to be mild and merciful ; " and of iii. 2, 32, 33—

> " Ay, but I fear you speak *upon the rack*,
>   Where men enforced do speak anything : "

they say : "it is pleasant to find Shakespeare before his age in denouncing the futility of this barbarous method of extorting truth. He was old enough to remember the case of Francis Throckmorton in 1584 ; and that of Squire in 1598 was fresh in his mind. See Lingard's *History of England*, vol. v. pp. 405, 558."

Elze thinks that the passage (in v. 1) on the music of the spheres may be taken from *Montaigne* (1, xxi.), and W. W. Lloyd is of opinion that the old *King Leir* (1594) furnished motives for a speech or two of our play.

---

[1] Elze, by the by, supposes that Shakespeare was in Italy in 1593, and to this journey he attributes the correct and vivid sketch of Venetian life and locality in our play, which he assigns to the following year (1594).

Malone laid great stress upon the likelihood of the lines, iii. 2, 48—53 :—

" Then music is
Even as the flourish when true monarchs bow
To a new crowned monarch," &c.

being suggested by the account of the Coronation of Henry IV. of France in 1594, as narrated in an English pamphlet translated from the French, and printed in London. The same commentator in his section on *King John*, reminds us that Lyly in 1592 and Ben Jonson in 1598 alluded to a fashionable affectation of sadness ; this may be compared with Antonio's peculiar disposition.

The description of Portia's suitors (cf. a similar scene in *Two Gentlemen of Verona*) has been supposed to be formed upon the proposals to Elizabeth. It may be added that the celebrated opening of Act v. Sc. 1 is (probably) imitated in the play called *Wily Beguiled*, which Mr. Fleay dates 1603, though Malone says it is alluded to by Nash in 1596.

The name Stephano, which is pronounced with an accentuated penultimate in this play, is correctly pronounced in *The Tempest;* Mr. Skottowe (*Life of Shakespeare*, vol. ii. p. 327, note) therefore thinks Shakespeare learnt the true pronunciation from the first draft of Ben Jonson's *Every Man in his Humour* (1598).

From a consideration of some of the comparisons here collected, the play will here be dated 1597—8 ; and this is supported by its being mentioned last among the comedies enumerated by Meres in 1598, and by the peculiar entry which was made in the Stationers' Register on 22 July, 1598, and which runs as follows :—

" James Robertes] a booke of the Marchaunt of Venyce, or otherwise called the Jewe of Venyse. Provided that yt be not prynted by the said James Robertes or anye other whatsoever, without licence first had from the right honourable the Lord Chamberlen."

The double name here given, seems certainly to imply
that the play was then "on the boards," and the proviso
would perhaps support this conclusion.

After what was said above with regard to an æsthetic and
metrical consideration of this play, nothing further need be
added in support of the date assigned beyond quoting
Hallam's remark that "in the language of this drama, there
is the commencement of a metaphysical obscurity, which
soon became characteristic ; but it is perhaps less observable
than in any later play." It may be added, however, that the
excellence of the play is proved by its ever-continued popularity, as well as by the fact that while Ulrici calls it "a
comedy of intrigue," Gervinus styles it "a comedy of character." The German hunt after the fundamental idea of
The Merchant of Venice is almost amusing ; Horn thinks it
is "Christian, conciliatory love," Hebler says it is "the
struggle against appearances" (cf. Gervinus), Ulrici is of
opinion that its motto is "Summum jus summa injuria,"
Rötsher thinks that the subject treated is "the dialectics of
abstract rights ;" Olze, after reviewing these opinions gives
his vote for "man's relation to wealth" (cf. Gervinus again),
while Kreyssig fairly gives up the search. English commentators, however, come to the rescue without much better
success, for while Mr. Fleay says the prevailing idea is
"Friendship," Mr. Furnivall gives it as "Vengeance over-
powered by Love and Mercy."

HAMLET.

"Reason in madness."—*King Lear.*

The sources, to which Shakespeare resorted, in writing
this celebrated drama, are :—

1. *The Historie of Hamblett,* a translation of one of
Belleforest's novels. The earliest existing edition is dated

1608; but it is known to have appeared much before that date. Belleforest was indebted to Saxo Grammaticus for the story.

2. Different passages in the play have been supposed to be founded upon parts of other works ; some of these will be mentioned below.

3. An older play upon the same subject has been thought to have existed ; the evidence for this will first be examined.

Three references to the older drama are usually quoted ; they are these : In *An Epistle to the Gentlemen Students of the Two Universities*, by Thomas Nashe (prefixed to Greene's *Arcadia*), of the date 1589, or perhaps even 1587, we have the following passage : " It is a common practice now-a-days among a sort of shifting companions that run through every art and thrive by none, to leave the trade of *Noverint* whereto they were born, and busy themselves with the endeavours of art that could scarcely latinize their neck-verse, if they should have need ; yet English *Seneca* read by candlelight yields many good sentences, as, ' Blood is a beggar,' and so forth : and if you intreat him fain in a frosty morning, he will afford you whole *Hamlets*, I should say, Handfuls of tragical speeches." [These words have even been thought to contain a personal reference to Shakespeare ; but we have no other hint of his connection with the subject at so early a date.] From an entry in Henslowe's Diary on June 9th, 1594, we learn that a play named *Hamlet* was performed at the Rose Theatre. Again, as Dr. Farmer first pointed out, Lodge in his *Wit's Miserie, or Devils Incarnate*, 1596, says one of the devils is a " foule lubber, and looks as pale as the vizard of the *ghost*, who cried so miserably at the theatre, *Hamlet, Revenge.*" But in addition to these references, the following hints seem to suggest the existence of an older play : The names Corambis and Montano (for Polonius and Reynaldo respectively) in the quarto of 1603, appear to be remnants of the earlier work ; especially if we remember that in the play *Prinz Hamlet aus Dännemark* (acted by

F 2

English players in Germany in 1603) we have a similar name
Corambus, and other marks of similarity, suggestive of a
common origin ; though it should be noted that Dr. Latham
has come to the conclusion that "the German play is the
play of Shakespeare corrupted, attenuated, shorn of its great
nobility, distorted, degraded, vulgarized " (*Two Dissertations*,
&c. p. 147). Again, the note in Henslowe's Diary, under
date July 7th, 1602, that Henry Chettle received 20 shillings
in part payment for a drama called *A Danish Tragedy*,
proves the existence of a tragedy other than Shakespeare's.
Once more, the entry made in the Stationers' Register, on
26 July, 1602, by James Roberts, although it undoubtedly
refers to the Shakespeare play ["as yt was latelie acted by
the Lord Chamberlayn his servants "], yet, by its title *The
Revenge of Hamlet*, seems to cast a glance back at the old
play mentioned by Lodge. Lastly,[1] either this old drama,
or an early draft by Shakespeare, seems to be shown, I think,
by the following facts : although the copyright of the *Hamlet*
of our author, as printed in the quartos, belonged to Ling
[for whom it was doubtless entered by Roberts], and although
it remained in the hands of Smethwicke (to whom Ling
assigned it on 19 Nov. 1607) until he joined in the publication
of the first folio, and afterwards too, for he brought out
quartos in 1631 and 1637 ; yet we find that Pavier was also
possessed of a *Historye of Hamblett*,[2] as we learn from a
transfer of his "right in Shakespeare's plays " to Edward
Brewster and Robert Birde on 4 Aug. 1626.

As to the connection of Shakespeare with the subject, the
following conclusion is arrived at by the Clarendon Press
editors : "that there was an old play on the story of *Hamlet*,
some portions of which are still preserved in the quarto of

[1] Jonson's *Cynthia's Revels* (Induction), referring to certain old plays, whose
revival on the Blackfriars stage had given great offence, speaks of "The 'umbra,'
or ghosts of some three or four plays, departed a dozen years since, have been
seen walking in your stage," &c. Perhaps one of these was *Hamlet*.

[2] That this could not have been the prose work which Pavier brought out in
1608, is proved by this mention of it among Shakespeare's *plays*, and still more
by its mention in the transference from Birde to Cotes on Nov. 8th, 1630.

1603; that about the year 1602, Shakespeare took this and began to remodel it for the stage, as he had done with other plays; that the quarto of 1603 represents the play after it had been retouched by him to a certain extent, but before his alterations were complete; and that in the quarto of 1604 we have for the first time the *Hamlet* of Shakespeare" (Preface to *Hamlet*, by Messrs. Clark and Wright), p. x. An attempt will however be made below, to throw back the first connection of our author with the play a year or two; of course, however, there were revisions of his work; this is proved by the title-page of the 1604 quarto ["Newly imprinted and enlarged to almost as much againe as it was, according to the true and perfect coppie"]; indeed Mr. Fleay claims to have proved that there was a revision after 1611; comparing some passages in a play called *Ram Alley* with lines in *Hamlet*, he says: "This shows that at the date of the acting of *Ram Alley* (published in 1611) the quarto form (Q$_2$) of *Hamlet* was acted: the alterations in the folio must be of subsequent date" (*Shakespeare Manual*, p. 19). We may here mention this critic's opinion that the early *Hamlet* of 1589 was written by Shakespeare and Marlowe in conjunction; and that portions of it can be traced in the first quarto as *Corambis' Hamlet* (*ib.* p. 41).

It was mentioned at the beginning of this section that certain parts of this play are supposed to be founded upon passages of other works; we may instance the following:—

(1) The names Marcellus, Cornelius, and Claudius (Clodius) may be due to North's *Plutarch;* and the supposition is rendered the more probable from certain classical allusions in the play, and from the fact (*vide infrà*) that Shakespeare at the time of his production of *Hamlet*, was probably reading for *Julius Cæsar.*

(2) The names of Rosencrantz and Guildenstern are found in the Council of Regency of King Christian of Denmark, the brother-in-law of James; and we may note that the

Stuart-monarch, in a letter on his wedding expedition, alludes to the carousals of the Danish court.

(3) Malone, in his *Second Appendix*, compares the celebrated expression in Act iii. Sc. 1, with these lines from Marlowe's *Edward II.*, published in 1598 :—

> " Weep not for Mortimer,
> That knows the world, and as a *traveller*
> Goes to *discover countries* yet unknown."

(4) Mr. R. Simpson, in a letter to the *Academy*, Dec. 19th, 1874, refers Act iii. Sc. 2, l. 264, " The croaking raven doth bellow for revenge," to these lines from the *True Tragedie of Richard III.* [1597 ?] :—

> *King to Lord Lovell.*
> " Methinks their ghosts come gaping for revenge,
> Whom I have slain in reaching for a crown."

> *Clarence*, &c.
> " The screeking raven sits croking for revenge,
> Whole herds of beasts come bellowing for revenge."

Mr. Furnivall, however, would refer the line in *Hamlet* to the old play mentioned by Lodge.

(5) Todd suggested that the speech of the player king is a burlesque of a passage in *The Comicale Historie of Alphonsus*, by R. G., 1599.

(6) Sir Thomas Overbury's *Characters* may have furnished Shakespeare with some lines ; for instance, his character of a " Melancholy Man " may have suggested certain points in Hamlet's character.   Compare also i. 3, 27, 28 :—

> " Do not believe his vows, for *they are brokers,*
> *Not of the dye which their investments show :* "

with Overbury's *Dissembler : " He dyeth his means and his meaning into two colours ;* he baits craft with humility, and his countenance is the picture of the present disposition. He allures, is not allured, by his affections, *for they are brokers of his observation.*"

(7) Some passages have been compared with corresponding ones in Montaigne's *Essays*. Florio's translation of these was entered at Stationers' Hall in the year 1599.

Certain passages in this play have been supposed to refer to matters of contemporary history; for instance, the well-known lines in iii. 2 about the causes of the "travelling" of the tragedians is generally allowed to be a reference to some events of the times, though it has been disputed as to what, Messrs. Clark and Wright point out, that in the 1603 quarto "the tragedians are driven to strolling because the public taste is in favour of the private plays and the acting of children; in the later quartos they are represented as being prohibited from acting in consequence of what is darkly called an 'innovation.' Both these causes are combined in the play as it stands in the folios, where the 'inhibition' and the 'aery of children'[1] are introduced to account for the tragedians having forsaken the city" (*Introduction*, p. xiii.) Malone referred the passage to the Order in Council of June, 1600; but this order was not enforced as late as the very end of 1601, when a second order was made. The Clarendon Press editors, after pointing out how often infringements were put upon stage exhibitions, and after noticing (*vide suprâ*) that the "innovation" is first referred to in the 1604 quarto, suggest that it is an allusion "to the license which had been given on 30 January, 1603—4, to the children of the Queen's Revels to play at the Blackfriars Theatre and other places." [I would draw attention to the fact that the 1603 quarto states that the play had been "divers times acted by His Highnesse servants in the Cittie of London: as also *in the two Universities of Cambridge and Oxford* AND ELSE-WHERE;" which (1) points to the "travelling" of the trage-dians, and (2) seems to require the date of the play to be thrown back a year or so. That Shakespeare was well-known as a dramatist, at Cambridge, before 1602, is proved

---

[1] The children were silenced from 1591 to 1599, when they again "berattled the common stages."

by the celebrated expression in *The Return from Parnassus*
(1602), where his superiority to Ben Jonson is so strikingly
asserted.]

Another somewhat similar passage a little further on, in
Act iii. Sc. 2, ["and let those that play your clowns speak
no more than is set down to them, &c."] has been supposed
to contain a special reference to the comedian Kemp, who is
thought (see Collier's *Memoirs*, &c.) to have deserted the
Lord Chamberlain's Company in 1600 for the Lord Admiral's
[see the Appendix on *Actors*, &c., p. 197].

Again, the allusion in the former passage, ii. 378, 379
["Do the boys carry it away? Ay, that they do, my lord ;
Hercules and his load too "] has, with great probability, been
taken as referring to the *Globe* Theatre, of which it was the
sign.   And it should be noticed that in the nearly contemporary plays of *As You Like It* and *Henry V.* similar references are made.

Mr. French, in his *Shakspereana Genealogica*, has a most
elaborate historical explanation of the *dramatis personæ ;*
and Mr. Simpson, in his paper on "the Political Use of the
Stage " (*N. S. S. Trans.*, 1874, vol. ii. p. 393), with the aid
of Mr. Mottley's *History*, finds " Burleigh " written in every
line of Polonius's face.

The account of the *Danish Carousals* in *Hamlet* has above
(p. 70) been referred to ; but it may be added that Mr.
Furnivall, in the *New Shakspere Society's Transactions* (1874,
vol. ii. pp. 512, 513) compares two passages on Danish (royal)
drunkenness from Stowe's *Annales*, under date July 14th,
1603.

Numerous allusions to, or quotations from, this play are
found in contemporary works ; it is not, however, mentioned
by Meres in 1598, and we may therefore take it as certain
that it had not appeared when the *Palladis Tamia* was
written.   The following are some of the allusions :—

(1) Mr. R. Simpson, in his edition of *A Larum for London*,
which he dates 1598 or 1599, [it was entered at Stationers'

Hall in 1600], says "that *Hamlet*, probably in the form of
the quarto of 1603, was in existence when that play was
written," and he compares passages from it with lines in
Hamlet, e.g. : "What should such fellows as I do crawling
between earth and heaven?"—(*Hamlet*, iii., 1, 129—131)
and :—

<blockquote>
"O woe is me
To have seen what I have seen, see what I see."
(iii. 1, 168, 169),
</blockquote>

compared with

<blockquote>
"What should we then do living?
Have you and I seen what we have seen,
And come to this?"
(*A Larum for London*, ed. Simpson, p. 71.)
</blockquote>

(2) A MS. note, by Gabriel Harvey, which may have
been written as early as 1598, was pointed out by Steevens.
As Malone remarked, however, it might not have been
written till 1600. It speaks of *Hamlet* as a performance
with which Harvey was well acquainted.

(3) Mr. R. Simpson, in a letter to the *Academy* on
May 8th, 1875, sees an allusion in Dekker's *Satiro-Mastix*
(written for Shakespeare's Company, and acted and published in 1602), to *Hamlet*. *Tucca* says, "My name's Hamlet
—Revenge," and he comes on the stage, "his boy after him
with two pictures under his cloak."

(4) In the *Malcontent* by Webster (before 1604) we have
the line : "Illo, ho, ho, ho ; art thou there, old Truepenny?"
which evidently refers to Hamlet's peculiar levity in the first
act.

(5) Again, in the same play, as augmented by Marston, in
1604, Sly the actor [see *Appendix*, p. 199] is introduced
quoting a line from Osrick in *Hamlet*. (J. O. Halliwell-
Phillipps.)

(6) Douce (*Illustrations*, &c. vol. ii., pp. 265, 266) quotes
the following sentence from Scoloker's *Diaphantus*, 1604 :
"Like friendly Shakespeare's tragedies where the comedian

rides, while the tragedian stands on tip-toe : faith, it should please all, like Prince Hamlet ; but in sadnesse then it would be feared he would runne mad."

(7) The same work contains several allusions to Hamlet ; cf. the line " O ! I would wear her in my heart's heart-core " with iii. 2, 77, 78 :—

> " And I will wear him
> In my heart's core, ay, in my heart of heart."

(8) In *Eastward Hoe!* by Chapman, Jonson, and Marston, 1605, one person asks another, whose name is *Hamlet*, " 'Sfoote, Hamlet, are you *mad?* "

(9) *Ratsie's Ghost* (1605) says : " I durst venture all the money in my purse on thy head to play Hamlet with him for a wager."

(10) In Dolarney's *Primrose*, by J. Reynolds, 1606 (reprinted for the Roxburgh Club in 1816) there is a singular imitation of Hamlet's soliloquy in the scene with the grave-digger ; and another stanza imitates a passage in the Ghost's address. (See the *Gentlemen's Magazine*, 1842, vol. i., p. 48.)

(11) Other references have been pointed out in later plays, such as *Philaster, Ram Alley, Two Noble Kinsmen*, &c.

A consideration of some of these references, a comparison with *Henry V., Julius Cæsar* (see p. 89), &c., seem strongly to suggest the date 1599—1600 for Shakespeare's first connection with this play ; [cf. the remark on the title-page of the 1663 quarto, as to the times and places of its performance before that year]. It was, of course, subsequently revised.

MUCH ADO ABOUT NOTHING.

" Jesters do oft prove prophets."—*King Lear.*

" Let's see: come, if it be *nothing*, I shall not need spectacles."
King Lear.

This play is generally supposed to have been written in the year 1599 or in the succeeding year; for while it is not mentioned by Meres in 1598 (unless it be granted to Mr. A. E. Brae that it is a revision of *Love's Labour Won*), it was twice entered in the Register at Stationers' Hall, in August, 1600, and a quarto edition appeared in the same year. The title-page of the quarto states that the play had been "sundrie times publikely acted;" but as the same statement is prefixed to almost every edition of Shakespeare's plays which appeared in, or after, 1600, nothing very definite can be deduced from the remark.

This date receives support from the following considerations :—

The allusion in the opening scene to a circumstance attending the campaign of the Earl of Essex in Ireland, during the summer of 1599, seems corroborated by the testimony of Camden and Moryson; see Chalmers's *Suppl. Apol.*, p. 381.

The character "Amorphus, or the one Deformed," in *Cynthia's Revels*, 1600, may be compared with "the one Deformed, a vile thief this seven year," referred to in our comedy (iii. 3, 34—38, 181—185).

The lines, iii. 1, 9—11,

" Like favorites
Made proud by princes, that advance their pride
Against that power that bred it,"

are certainly very striking and rather forced. The case of Essex, from the latter part of 1599 till his death, should of course be compared ; though Mr. Simpson (*Academy*, Sept. 25th, 1875) would refer the words to Cecil.

Turning to the sources of the play, it may be first stated that the story of the interrupted marriage, &c., may be traced to Ariosto's *Orlando Furioso*, and that this had been done into English by Beverly in 1565 [a second edition appearing in 1600] and again by Harrington in 1591. Shakespeare, however, was probably indebted to Belleforest's translation (1594) of a tale by the Italian novelist Bandello ; though it should be added that there are several indications that he may have consulted some old drama, or other work, on the same subject ; it has been pointed out, for instance, by Cohn, that Jacob Ayrer's *Beautiful Phœnicia* is also founded upon Bandello's tale, while it has, in common with *Much Ado About Nothing*, some points not met with in the story. Professor Ward (*u. s.*, p. 403) says : " As the date of Ayrer's piece is not known—it may have been written before or after 1600—and as that of Shakspere's is similarly uncertain, it is impossible to decide as to their relative priority. That, however, Ayrer did not copy from Shakspere seems, as Simrock points out, clear from the names of the characters in his play which follow Bandello, while Shakspere has changed all the names except those of Don Pedro and old Leonato."

Steevens thought that the instructions which Dogberry and Verges give to the watch might "be intended as a burlesque on *The Statutes of the Streets*, imprinted by Wolfe, in 1595 ;" I may add that Dogberry calls them "the Statues." There is no doubt an allusion to these celebrated characters in the following extract from the Induction to Ben Jonson's *Bartholomew Fair* (1614) : "*I am an ass! I! . . . .* as though it had cost him *nothing!* and then a substantial watch to have stolen in upon them, and taken them away, with mistaking words, as the fashion is in the stage practice ;" though it should be added that the watch-men were a favourite object of ridicule then-a-days.

It has been conjectured that this play may have some reference to the difficulty of inducing the Earl of Pembroke to "marry and settle."

The assumed date is confirmed if we observe the advance upon some of the earlier comedies ; notice the brilliancy and polish of the wit of the ladies and gentlemen introduced, and contrast Beatrice and Benedick with Rosaline and Birowne ; mark, too, how, while the clown, or fool, is avoided, the most delightful fun is caused by the introduction of the incomparable watchmen.   Again, the mixture of comedy and tragedy is managed with fine effect ; " Perhaps," says Hazlitt, "the middle point of comedy was never more nicely hit, in which the ludicrous blends with the tender, and our follies, turning round against themselves, in support of our affections, retain nothing but their humanity ; " whilst, it may be added, as to the tragical catastrophe (which in less skilful hands might easily have been too severe) the edge is taken off by our foreknowledge of the heroine's innocence.

As to the style, it may be remarked that while at times it has the appearance of comparatively early manner (see, for instance, Act v., Sc. 3 ; though this may be due to the fact that the company, at the time of the production of this drama, evidently had a good musician or two), at other times the diction is of the highest order (see, for instance, Act iv., Sc. 1, lines 226—232, than which Shakespeare never wrote anything finer).

The metrical tests tell the same tale ; the double endings place it comparatively early, the rhymes put it later ; while the classical allusion test gives doubtful results.

AS YOU LIKE IT.

"The green leaves quiver with the cooling wind,
And make a chequered shadow on the ground."
Titus Andronicus.

There can scarcely be a doubt that this play was produced in the year 1599, as the following remarks will show :—

It is not mentioned by Meres in 1598; it was entered (with a proviso) on the Stationers' Register on August 4th, 1600 (the year of the entry is not given, but there can be no doubt about it). In iv. 1, 154, 155, we have the expression "I will weep for nothing, *like Diana in the fountain;*" as Malone pointed out, this doubtless refers to a statue mentioned by Stowe, in the first edition of his *Survey of London*, 1598, as set up in that year in Cheapside; in the second edition of the same work in 1603, he tells us that the statue of Diana was then decayed ; the allusion would of course be "telling" in 1599. Malone also pointed out the lines, iii. 5, 82, 83 :

"Dead shepherd, now I find thy saw of might,
'Who ever loved, that loved not at first sight?'"

The line quoted in this extract is from Marlowe's *Hero and Leander*, where we find :

"Where both deliberate, the love is slight.
Who ever loved, that loved not at first sight?"

Hero and Leander was first printed (as completed by Chapman) in 1598, five years after Marlowe's death.

In reference to the celebrated lines, in Act ii. Sc. 7, beginning "All the world's a stage," it may be remarked that the sentence "Totus mundus agit histrionem" is said to have been inscribed over the Globe Theatre, and it might almost be imagined that the opening of that house in the end of 1599 was quickly followed by the play containing these appropriate lines.

A tradition says that Shakespeare supported a character (Adam) in this drama ; now as the only definite records of his acting [viz. : in *Every Man in His Humour* (1598) and *Sejanus* (1603)] give just the same limits as those in the remarks on the sentence "like Diana in the Fountain," we may make somewhat the same deduction.

The plot of this play is taken from a novel by Thomas Lodge, entitled *Rosalynde, Euphues' Golden Legacie,* &c. Mr. Collier has noticed that the editions, which appeared between 1592 and 1598, have not the name Rosalynde on the title-page ; whilst in the 1598 and in subsequent editions it reappears ; the reason he assigns is that the success of Rosalind in *As You Like It* caused the reproduction of what would be an attractive title. But is it not more probable, considering the remarks made above upon the date, that Shakespeare was using one of the new editions? It is perhaps reasoning in a circle to say it, but this seems to add another proof of the correctness of the ordinarily received date.

Touchstone, in Act v. Sc. 4, in his remarks upon quarrels and lies, apparently refers to Saviolo's *Treatise on Honour and Honourable Quarrels,* 1595 ; some "books for good manners" (to which the same "rare fellow" perhaps alludes a little further on in the scene) have also been pointed out of a somewhat earlier date.

Tieck thought the title of this comedy might be due to the last line in the epilogue to *Cynthia's Revels* (1600) ; this would, however, clash with the date assumed above, as well as with an endeavour made, in the Appendix (p. 177), to show that Ben Jonson in writing that epilogue had our author in view. The title may be due, as Simrock thinks, to Lodge's prefatory remark " If you like it, so ;" or to a remark, in Shakespeare's own epilogue, "like as much of this play as please you."

Tieck also thought that Jacques was akin to Asper, Ben Jonson's portrait of himself in *Every Man Out of Hi Humour,* 1599.

Several works published in the year 1594, contain passages parallel to some in this play :

(1) "And thou, thrice-crowned queen of night, survey
     With thy chaste eye, from thy pale sphere above," &c.
                                        (iii., 2, 3, 4.)

Compare the following lines, from one of Chapman's Hymns *In Cynthiam* (1594) :

"Nature's bright *eye-sight*, and the *Night's* fair soul,
 That *with thy triple forehead* dost control
 Earth, seas, and hell."

(2) "Sans teeth, sans eyes, sans taste, sans everything."
                                        (ii., 7, 166.)

Compare the following lines from Garnier's *Henriade* (1594) :

"Sans pieds, sans mains, sans nez, sans oreilles, sans yeux,
 Meurtri de toutes parts."

(3) The name Celia may be due to some *Sonnets to the Fairest Celia*, by W. Percy (1594). The same character in Lodge is called "Alinda."

(4) The allusion to Gargantua, in ii. 2, 238, may be due to "a booke entitled the *Historie of Gargantua*," entered in the Stationers' Register in 1594. (There is a somewhat similar entry in 1592; and an English translation of Rabelais's work had appeared in 1575.)

(5) "And so, from hour to hour, ripe and ripe ;
     And then, from hour to hour, we rot and rot,
     And thereby hangs a tale."—(ii., 7, 26, 27.)

may be a parody on the following lines in T. Kyd's *Spanish Tragedy* (published 1594) :

"At last it grew and grew, and bore and bore,
 Till at length it grew a gallows."

Some of these allusions are due to Mr. J. O. Halliwell-Phillipps.

Mr. W. W. Lloyd (*Critical Essays*, &c., p. 112) thinks that the contemporaneity of *The Merchant of Venice* and *As You Like It* is suggested by Portia's remarks to Nerissa on their intended disguise (iii. 4, 60—76); especially as "the scheme of impersonation is so different to that really carried out." The contiguity of the two plays in the folio edition may also be noticed.

Chalmers sees one or two imaginary historical allusions in the play, and points out that it is imitated by Drayton in *The Owl*, 1604.

The various metrical tests (for example, the rhyme-test and the double-ending test) relatively confirm the assignment of this play to the last year of the sixteenth century; and, as Mr. Hallam remarks, "in no other play do we find the bright imagination and fascinating grace, of Shakespeare's youth so mingled with the thoughtfulness of his maturer age." Following up another remark of the same writer's, the Rev. C. E. Moberly (Rugby Edition of this play) thinks that "*As You Like It* was one of the earliest attempts of the poet to control the dark spirit of melancholy in himself, by a process which a great writer [Johnson (*Boswell*, 1776)] has described as hopeless, that of thinking it away;" but surely the general impression received by perusing this delightful play (which Professor Wilson has termed *The Romance of the Forest*) is anything but sad or sorrowful; Adversity here is not a Fury, she is a fourth Grace [see *Guesses at Truth*], and if it be Jacques, upon whom the hypothesis is built, better would it be to clothe him, as Ulrici does, in motley, than to miss for one moment the graceful charm of Rosalind ("who after Portia is the most gifted of Shakespeare's heroines," and "who, in the true spirit of comedy, is rightly made the centre-piece" of the drama), or to lose for one second the delightful freshness of those Arden glades, of which Gray doubtless thought when he wrote among his lines on Shakespeare in his *Ode on the Progress of Poesy:*

G

"This pencil take (she said) whose colours clear
Richly paint the vernal year."

Professor Dowden (*ut supra*, p. 76) says : "Shakspere, when
he had completed his English historical plays, needed rest
for his imagination ; and in such a mood, craving refresh-
ment and recreation, he wrote his play of *As You Like It*.
To understand the spirit of this play, we must bear in mind
that it was written immediately after Shakspere's great series
of histories, ending with *Henry V.* (1599), and before he
began the great series of tragedies. Shakspere turned with
a sense of relief, and a long easeful sigh, from the oppressive
subjects of history, so great, so real, so massive, and found
rest," &c., in this comedy. [An attempt will, however, be
made in the Appendix on "Classical allusions," to show that
As You Like It preceded *Henry V.*]

HENRY V.

"True nobility is exempt from fear."—2 *Henry VI.*

The date of this play can be fixed by the striking historical
allusion in the chorus to Act v. ; it has indeed been asserted
by Pope, Warburton, Chalmers, and others, that the choruses
and some other parts of the drama were inserted at a later
period ; this conclusion they ground on the omissions in the
quartos, and on supposed historical references (see Chalmers's
Supplemental Apology, vol. ii., pp. 334—343) ; but let any
one consider the important relation which these choruses
bear to the rest of the play (a point which Garrick felt when,
in his production of the drama, he himself recited them), and
notice the intimate connection between them and the body
of the work [could any one, for instance, suppose that the
chorus to Act iii. can be separated from the spirited scene
which opens that act ?], and the conclusion must surely be

that the whole was written at the same time. At any rate, the allusion above referred to was penned in the summer of 1599; it is this :

> "Were now the general of our gracious empress,
> (As in good time he may,) from Ireland coming,
> Bringing rebellion broached on his sword,
> How many would the peaceful city quit,
> To welcome him !"—Act v. Prologue, l. 30—34.

Camden (*Kennet*, vol. ii., p. 614) tells us that "about the end of March [1599] the Earl of Essex set forward for Ireland, and was accompanied out of London with a fine appearance of nobility, and gentry, and the most cheerful huzzas of the common people." Chalmers points out, too, as a proof of the popular applause with which the allusion would be received, that the Queen at the same time issued a Proclamation "declaring her princely resolution, in sending over of her army into the realm of Ireland," and ordered a Public Prayer "for the good success of her Majesty's forces" there.

Essex returned, disappointed and disgraced, in the following September.

The play [which, by the by, is not mentioned by Meres in 1598] had indeed been promised in the Epilogue of 2 *Henry IV.;* but a comparison of the plan there laid down and of the details here presented will show that some considerable period must have elapsed between the production of these two plays.

On consulting the Stationers' Register, we find, August 4th [1600], the entry "Henry the Ffift, a book," with the injunction that this and the two others are "to be staied;" again under August 14th, 1600, we have "Thos. Paryer] *The Historye of Henrye the Vth. with the Battel of Agencourt.*" In the same year (1600), T. Creede printed, for T. Millington and T. Busbie, a quarto edition of *Henry V.;* and, in 1602, the same printer produced another quarto, which was published by T. Pavier ; a third appeared in 1608. These, however, are all mangled editions, and it may be added, in support of the argument mentioned above, that the author's name does not appear upon the title-page.

In writing the play, Shakespeare made use of Holinshed's *Chronicle*, and an old play called *The Famous Victories of Henry the Fifth;* this, as Collier states (in his *Six Old Plays*, &c.), was acted prior to 1588, was probably published in 1594, and was certainly printed in 1598 : he notes, too, that a *Henry the Fifth* is entered in Henslowe's *Diary*, Nov. 25th, 1595.

In the prologue to Ben Jonson's *Every Man in his Humour* [the play was ¡ written in 1598, but the prologue was not added till after 1601], there seems to be an allusion to *Henry V.;* the lines are :—

> " He rather prays, you will be pleased to see
> One such, to-day, as other plays should be ;
> *Where neither chorus wafts you o'er the seas*," &c.

Again, in the same dramatist's *Poetaster*, 1601, some passages in our play seem to be ridiculed (see p. 177).

Chalmers, in endeavouring to antedate the drama by a year or two, refers :—

(1) The Archbishop of Canterbury's speech concerning the Bill about Church property (i. 1, 1—19), to the two Church Property Bills submitted to Parliament in November, 1597.

(2) Certain remarks about the French and Scots, to events which happened in the same year : and

(3) Falstaff's dying remark about "devils incarnate," (ii. 3, 33, 34), to Lodge's *Devils Incarnate*, which appeared in 1596.

At the beginning of the section upon this play, attention was drawn to the striking and peculiar adoption of the chorus in the drama, and the point will be again referred to in the Appendix upon the *Prologues*, &c.; so that it need only be here added that Hartley Coleridge says : " Of all Shakespeare's dramas, *Henry V.* is, in its serious parts, the least truly dramatic ; it abounds above all his work, in description" [*Marginalia*, ii. p. 60] ; while Schlegel remarks that the choruses "unite epic pomp and solemnity with lyrical sublimity."

Æsthetic critics of Shakespeare have repeatedly remarked how fascinated he seems to have been by the character of Henry V., who is perhaps his ideal of highest manhood, or rather, to adopt Dowden's correction of Gervinus, of highest *practical* manhood ; and they have observed how fitting a climax it is to the grand series of historical plays of which it is, chronologically, the last.

JULIUS CÆSAR.

" A way, I think, to liberty."—Cymbeline.

The older commentators, Malone, Chalmers, and Drake, unanimously dated this play in the year 1607, and this date was generally accepted till comparatively lately ; gradually, however, the chronological connection of this with the other Roman plays was severed ; Gervinus dwelt upon the internal connection with *Hamlet;* Craik, by a metrical test, showed its priority to *Antony and Cleopatra*, and *Coriolanus;* Collier and Halliwell by their researches showed its early date.

An allusion, which was first pointed out by Mr. Halliwell-Phillipps, may as well be at once given. He says (Introduction to *Julius Cæsar*) that this play was written by Shakespeare "in or before the year 1601, as appears from the following lines in Weaver's *Mirror of Martyrs*, printed in that year, lines which unquestionably are to be traced to a

recollection of Shakespeare's drama, not to that of the
history as given by Plutarch :—

> " The many-headed multitude were drawne
> By Brutus' speech, that Cæsar was ambitious :
> When eloquent Mark Antonie had showne
> His virtues, who but Brutus then was vicious ? "

I have myself noticed the following apparent allusion to
a passage in this play, in a collection of poems on the death
of Elizabeth entitled *Sorrowes Joy*, published by John Legat
in 1603 :—

> " UPON THE DEATH OF OUR LATE QUEENE.
> They say a *comet* woöteth to appeare,
> When *Princes* baleful destinie is neare ;
> So *Julius* starre was *seene* with fiery crest,
> Before his fall to *blaze* among the rest ; " &c.

With this extract compare the lines 31, 32 in Act ii. Scene
2 of *Julius Cæsar :—*

> " When beggars die there are no *comets seen ;*
> The heavens themselves *blaze* forth the death of *princes*."

There are several plays upon the subject of Cæsar published about this time ; some of these, and especially Lord
Stirling's (though there do not seem to be any grounds for
the assumption), have been thought to throw light either
upon the production, or upon the reproduction of Shakespeare's tragedy ; the following is a list of them :—

Julius Cæsar, acted at Whitehall, Feb. 1st, 1562.

Cæsar and Pompey, mentioned by Stephen Gosson, in
1579.

Epilogus Cæsaris Interfecti, by Dr. Richard Eades, acted
in Oxford in 1582.

The Tragedy of Cæsar and Pompey ; or, Cæsar's Revenge
[Malone speaks of two editions, one of 1607, and " one
without date but probably earlier ; in the running title it is
called *The Tragedy of Julius Cæsar ;* perhaps the better to

impose it on the public for the performance of Shakespeare."
Craik says it "appears to have been first produced in 1594"
(see Henslowe's *Diary*, by Collier, p. 44)].

Cæsar's Fall. From Henslowe's *Diary*, we learn that
Munday, Drayton (*vide infra*), Webster, and others were
jointly engaged upon a play of this name in 1602.

Julius Cæsar, by William Alexander, afterwards Lord
Stirling ; printed in Scotland in 1604, in London in 1607.

Julius Cæsar, a droll or puppet-show, mentioned by
Marston in 1605, and by Jonson in 1609.

Cæsar's Tragedy, mentioned in the Vertue MS., as acted
at court before the 10th of April, 1613. "This (says Malone)
was probably Shakespeare's *Julius Cæsar*, it being much
the fashion at that time to alter the titles of his plays ; "
cf. *Henry VIII.*, &c.

But there is no proof that Shakespeare owed anything to
any of these plays ; and the numerous allusions in his works
to Cæsar, show that he often thought upon the subject.
I have endeavoured above (see Introduction) by the aid of
these allusions to arrange the relative positions of certain
of the plays.

The following apparent references to phrases or scenes
in our drama may now be noticed.

In *A Warning for Fair Women*, printed 1599, occur the
following lines :—

> "I have given him fifteen wounds,
> Which will be fifteen mouths that do accuse me ;
> In every mouth there is a bloody tongue,
> Which will speak although he holds his peace."

With this compare :—

> ["Show you sweet Cæsar's wounds, poor poor dumb mouths ;
> . . . . And put a tongue
> In every wound of Cæsar."—(iii. 2, 229, 232).

In Dr. Eades's Latin play ; in *The True Tragedie of
Richard, Duke of Yorke*, first printed in 1595 [though it may

be here noted the expression is not retained in 3 *Henry VI.*];
in the *Mirrour of Magistrates;* the celebrated exclamation
" Et tu, Brute !" is found. It is not in Plutarch. We also
find in a poem by S. Nicholson, entitled *Acolastus his
Afterwit*, printed in 1600, we have the line : " Et tu, Brute !
Wilt thou stab Cæsar too ?" (This is pointed out by Craik,
The English of Shakespeare, p. 224.)

In Drayton's *Barons' Wars*, 1603 (a version of *Morte-
merias*, 1596, *in which the passage does not appear*) there are
some lines similar to v. 1, 73—75 :—[1]

" His life was gentle, and the elements," &c.

That Drayton borrowed the expressions from Shakespeare
is rendered certain by the still greater resemblance in the
edition of 1619. With iv. 3, 218—221 :—

" There is a tide in the affairs of men,
Which taken at the flood leads on to fortune :
Omitted, all the voyage of their life
Is bound in shallows and in miseries,"

compare Bacon, *Advancement of Learning*, 1605 : " In the
third place, I set down reputation, because of the peremptory
tides and currents it hath, which if they be not taken in due
time, are seldom recovered ; it being extremely hard to play
at an aftergame of reputation."

Malone pointed out that the celebrated quarrel scene
between Brutus and Cassius is imitated in Beaumont and
Fletcher's *Maid's Tragedy*, cir. 1608. It has several times
been suggested that *Julius Cæsar* was written not without
reference to the rebellion of the Earl of Essex ; and Mr.
Furnivall (in a letter to *The Academy*, Sept. 18th, 1875)
" would note how closely Shakespeare's *Julius Cæsar* (1601)
would come home to the ears and hearts of [a] London
audience of 1601, after the favourite's outbreak against his

[1] Cf. also Ben Jonson's *Cynthia's Revels* (1600), "a creature of a most perfect
and divine temper; one in whom the humours and elements are generally met
without emulation of prophecy" (ii. 3).

sovereign. 'Et tu, Brute!' would mean more to them than to us.   Indeed it is possible that the conspiracy against Elizabeth may have made Shakspere choose 1601 as the time for producing, if not writing, his great tragedy, with its fruitful lesson of conspirators' ends."

As before remarked, Craik and others have given reasons for assigning this play to a much earlier date than the other Roman plays ; and the same point is conclusively proved by the "weak-ending" test (see Prof. Ingram's statistics) ; while it is confirmed by the position of the plays as arranged in the folio edition.   As to the other metrical tests, the evidence is to a certain extent divided ; and Mr. Fleay, while admitting an early date for the production of the play (1600), argues that it must have been revised and "abridged for theatrical purposes."   [This, he thinks, was done by Ben Jonson.]   " The paucity of rhymes, the number of short lines, and the brevity of the play are conclusive as to its not having been produced in its present state at that date " (Fleay).   Mr. Fleay also thinks that 'the play was brought out a second time in 1607, and in an abridged form, as we have it, after 1613.

The great similarity of style between this play and *Hamlet* and *Henry V.* has been pointed out by Gervinus, Spedding, Dowden, Hales, and others, and, I suppose, must have been felt by nearly every reader.   It is not only shown by the many allusions to Cæsar in these plays [allusions, by the by, which show a co-ordinate estimation of his character] but by "the minor relations" of these plays.   This point is so strong that, taking into consideration some of the references mentioned above, there can scarcely be any doubt that the original production of this play must be placed in 1599—1600. It may have been revised afterwards, and the appearance of several works bearing similar titles in 1607 suggests, as Mr. Fleay says, its reproduction at that date.

88 .

MERRY WIVES OF WINDSOR.

" Hence this Jack, and whip him."—Antony and Cleopatra.

The reasons which favour an early date may first be stated (1592 or 1593) ; they are due to Mr. Halliwell, C. Knight and others. [It may be premised that a subsequent revision is admitted, and that a quarto edition (of what is generally thought to be a first sketch) appeared in 1602]. Remembering the Elizabeth tradition (*vide infra*), attention is drawn to the festivities, including masques, given by the Queen at Windsor Castle at the commencement of 1593 (compare iii. 2, 63).

Again in 1592, Duke Frederick of Würtemburg and Teck visited Windsor, and the fact that free-post horses had been granted to him, through a pass of Lord Howard's, seems to be alluded to in a short, but peculiar, scene (the 3rd) of Act iv.

Reference is also made to the Duke, in iv. 5, 72, in connection with the impositions practised upon the host of the Garter by some German travellers, which facts are also referred to about the same period. [I may add that the allusion in this passage, "the three Doctor Faustuses," as well as the mention, in i. 1, 132, of Mephistopheles, would have more point at an early date than later on.[1]]

Malone contended that the line (i. 3, 89), "Sail like thy pinnace to *those golden shores*," shows that the earliest edition was written after Sir Walter Raleigh's return from Guiana in 1596 ; but Mr. Knight answers that the line quoted contains only a general statement, while certain lines subsequently inserted (*e.g.*, i. 3, 76, "She is a region in Guiana,

[1] I may take this occasion, too, of noting that, in iv. 5, 69, a local allusion, as well as a pun, is lost in all editions of Shakespeare, by not printing the word "Slough" with a capital letter. Cf. the mention of Windsor, Eton, Maidenhead, Reading, and Colebrook in adjacent passages.

all gold and bounty," which appears in F₁, but not in Q₁,)
show that the sketch was written before Raleigh's return ;
the finished play after Guiana was known and talked of.

Again, Chalmers contends that *The Faery Queen*, 1596,
is "plainly" alluded to in several places ; but here, also,
Mr. Knight answers that there are only *general* allusions to
fairies in the early sketch, while in the folio edition *The
Faery Queen* is three times presented to the audience as a
familiar name.

It may be added that the resemblance in this play to
Lyly's *Endimion* (1591) [iv. 3, *Song by Fairies*, pointed out
by Prof. Ward, *ut suprà*, p. 165, note 2] would be more
pointed at an early date.

Before proceeding further, it may be remarked that
Chalmers, who was strongly of opinion that this comedy
preceded the plays on Henry IV., in arguing for the date
1596, urged, beside the above allusion, his favourite reference to Lodge's *Incarnate Devils*, 1596 ; cf. v. 5, 20—24,
where, says Chalmers, "the' very language" of the Devil
Luxury is quoted.

The *sources* of the play do not aid us in settling the
chronology of the play ; unless, indeed, they be held to
favour the early date ; they are, as Mr. Malone pointed out
(*Appendix I.*, pp. 689—697) the story of *The Two Lovers
of Pisa* in Tarlton's *News of Purgatorie* ["about 1590,"
Halliwell] ; and, it may be, *The Fishwife's Tale of Brainford*
in *Westward for Smelts*, though this was not published till
1620 (or according to Steevens, 1603).

Much discussion has arisen as to the relative (chronological) order of this comedy, and the historical plays in
which Falstaff appears ; it has been contended that *The
Merry Wives* must have preceded 2 *Henry IV.*, in which
the fat knight is disgraced, and it has been still more strongly
urged that it must have been produced before *Henry V.*
in which Falstaff's death is recorded. But it is now pretty
generally agreed that the inconsistencies as to the characters

which are common to this comedy and to the historical
plays are so great, that *The Merry Wives* cannot be considered as one of the *Henry IV.* and *V.* series ; so that it
must, to a great extent, be considered independently ; still
the appearance of Falstaff in the comedy is almost un-
deniably that of a *known* character,[1] and the first and second
parts of *Henry IV.* are so intimately connected together[2]
and so evidently were almost contemporary, that it seems
impossible to consider *The Merry Wives* as anterior to either
of these parts. The question then remains, whether the
comedy preceded or succeeded *Henry V.?* As remarked
above, it is perhaps impossible to answer this question by a
mere comparison of the characters common to the two
plays ; but the following considerations seem to justify us
in assigning the priority to *The Merry Wives*, and dating it
1598—1599.

The epilogue of 2 *Henry IV.* had promised a continuation
of the story "with Sir John" in it : now, it is scarcely
possible that that epilogue can be Shakespeare's, so that we
must not press too closely the details of the promise
there made ; still some weight must be allowed to that
statement, and perhaps also to the tradition that the Queen
had desired to see Falstaff in love. The grand historical
play of *Henry V.*, with its marvellous use of the chorus
(which Garrick so well appreciated), of course precluded the
combination of "Sir John" and French affairs which the
epilogue promised, so that we cannot wonder that Shakespeare separated the comedy from the history ; and that *The
Merry Wives* came out before *Henry V.* seems proved,
among other reasons, by the following point : Sir Hugh
Evans, in Act iii. Sc. 1, jumbles up, in his singing, part of
an excellent pastoral song of Marlowe's with a line or two
from the old version of the 137th Psalm. Misled perhaps

---

[1] And notice that he is here *Falstaff* pure and simple. No hint, external or
internal, speaks of Sir John Oldcastle.

[2] See page 54.

by this quotation, William Jaggard, when he brought out *The Passionate Pilgrim* in 1599, included *Live with Me and be My Love*, as one of Shakespeare's productions ; the following year (1600), however, it was rightly attributed to Marlowe in the collection of poems, entitled *England's Helicon*. This seems to suggest that *The Merry Wives* had been brought out early in 1599, or late in the preceding year. And this date is supported by a general consideration of the style and versification of the play, for while (as Warton says) it is perhaps "the most complete specimen of Shakespeare's comic powers," and while (as Dr. Johnson observes) "it is remarkable for the variety of its characters," still there are several points about the comedy that prevent us from placing it too late in the chronological order ; Lloyd notices, for instance, "the little hint there is, of any subjective difference between the pair of merry wives," and in spite of the marks of "maturity of power, the little scope there is for full play of the power."

That this comedy was revised in the reign of King James is evident from the following alterations and additions, as shown by a comparison of the quarto and folio editions.

(1) Chalmers says that in the amended edition, Slender is altered from a swaggerer to a simpleton in accordance with the act of Parliament (3 Jac. I. c. 21) for "preventing the abuse of the holy Name of God."

(2) The same commentator thought that Mrs. Page's remark : " I will exhibit a Bill in Parliament " (ii. 1, 30) was a " sarcasm on the many bills which were unadvisedly moved in the Parliament which began Nov. 5th, 1605, and ended May 26th, 1606."

Malone, also, called attention to the following points :—

(3) ii. 2, 63, " When the court lay at Windsor " may refer to July 1603 : it was usually held at Greenwich in the summer.

(4) ii. 2, 66, " Coach after coach " is hardly likely to have been used before coaches came into *general use* in 1605 ; [but Chalmers demurs to this date].

(5) i. 1, 112, 113, "You complain of me to the *council*," (afterwards altered to "*the king*") supports the statement made above.

(6) ii. 1, 79, "These knights will hack," may have reference to the numbers knighted by James on his way from Scotland to his new metropolis.

(7) i. 1, 91—99, with the line "I heard say he was outrun on Cotsall," may be an insertion, containing an allusion to the founding (or the reviving) of the Cotswold games by Mr. Dover.

These alterations and insertions certainly seem to prove an amended edition in King James's reign, but there is nothing to particularise the year in which the comedy was revised.

For the registration and publication of the play, see *Appendix* (pp. 179, 180). ·

TWELFTH NIGHT; OR, WHAT YOU WILL.

"What a brawling dost thou keep."—1 *Henry IV*.

"They'll so whip me with their keen jests."
Merry Wives of Windsor.

The older commentators classed this play among Shakespeare's latest works; the reason assigned, besides the perfection of style in certain parts, being supposed allusions to various contemporary events. These need not be mentioned, for they can be found in Malone, Chalmers, or Drake; they are very general, and the date is now known to be earlier. In the diary of a member of the Middle Temple (John Manningham), discovered by Mr. Hunter, we find the following memorandum :—

"Feby. 2, 1601 [2]. At one feast we had a play called *Twelfth Night, or What You Will*, much like the *Comedy of Errors* or *Menechmi* in Plautus; but most like and near to that in Italian, called *Inganni.* A good practice in it to make the steward believe," &c.

The beginning of 1602 is thus an undoubted *terminus ad quem;* while in the other direction a limit is supplied as well by the non-mention in Meres, as by the allusion in the following passage in the play : " He does smile his face into *more lines* that is in *the new map with the augmentation of the Indies*" (iii. 2, 84—86) ; there is here, as Steevens pointed out, " a clear reference to a map engraved for Linschoten's *Voyages,* an English translation of which was published in 1598. This map is *multilineal* in the extreme, and is the first in which the East Indies are included."

Mr. Hunter, in his *New Illustrations,* &c., was of opinion that the treatment of Malvolio, in Act iv. Sc. 2, was fou....'~d upon the exposure of the exorcism practised by the Puritans (who, by the by, are held up to so much ridicule in this comedy) by Dr. Harsnet, in his tract *A Discovery of the Fraudulent Practices of John Darrel,* 1599. It should be remembered that Shakespeare undoubtedly consulted another of this writer's tracts, when, a few years after, he was preparing his *Lear.* But, again, the following passage from the end of Act iii. Sc. 1, of Ben Jonson's *Every Man Out of His Humour,* 1599, has been supposed to furnish another posterior limit for the date :—

" The argument of his comedy might have been of some other nature, as of a duke to be in love with a countess, and that countess to be in love with the duke's son, and the son to love the lady's waiting-maid ; some such cross wooing, with a clown to be their serving-man, better than to be thus near, and familiarly allied to the time."

This could scarcely, however, refer to our play, if we consider the time and the place of the performance of Ben Jonson's piece, as well as the generality of the remarks on the one hand, and the want of agreement in detail (with *Twelfth Night*) on the other.

We have above remarked that the Puritans are held up to

some ridicule in this play (and the same may be said of the nearly contemporary *All's Well that Ends Well*). Now it has been pointed out that in 1600 the puritanical city magistrates obtained an order from the Privy Council restricting stage performances. In these passages then, and in the character of Malvolio, we may have some good-humoured and gentle retaliation (see W. W. Lloyd, *Essays*, &c., p. 155, 156).

In Act iii. Sc. 2, Sir Toby Belch, when urging Sir Andrew to send a challenge to Viola, says : "if thou *thou'st* some thrice, it shall not be amiss ;" Theobald and others see in this advice, which, by the by, Aguecheek follows, an allusion to Cooke's insulting remarks at Raleigh's trial : "at thy instigation, thou viper, for I *thou* thee, thou traitor ; " but the reference is in itself unlikely, and is of course put out of court by Manningham's memorandum.

The line, i. 5, 275 :—

" With groans that thunder love, with sighs of fire,"

may be intended to satirize a passage in Lodge's *Rosalynde*, (which we know Shakespeare had so lately used) :—

> " The winds of my deep sighs
> That thunder still for nought."

Guided by some of these allusions, and especially by Manningham's detailed description of what was apparently a comparatively new play in the beginning of 1602, the play will here be assigned to the year 1601 ; a conclusion which we shall find is supported by a consideration of the style and versification. It should, however, be here remarked that Mr. Fleay, in his paper on "Certain Plays of Shakespeare of which portions were written at different periods of his life" (*N. S. S. Trans.*, 1874, vol. ii.) has included this comedy, parts of which he assigns to the year 1593—4, chiefly on account of the freshness of style they exhibit. These views are combated in the *Transactions* referred to ;

and we may quote the following extract from a letter to the *Academy* of June 20th, 1874, by Mr. C. Eliot Browne, who supplied fresh evidence that no part of *Twelfth Night* was written before 1598.

" Shakspeare was, probably, indebted for the names of the heroines of *Twelfth Night* to the first part of Emanuel Forde's *Parismus, the Renowned Prince of Bohemia*, Lond. 1598, for neither Olivia nor Viola occurs in the *Ingannati* from which Shakspeare is believed to have borrowed the plot. In the romance, Olivia is Queen of Thessaly ; and Violetta, the name of a lady, who unknown to her lover, disguises herself as a page to follow him, and she also, like Viola, is shipwrecked. If this conjecture be correct, the negative evidence that *Twelfth Night* was written after 1598 afforded by its omission in Meres's list is confirmed."

Mr. Browne then gives one or two other reasons for thinking that Shakespeare was acquainted with the romance in question.

The reasons which Mr. Fleay brings forward in favour of an early date for parts of this play, will probably, apart from considerations urged above, convince us that the very late date formerly assigned must be wrong ; whilst, on the other hand, the opinion of those commentators, in so far as it was grounded upon a study of the style, will favour the date assumed in a former part of this section.

TROILUS AND CRESSIDA.

" Tragical—comical—historical."—*Hamlet.*

" O above-measure false ! "—*Cymbeline.*

In a play which presents so much difficulty as this, it is perhaps best to commence by stating simply the external evidence, which bears, or is supposed to bear, upon the subject.

H

1599. From entries in Henslowe's Diary, it appears that Dekker and Chettle were preparing a drama, which was at first called *Troyelles and Cresseda*,[1] but afterwards *The Tragedy of Agamemnon*. This was licensed by the Master of the Revels, on June 3rd, 1599.

1603. Feb. 3rd. The Stationers' Register has the following entry :—

" Mr. Roberts]. The booke of Troilus and Cresseda, as yt is acted by my Lo. Chamberlens men."

1609. Jan. 28th. The same source supplies us with the following record :—

" Rich. Bonion and Hen. Whalleys] entered, &c., a booke called, the History of Troylus and Cressula."

1609. In the same year there appeared two quartos ; the difference of the title-pages should be noticed :—

Q_1 " The Famous Historie of Troylus and Cresseid. Excellently expressing the beginning of their Loves, with the conceited wooing of Pandarus, Prince of Lucia. Written by William Shakespeare. Imprinted by G. Eld, for R. Bonian and H. Walley, 1609." [This Quarto contains a very remarkable Preface, which says, among other things, " You have here a new play, never staled with the stage, never clapper-clawed with the palms of the vulgar, and yet passing full of the palm comical . . . . Refuse not, nor like this the less for not being sullied with the smoky breath of the multitude ; but thank fortune for the scope it hath had amongst you, since by the grand possessors' wills I believe you should have prayed for them rather than been prayed."]

Q_2 [Same title as Q_1, but the word *Famous* is omitted, while the following is added, " As it was acted by the King's Majesties Servants at the Globe."]

No other edition appeared until the folio came out in 1623.

---

[1] Mr. Fleay says, Dekker and Chettle's *Troylus and Cressida* was written in 1592, and reproduced in a revised form as *Agamemnon* in 1599. But he does not give his authority for the statement.

The position, pagination, and title of the play in this volume deserve notice ; on inspection it will be noticed that the last page but one of *Romeo and Juliet*, among the *tragedies*, is numbered 76, and that the last page is numbered 79. Now, as Knight pointed out, *Troilus and Cressida* (although still styled "a tragedy") is placed at the end of the *histories*, and is not paged at all, with the exception of the second and third pages which are numbered 79 and 80. This seems to show that it had been intended to follow *Romeo and Juliet*, which it would exactly do, if the last page of that play had been correctly[1] numbered ; and it has been suggested that the difficulty of classing the play led to the rearrangement ; [it may be added, to show the complete perplexity on this point, that the writer of the remarkable preface to the first quarto seems to regard it almost entirely as a "comedy ;" and that in the catalogue of the folio it is not mentioned at all].

Amongst the external evidence must also be classed the following undoubted allusion to an incident in *Troilus and Cressida;* the passage is taken from a play, entitled *Histrio-mastix, or the Player Whipt*, (the date[2] of which is not known, though it was certainly produced before the death of Queen Elizabeth) :—

> " *Troy.*   Come, Cressida, my cresset light,
> Thy face doth shine both day and night.
> Behold, behold *thy garter blue*
> *Thy knight his valiant elbow wears,*
> That when he SHAKES his furious SPEARE,
> The foe in shivering fearful sort
> May lay him down in death to snort."
>
> " *Cres.*   O knight, with valour in thy face,
> *Here take my skreene,* wear it for grace ;
> *Within thy helmet put the same,*
> Therewith to make thy enemies lame."

---

[1] There is no greater instance of the carelessness of the first folio editors than the fact that in the volume, containing the tragedies, page 257 succeeds page 156, the intervening 100 numbers being omitted.

[2] There seems to be an allusion to it as well-known in Ben Jonson's *Every Man Out of his Humour* (iii. 1), 1599.

This must surely refer to Shakespeare's work, as was observed by the early commentators, although they missed the "buried-city" mention of our author's name.

Now the only way of reconciling this early allusion with the declaration, in the preface to the first quarto, that it was then "a *new* play, never staled with the stage;" of accounting for the marked difference of opinion as to the date, as evidenced, for instance, by Dryden's classing it among Shakespeare's "first endeavours," while Pope thought it one of his latest; and of affording a reason for the difficulty, which the early editors felt, as to the dramatic order in which it should be placed—the only way, it may be thought, out of these difficulties is by supposing that the play, as we now have it, was composed at different periods of time. This theory (which has been advanced by several writers, and has lately been elaborated by Mr. Fleay) is supported by various pieces of internal evidence, such as the marked differences of style and language in different parts of the play, and by certain discrepancies in the editing and the printing. Two examples of the discrepancies, pointed out by the Cambridge editors and Mr. Fleay, may be mentioned; "in Act i. Sc. 2, Hector goes to the field and fights, in Act i. Sc. 3, after this, we find him grown rusty in the long-continued truce;" again the rhyming couplet, v. 11, 33, 34, which (almost) terminates the last scene, is by the folio editors repeated at the end of Act v. Sc. 3, which fact strongly suggests that Scenes 6—11 are a later insertion.

Mr. Fleay thinks the play is formed of three parts, written at different intervals; viz. (1) the Troilus and Cressida Story (1594), the Hector Story (1595), and the Thersites and Achilles part (1607). Since these divisions are made almost entirely upon internal evidence, it would certainly be strange if this arrangement were strictly correct; for it seems extremely unlikely that the difference of one year only could be discriminated by metrical tests; and, I would venture to add, that some parts which Mr. Fleay places in group 2, seem, in my opinion, contemporary with parts of his third group.

At the same time, as said above, the marked difference of style seems certainly to point to *two* different parts, written at different periods—the Love Story, and the Camp Story. I would support this division by the following application of the "classical allusion" test ; by which, I think, it will appear that any allusions in other plays to characters appearing in this drama vary in their tone according as they were written when "the Love Story" only was extant, or when "the Camp Story" had been joined to it. It may be first remarked that such allusions as occur in *Henry VI.* in *The Taming of the Shrew*, and in *Titus Andronicus*, will not affect our argument, as we have reason to think they are not entirely from Shakespeare's hand (a fact which appears the more probable—though to say so here may seem perhaps to be reasoning in a circle—from the tone of the references). Let the examples, however, speak for themselves :—

> "The Greeks upon advice did bury *Ajax*,
>   That slew himself ; and wise *Laertes' son*
>   Did graciously plead for his funerals."
>   (*Titus Andronicus*, i. 1, 379—381.)

[The term "wise" is hardly applicable to Shakespeare's Achilles.]

> "Five-and-twenty valiant sons
> Half the number that kind Priam had."—(i. 1, 79, 80.)

["The Love Story" of *Troilus and Cressida* represents Priam as the father of fifty-one sons (i. 2, 176, *Globe Edition*).]

> "A second Hector, for his grim aspect,
>   And large proportion of his strong-knit limbs."
>   (1 *Henry VI.*, ii. 3, 20—21.)

> "Nestor-like aged in an age of care."—(ii. 5, 6.)

[These scarcely describe either the counsellor or the warrior of "the Camp Story."]

" And now, like Ajax Telamonius,
On sheep and oxen could I spend my fury."
(2 *Henry VI.* v. 1, 26, 27.)

[Contrast this with the Ajax of Shakespeare's play.]

" Whose smile, and frown, like to Achilles' spear,
Is able with the change to kill and cure."
(v. 1, 100, 101.)

[This does not read like Shakespeare-mythology.]

3 *Henry VI.*, iii. 2, 188—193 ; iv. 2, 19—21 ; &c.

[These allusions to Ulysses, Diomede, &c., regard the Trojan story far more classically than Shakespeare does in his original works.]

Love's Labour's Lost, iv. 3, 7 ; iv. 3, 177 ; &c.

[It is perhaps superfluous to prove that this play preceded *Troilus and Cressida.*
It may also be noticed that the contemptuous use of the word *Trojan* in this play and in *Henry IV.* was dropped before "the Camp Story " appeared.]

" Though Nestor sware the jest be laughable."
Merchant of Venice.

[The Nestor of "the Camp Story " could appreciate " a *sportful* combat " (i. 3, 375).]

" In such a night
Troilus methinks mounted the Trojan walls
And sighed his soul toward the Grecian tents
Where Cressida lay that night."—(v. 1, 3—6.)

[A consideration of this passage seems to imply that " the Love Story " had already attracted Shakespeare's attention, but that he had not yet undertaken the work itself.]

" Troilus had his brains dashed out with a Grecian club, and yet he did what he could to die before, and he is one of the patterns of love."—(*As You Like It,* iv. 1, 97—100.)

[This was written before " the Camp Story," at any rate.]

[*Pistol*] " And from the powdering tube of infamy
     Fetch forth the larger kite of Cressid's kind."
                    (*Henry V.*, ii. 1, 79, 80.)

" Like a base Pander hold the chamber door."—(iv. 5, 14.)

[*Pistol*] " Shall I Sir Pandarus of Troy become
     And by my side wear steel? Then Lucifer take all."
           (*Merry Wives of Windsor*, i. 3, 83, 84.)

" To whom you should have been a Pander."—(v. 5, 176.)

" In loving, Leander the good swimmer, Troilus the first
employer of *panders*, and a whole bookful of these quondam
carpet-mongers, whose names yet run smoothly in the even
road of a blank verse, &c."—(*Much Ado About Nothing*, v.
2, 30—34.)

[These passages, in these nearly contemporary plays, show
that Shakespeare's attention had certainly been drawn to
" the Love Story." To dwell much upon Pistol's expressions
were perhaps " to inquire too curiously." " The Camp
Story" had surely not been written before the last quotation,
in which, by the by, there may be a reference to the writings
of Dekker and Chettle and others.]

" I would play Lord Pandarus of Phrygia, sir, to bring a
Cressida to this Troilus . . . . . Cressida was a beggar."
—(*Twelfth Night*, iii. 1, 58, &c.)

[Shakespeare had been reading Chaucer. (Note the inserted stage direction which occasioned the last part of the
quotation).]
           " I am Cressid's uncle
     That dare leave two together."
       (*All's Well That Ends Well*, ii. 1, 100, 101.)

[This is just what would be said as a *remembrance* of "the
Love Story."]

         " None of these rogues and cowards
   But Ajax is their fool."—(*Lear*, ii. 2, 131, 132.)

"O, he is more mad
Than Telamon for his shield."
(*Anthony and Cleopatra*, iv. 13, 1, 2.)

"The seven-fold shield of Ajax cannot keep
The battery from my heart."—(iv. 13, 38, 39.)

[These imply a study of the Trojan war, though Shakespeare had not used these particular materials.]

"Thersites' body is as good as Ajax
When neither are alive."
(*Cymbeline*, iv. 2, 252, 253.)

[This seems (said Malone) to impart a precedent knowledge of Ajax and Thersites, and in this light may be regarded as a presumptive proof that *Troilus and Cressida* was written before *Cymbeline*.]

From a consideration of these allusions and other internal evidence, and a comparison of the external data above, the following opinion is offered, with hesitation ; that *about* 1599 Shakespeare composed a *Troilus and Cressida*, consisting of the parts above called "the Love Story," which was alluded to by *The Histriomastix*, and rivalled by Dekker and Chettle's work ; that *about* 1602, "the Camp Story" was added to this, forming the long play we now have, and alluded to by Roberts, who wished to print it, early in 1603, "as yt *is* acted by my Lo. Chamberlens men ;" this company however doubtless prevented[1] the publication of the work, until a surreptitious copy, with a talkative preface, having appeared in 1609, they came to an arrangement with the publishers of that quarto, by which the remainder of the edition was printed without the preface about its being "a *new* play, never staled upon the stage," and with the remark that it is here presented "as it *was acted* by the King's Majesties Servants." That "the Camp Story" cannot be so late as

---

[1] See the proviso to an entry of Roberts's in the Register of the Stationers' Hall, under date July 22, 1598, and compare the Preface to *Troilus and Cressida* (Q₁) *sub fine*.

1608, or even as 1607, is proved conclusively by an application of the " weak-ending " test, which on such a point as this is decisive (see Prof. Ingram's table of the weak and light endings), and that the " comedy " part of it at least is not so late as 1606, is, I would point out, shown pretty certainly by the occurrence, in i. 2, 228, of the oath " by God's lid " (see Act of Parliament, 3 Jac. I. c. 21), so that the remarks of the preface-writer, about *Troilus and Cressida* being a " new play . . . passing full of the palm comical " must be taken for what they are worth.

In 1597, Chapman's *Homer* (first seven books) had appeared, and to this Shakespeare was perhaps indebted for some of his facts ; indeed Augustus Hare (*Guesses at Truth*, pp. 356—358) suggests that the key to the peculiar diction and style of *Troilus and Cressida* is to be found in the fact that Shakespeare knew Homer only through Chapman ; and he thinks that the dramatist " taking offence at such pompous phraseology in the mouths of simple warriors," thereupon wrote what *Tieck* calls " a heroic comedy, a tragic parody." He adds, that " though Agamemnon and his peers were certainly not meant as a satire on James and his court, yet they have sundry features in common." One or two passages derived from other works may be noticed. The expression, " and devil envy say ' Amen ' " (ii. 3, 23), has been referred by Mr. R. Simpson (in a letter to the *Academy*, April 29th, 1876) to the play *Mucedorus* [1610 ?][1] where at the end of the address to the king, we find :—

" *Comedy.*   Be blessed then
     Who other wishes, let him never speak.
" *Envy. Amen.*"

The words, v. 2, 55—57, " How the Devil Luxury, with fat rump and potatoe finger, tickles these together ! Fry, Lechery, fry ! " are due (says Chalmers, of course) to Lodge, *Incarnate Devils*, 1596.

---

[1] I have not had an opportunity of consulting the early editions of this play, nor have I seen Lodge's *Devils Incarnate.*

Dr. C. M. Ingleby (*Shakespeare Allusion-Books*) *N. S. S.*, p. viii.) compares i. 3, 119—124, beginning " Then everything includes itself in power," &c., with a passage in Greene's *Groatsworth of Wit* (*ut suprá*, p. 29) ; and Dr. R. G. Latham has since pointed out that this passage is really in heroic verse, and may be an extract from Marlowe.

The misapplied anachronism, in ii. 2, 165—167 :—

> " Not much
> Unlike young men, whom Aristotle thought
> Unfit to hear moral philosophy,"

has been compared (see Bacon's works, ed. Ellis and Spedding) with the following passage in the Second Book of the *Advancement of Learning* (1605), " Is it not the opinion of Aristotle worthy to be regarded, where he saith that young men are not fit auditors of moral philosophy?"

We can scarcely wonder that in a play of so strange a nature ; composed, as we have supposed, at different periods of time ; consisting, as it does, of nearly every kind of dramatic writing ; and clothing, as to a certain extent it does, the beings of old with the habits of to-day ; there should be certain peculiarities and even certain discrepancies. Dryden, long ago, tried to improve it ! Coleridge, some time since, " did not know what to do with it !" and, now Prof. Dowden shirks it altogether ! And yet, I suppose, there is no one but will agree that in this play there occur some of the finest expressions and some of the noblest thoughts that Shakespeare ever uttered.

MEASURE FOR MEASURE.

" My sceptre for a palmer's walking staff."—*Richard II.*

This tragedy was not entered at Stationers' Hall, nor was it printed till 1623 ; Meres does not mention it, and the only direct allusion to it in Shakespeare's time—an entry on the

Revels Records, in 1604—has been declared to be a forged insertion. Still the style and versification, as well as the allusions which will be pointed out, seem to agree pretty conclusively with the generally assumed date, 1603.

Tyrwhitt and *Malone* have conjectured that two passages in this play offer "a courtly apology for King James I.'s stately and ungracious demeanour on his entry into England." *Chalmers* points out various points of likeness in the characters of the duke and James. *Lloyd* "fortifies the parallel by note of the coincidences of his Majesty's expedition to Norway for a bride in 1589; when he slipped away privately without knowledge of the nation," having delegated his authority to one of his chief nobles. Prof. *Ward* accepts Malone's conjecture, "the more so that there is something in the sentiment of the passages not ill according with the tendency towards shrinking from an unnecessary publicity, which we may fairly suppose to have been an element in the poet's own character." The passages referred to are :—

> "I'll privily away. I love the people,
> But do not love to stage me to their eyes.
> Though it do well, I do not relish well
> Their loud applause, and arts vehement."
> (i. 1, 68—71.)

> "The general, subject to a well-wished king,
> Quit their own part, and in obsequious fondness,
> Crowd to his presence, where their untaught love
> Must needs appear offence."—(ii. 4, 27—30.)

Malone also pointed out the following historical allusions : "Heaven grant us its *peace!* . . . what with the *war*, what with the *sweat* . . . I am custom-shrunk" (i. 2, 4, 83, 84).

James had early announced his intention of bringing to an end the *war* with Spain, which England was involved in when he ascended the throne; *peace* was concluded in the autumn of 1604. The year before, as Capell pointed out, a *plague* had carried off more than 30,000 people in London alone ; that is one-fifth of the then population of the metropolis.

Of ten prisoners, whom the clown names in Act iv., Sc. 3, four are *stabbers* and duellists ; according to Wilson the historian, such enormities were committed in 1604 by roaring boys, bravadoes, roysters, &c., that the "*Act of Stabbing*" (1 Jac. I. c. 8) was passed to restrain them.

Referring to Escalus's forced and somewhat rude pun about "the biggest thing about" Pompey (ii. 1, 228, 229), Steevens says : " In consequence of a diligent inspection of ancient pictures and prints, it may be pronounced that this ridiculous fashion appeared in the early part of Queen Elizabeth's reign, then declined, and *recommenced at the beginning of that of James I.*"

Chalmers endeavoured to fix the date of the proclamation referred to, in i. 2, 95, but in his efforts to differ from "the commentators," he seems to have become somewhat con- fused.

The allusions, however, mentioned above do not seem forced, and, when taken with a general consideration of the style and versification, appear pretty convincingly to fix the composition of *Measure for Measure* in the year 1603—4.

This date is confirmed, or rather is not contradicted, by the following remarkable and interesting comparison :—

" So play the foolish *throngs* with one that *swoons* ;
   Come all to *help* him and so stopt the *air*
   By which he should revive."
                    (*Measure for Measure*, ii. 4, 24—27.)

" And like as when some sudden extasie
     Seizeth the nature of a sicklie man ;
   When he's discerned to *swoone*, straight by and by
     Folke to his *helpe* confusedly have ran ;
   And seeking with their art to fetch him backe,
   So many *throng*, that he the *ayre* doth lacke."
                    (*Myrrha, the Mother of Adonis.*)

Now the author of this poem, William Barksted, who by the by (as Malone points out) at the end of his piece expressed his personal regard for Shakespeare and his admiration for his writings, was an actor in our author's company, and so doubtless either heard the piece acted or saw the play-book—for it will be remembered that *Measure for Measure* was not printed during Shakespeare's lifetime. But I may go a step further. Barksted was also one of the children of the Revels, and therefore we may presume in acting for the King's Company would take a woman's part. Is it improbable, then (seeing the impression this passage made upon him), that we have in the author of *Myrrha, the original Isabella?* He would be listening, for they were the cue-words.

A few words upon the æsthetic and metrical tests : as for these latter, they all support the position here assigned to the play ; see the rhyme-test, the feminine-ending test, the classical allusion test, and, as Mr. Fleay remarks (*Shakespeare Manual*, p. 46) "the play is the central one for the metre of the third period ; it has more lines with extra syllables before a pause in the middle of a line than any other. It is freer in rhythm than any play in the first and second period."

Although the subject is undoubtedly a painful one, and the play itself has scarcely ever been a popular one, yet when we think of the many marvellous passages which it contains, when we remember the wonderful delineation of character which it exhibits, and when we compare the drama as Shakespeare produced it with the original[1] upon which

[1] The plot of this piece is taken from the *History of Promos and Cassandra* translated by G. Wheatstone from one of Cinthio's novels, and afterwards dramatised by the translator in 1578. Collier suggests that the title of Shakespeare's play may have been suggested by the following lines from the old drama:—

"Who others doth deceyve,
Deserves himself *like measure* to receyve."

Malone compared the following passage from *A Warning for Faire Women*, 1599:—

"The trial now remains, as shall conclude
Measure for Measure, and lost blood for blood."

But surely the expression was then, as now, a proverbial one : it is used in 3 *Henry VI.* (ii. 6).

he founded it, we must feel that we are watching our author
as he is leaving the mirth of his younger days and drifting
into that frame of mind in which he evolved those marvellous tragedies poured forth in his later years.

ALL'S WELL THAT ENDS WELL.

" Love sought is good, but given unsought is better."
                                        Twelfth Night.

" What should such a fool
Do with so good a wife ? "—*Othello.* [1]

Coleridge, Tieck, Collier, Dyce, Gervinus, von Friesen,
Fleay, and others have pointed out two distinct styles of
composition in this drama ; and, though the fact is denied
by Delius, Hertzberg, and others, yet a careful consideration
of the play seems incontestably to lead to the conclusion
that we have here a late revision of an early play.

It undoubtedly contains some parts of very early work,
as is proved by the frequent rhymed passages, by the sonnet-
letter in Act iii. Sc. 4, by the occasional alternates, and by
the lyrical, non-dramatic form of certain portions, as well as
by some peculiar and early grammatical constructions.   Mr.
Fleay has picked out the parts which he considers to be of
early date ; " boulders from the old strata imbedded in the
latter deposits," as he so aptly calls them.   (See *New
Shakspere Society's Transactions,* 1874, vol. ii.)

As to the particular time at which Shakespeare first worked
upon the subject, we are helped by the very probable conjecture that we have in *All's Well* a remodelling of the play
mentioned by Meres under the title of *Love's Labour's Won.* [1]

---

[1] Mr. Hunter identified the play named by Meres with *The Tempest,* Mr.
A. E. Brae argues for *Much Ado,* &c., while Craik and Hertzberg think that the
Taming of the Shrew is the play meant.   But we know that *some* of Shake-
speare's plays were (generally or occasionally) known by different names (*e.g.
Twelfth Night,* or " What You Will ; " the *Merchant of Venice,* or the " Jew
of Venice ; " *Merry Wives of Windsor,* or " Sir John Falstaff ; " *1 Henry IV.,*

Shakespeare obtained the plot of his story from Paynter's *Palace of Pleasure;* which, it is to be noted, he doubtless consulted at about the same time in preparing his *Romeo and Juliet.*

He may also have obtained passages or hints from the following works : *Tom Drum's Vants*, &c., in *Gentle Craft* (ii. 8), 1598 ; Mendoza's *Theorique and Practice of Warre*, translated by Hoby, 1597 (cf. iv. 3, 160—165) ; *Life of Jack Wilton*, 1594 (cf. Parolles's adventure with " the examination of one of Henry VIII.'s captains, who had gone over to the enemy.")

On the expression, in ii. 3, 47, " *Lustig*, as the Dutchman says," Capell remarks : " An old play, that has a good deal of merit, called *The Weakest Goeth to the Wall* (printed in 1600, but how much earlier written or by whom written, we are nowhere informed), has in it a Dutchman, called Jacob van Smelt, who speaks a jargon of Dutch and our language ; and upon several occasions uses this very word, which in English is lusty." Compare the expression " *Veal*, quoth the Dutchman," in *Love's Labour's Lost*, v. 2, 847.

Commenting on v. 3, 83—87, Elze compares the [disputed] similar gift of a ring by Elizabeth to Essex, when the latter departed for Cadiz, in 1596. He adds : " The circumstance of the ring is strangely not referred to till this last scene ; and may have been introduced into the fifth act (somewhat in the same way as Maudlin Lafeu) at a remodelling in 1597 say (or—with Gervinus—in 1605—6 [or, as above, in 1604]), when Shakespeare would know of the Essex-incident." It may be remarked that nobody could possibly imagine that the lines containing the ring-incident (v. 3, 76, &c.), were written at the same time as the preceding lines (v. 3, 60—72).

or " Hotspur; " *Henry V.*, or " Agincourt; " *2 and 3 Henry VI.*, or "York and Lancaster," &c. ; *Henry VIII.*, or " All is True; " *Much Ado*, &c., or " Benedick and Beatrice; " *Julius Caesar*, or "Caesar's Tragedy: " *Othello*, or " The Moor," &c.). The occurrence in the context, twice or thrice, of the proverbial phrase *All's Well*, &c., may have suggested the title. See also Act v. Epilogue, l. 336.

The clown's remarks upon Puritanism (i. 3, 98—100), Steevens referred to Elizabeth's reign, while Malone thought them particularly appropriate to the time of James, who hated the Puritans.

The play was evidently intended, according to Meres, to be a companion-play to *Love's Labour's Lost;* and a consideration of the style of such parts as seem to remain of the older edition justifies the adoption of a corresponding date, say about 1592 ; Knight indeed would even date it before 1590, and Ulrici contends for an early year.

The date, at which the revision was made (assuming that there was only one), is also a problem to be determined by internal evidence. Von Friesen and Elze have pointed out similarities with *Hamlet,* while Lloyd and Fleay, as well as Von Friesen, have dwelt upon similarities with *Measure for Measure.* The uncertainty of the date of the different parts of *Hamlet* prevents the analogy from helping us in settling the chronology of this play ; but the resemblance, both in incidents and tone, to *Measure for Measure* is so striking, that we can scarcely be far wrong if about the same date assigned to that play be given for the revision of this (1604). This is supported by the various metrical tests, especially if the separation proposed by Mr. Fleay be adopted ; the "light-ending" test, which is generally very accurate, confirms the result (see Prof. Ingram's table).

It is a rather remarkable fact, that of the two actors whom Mr. Halliwell Phillipps mentions as taking part in this play, the one, Robert Goughe, is not known to have acted much after the early part of Shakespeare's career ; the other, William Ecclestone, is not known to have performed till late in our author's time.

We have above supported the date here given on various metrical and other grounds ; it needs therefore only to be remarked that the comic characters are probably in conception, as well as in execution, due to Shakespeare himself ; that Parolles has been called, by Ulrici and Schlegel, " the little appendix of the great Falstaff;" and that the following general remark of Mr. Ruskin's is particularly applicable to this play : "The catastrophe of every play is caused always by the folly or fault of a man ;[1] the redemption, if there be any, is by the wisdom and virtue of a woman, and, failing that, there is none." (*Works, Edition* 1871, vol. 1, pp. 78—81.)

OTHELLO, THE MOOR OF VENICE.

" A man more sinned against, than sinning."—*King Lear.*

This tragedy was formerly placed among the latest of our author's works ; Warburton and Malone (in early editions) dating it 1611, Chalmers 1614, and Drake 1612 ; but in his last edition Malone cursorily assigned it to the year 1604, and reasons for adopting an early date will be given below.

The arguments for a late production may however be first stated.

The lines, iii. 4, 46, 47 :—

> " The hearts of old gave hands ;
> But our new heraldry is hands not hearts,"

were thought by Warburton, Chalmers, Douce, Drake, and others to refer to the arms of the order of Baronets, instituted by King James in 1611 ; but to what particular period, or to what particular grant of arms, was disputed ; their opinions and dates may be seen in their respective works.

Steevens thought he saw an allusion to this play in Ben

---

[1] Of course Mr. Ruskin would tell us that the line, ii. 4, 315,

" A young man married is a man that's marr'd,"

is spoken by *Parolles* to *Bertram.* It may here be noted as a strange fact that n ne of the " picklocks," who can read Shakespeare's life written between the lines of his writings, have applied this line to the great dramatist himself. The passage of nearly doggerel rhyme in which it occurs, and the forced pun which it contains, are almost certain signs that it was written among his earliest productions.

Jonson's *Alchemist*, first produced in 1610 or 1612 ; but Malone disputes this. The passage referred to is :—

Lovewit. " Didst thou hear a cry, say'st thou ?"
Neighb. " Yes, sir, like unto a man that had been strangled an hour and could not speak."

The MS. of an attendant on the Duke of Wurtemberg, in his second visit to England in the year 1610, says : " S. E. alla au Globe, lieu ordinaire ou l'on joue les commedies ; y fut representé l'Histoire du More de Venise " (April 30th, 1610).

Again, the MS. of Mr. Vertue tells us that the play was acted at court before King James in the early part of the year 1613.

Randon Brown, as cited by Simrock and Ward, suggested that Shakespeare received the story from the personal communications of the Venetian embassy which visited London in 1613—16. As a set-off against this the following observations may be quoted from Dr. Karl Elze (English Translation, p. 300) : " The difference between Shakespeare's earlier and his later Italianising comedies is so striking, that this (also) points to the supposition of a journey intervening between them as the only satisfactory explanation. We cannot help agreeing with Knight, who assigns the supposed journey to Italy to the year 1593, so that the *Merchant of Venice, Othello,* and perhaps also the *Taming of the Shrew* (if the latter must not be referred to an earlier date) would have directly followed the poet's return, when he was still filled with the impressions he had received, and when the whole charm of Italy and its sky unconsciously guided his pen."

Emilia and Lodovico, two of the characters in this play, are likewise two of the persons represented in *May-Day,* a comedy by Chapman, first printed in 1611 (Malone).

Again, this tragedy was not entered on the books of the Stationers' Company till Oct. 6th, 1621, nor printed till the following year. I may add, that Underwood, who is said to have acted in *Othello*, does not appear to have joined the King's Company much before 1610 (see *Appendix*, p. 200); and Field and Swanston, who also appeared in this tragedy, did not join the company till a late date.

On the other hand, in favour of an earlier date we may adduce the following points :—

On the authority of the Mainwaring MS. among the Egerton papers, Mr. Collier has stated that "Burbidge's players" performed *Othello* before Queen Elizabeth, on August 6th, 1602, at Harefield ; but this document has been pronounced a forgery.

Gervinus, without giving any reasons for the statement, dates the play in the year 1600 (Bunnett's English Translation, vol. i., p. 481).

Mr. Halliwell-Phillipps points out that the celebrated lines in iii. 3, 157, &c., "Who steals my purse," &c., are closely paralleled by an expression in *The New Metamorphosis* by J. M. (MS. dated 1600); the thought, however, is comparatively a trite one.

Again, the lines in Othello's speech, i. 3, 142, &c. :—

> "—The cannibals that each other eat,
> The Anthropophagi, and men whose heads
> Do grow beneath their shoulders,"

have been referred to Raleigh's *Discovery of Guiana*, 1600.

Malone, in his last edition, thought that the passage above quoted from iii. 4, about "our new heraldry," may have been suggested to Shakespeare by a passage from Cornwallis's *Essays*, 1601 (Variorum Edition, 1821, vol. ii. pp. 403, 404).

He was of opinion, too, that the simile of the Pontic Sea, in Act iii. Sc. 3, might be an allusion to Holland's *Pliny*, 1601.

It may be remarked, also, that Shakespeare was evidently acquainted with Cardinal Contareno's *Commonwealth of*

I 2

Venice, Lewkenor's Translation, 1599. Cf. the statement as to "the double voice of the duke" (i. 2, 13, 14).

The *Willow Song* (iv. 3) is referred to in Middleton's *Blurt, Master Constable* (1601); but references to this are pretty frequent.

Malone abruptly concluded his remarks on the chronology of this play by saying : " We know that it was acted in 1604." Boswell "laments deeply that he was not able to discover upon what evidence" Malone knew this. It was probably due to a statement in the *Accounts of the Revels at Court* (see Cunningham's edition), viz. :—

By the Kings   "Hallamas Day, being the first of Nov.,
Ma^{tis} Plaiers.   A play at the banketinge House att
                     Whitehall, called the Moor of Venis [1604]."

This, and other entries, however, have been considered by some as spurious ; still Malone's statement leads me to adopt the date 1604 ; and it may be noted that the names of some of the characters in this play are adopted in a work, entitled *The History of Enordamus*, published in 1605. That it was written before the year 1606 is, I may observe, proved by the following minute detail : in the fourth line of Act i. Sc. 1, in the quarto edition of 1622, we have the expression "'Sblood ;" now this oath is omitted in the folio edition ; it seems to me that the folio edition of this play was printed from a copy made before the Act of Parliament (3 James I. c. 21) issued in 1606 against the abuse of the Holy Name in plays, &c. Cf. also "'*Zounds*" and "*by tne Mass*" (ii. 3).

The date above assigned will now be tried by various metrical and æsthetic tests.

It is pretty generally assumed that *Othello* must be grouped with *Lear* and *Macbeth ;* and to the "internal" arguments of style, &c., usually adduced in proof of this, I may add the remarkable absence of "classical allusions" in these three plays.

Professor Dowden points to the fact that while *Othello*,

Lear, &c., end in confusion and sorrow, *The Tempest, Cymbe-line,* and *Winter's Tale* close with reconciliation and peace ; he adds : "It is not, as in the earlier comedies—*The Two Gentlemen of Verona, Much Ado About Nothing, As You Like It,* &c.—a mere *dénouement;* the resolution of the discords in these latest plays is not a mere stage necessity, or a necessity of composition resorted to by the dramatist to effect an ending of his play, and little interesting his imagination or his heart ; its significance here is ethical and spiritual, it is a moral necessity."

The position of these plays in the third, out of the four periods, into which the production of Shakespeare's dramas is usually divided, is confirmed by the various metrical tests ; for instance, the rhyme-test (see p. 174) places them together, if allowance be made for the peculiar case of *Macbeth;* they are fairly near, according to the double-ending test, if the shortness of *Macbeth* be taken into account ; compare, too, the weak-ending test, as applied by Prof. Ingram (*New Shakspere Society's Transactions,* 1874, p. 450) from whose table the following statistics are taken :—

	No. of Light Endings.	No. of Weak Endings.
Othello	2	0
Lear	5	1
Macbeth	21	2

These numbers should be contrasted with those of the plays of the fourth period (see p. 176) ; they support, too, the precedence of *Othello* adopted above.

Dr. Drake (*Shakspeare and His Times,* ed. 1817, vol. 2, p. 529) says : "The tragedy of *Othello,* certainly *one* of the first-rate productions of its author, is yet, in our opinion, inferior, in point of originality and poetic wealth, to *Macbeth,* to *Lear,* &c." Although this last remark favours the chronological arrangement here adopted, the statement is not indorsed ; the fact is, that Shakespeare had now, by his

intuitive power and by his acquired skill, arrived very nearly
at poetic and artistic perfection, and chronological criticism
must be content, or almost so, to limit itself to external
evidence, and to such mental tests as are independent of the
consciousness of the author.   It would be hard to name any
play, upon which more congratulatory wreaths have been
thrown by men themselves eminent in literary walks.
Wordsworth, in one place, has an exquisite reference to
"the gentle lady wedded to the Moor ;" in another, he says :
" The tragedy of *Othello*, Plato's records of the last scenes
of the career of Socrates, and Isaac Walton's *Life of George
Herbert*, are the most pathetic of human compositions"
(*Memoirs*, by C. Wordsworth) ; Johnson and Coleridge we
will not now cite, they are professed Shakespeare critics ;
but turn to Augustus Hare who, contemplating Iago, declares
him to be a product of " the mature manhood of the mightiest
intellect that ever lived upon earth " (see *Guesses at Truth*,
ed. 1871, pp. 420, 421, where this sentence is succeeded by
one of the finest similes in that marvellous work) ; to cap a
climax, Macaulay gives it as his opinion that *Othello* "is
perhaps the greatest work in the world " (*On the Principal
Italian Writers*).

KING LEAR.

" The silence often of pure innocence
Persuades where speaking fails."—*Winter's Tale.*

In dealing with this play we may at once limit our inquiry
by stating a *terminus a quo*, and a *terminus ad quem*.
    It could not have been produced *earlier* than 1603, when
there appeared Harsnett's *Declaration of egregious Popish
Impostures;* from which Shakespeare borrowed, among other
things, the fantastic names of spirits in Act iii., Scene 4.
    It could not have been produced *later* than December

26th, 1606; as we learn from the entry, made on the *Stationers' Register*, November 29th, 1607, which is as follows : " Mr. Willm. Shakespeare his Historye of Kinge Lear ; as it was played before the King's Majestie at White - hall upon St. Stephen's night at Xmas last, by his Majesty's servants, playing usually at the Globe on the Bankside." This is produced on the title-pages of the two quarto editions of the play which were published in the following year (1608).

In giving the evidence, upon which the date may be still more closely ascertained, we will begin with a list of the sources to which Shakespeare may have been indebted for the plot and the various details of his drama. Besides earlier works, there have been suggested, Holinshed's *Chronicle* (ed. 1577), *the Mirror of Magistrates* (ed. 1594), Harvey's *Defence of Brutes and Brutans History* (ed. 1593), *The True Chronicle Historie of King Leir* (vide infra), Spenser's *Faerie Queene* [whence Shakespeare probably obtained the name Cordelia (see *The Passionate Pilgrim*, viii., 109, &c.)], a ballad (printed in Percy's *Reliques*) entitled *The Death of King Leir* and his *Three Daughters* (date uncertain, probably later than our drama), Sidney's *Arcadia*, [ed. 1598, (ii. pp. 133—138) whence the conception of Gloster may be borrowed], Warner's *Albion's England*, and Camden's *Remaines* (ed. 1605).

· In the last-mentioned work, Ina, King of Wessex, similarly tests his daughter's love ; and, when it is re- membered that Shakespeare undoubtedly borrowed expres- sions from this work in his *Coriolanus* (see p. 148), it certainly is not improbable that he may from the same volume, have borrowed the idea which, with the aid of other books, he has worked up into his *King Lear;* Professor Ward (*u.s.*, vol. i., p. 417) seems to state the contrary opinion too dogmatically.

Malone (Variorum ed., vol. ii., pp. 404, 405) well remarks : " It seems extremely probable that its first appearance was

in March or April, 1605 ; in which year the old play of
King Leir, that had been entered at Stationers' Hall in 1594,
was printed by Simon Stafford, for John Wright, who, we
may presume, finding Shakspeare's play successful, hoped to
palm the spurious one on the public for his.   The old *King
Leir* was entered on the Stationer's books, May 8, 1605, as it
was *lately* acted."   It may be added that this old drama
(which had been performed by Henslow's company in 1593)
was again entered on the *Stationers' Register* in 1607.

Various passages in the play will now be examined.[1]

" Seek him out upon the *English* party," iv. 6, 255, 256, is the
folio reading where the quarto has " British."   England and
Scotland were proclaimed " Great Britain," Oct. 20th, 1604 ;
therefore (says Mr. Wright) we might think the folio MS.
was written before Oct. 1604, and afterwards corrected
before printing in 1608 ; but Shakespeare may inadvertently
have used the familiar word " English."

Compare iii. 4, 189, 190—

> " Fie, foh and fum,
> " I smell the blood of a British man."

[Steevens endeavoured (with Drake's approval) to throw
back the " terminus " above assumed, from the Proclamation
of Oct. 1604 (which Malone had dwelt upon) to a Proclamation in May, 1603 ; supporting his idea by quotations
from Daniel and Drayton.]

> " These late eclipses in the sun and moon portend no good
>   to us." i. 2, 112, &c.
> " O these eclipses do portend these divisions."   147.
> " I am thinking, brother, of a prediction I read this other
>   day, what should follow these eclipses."   152, &c.

There was a great eclipse in Oct. 1605 ; and Mr. Wright
quotes from a book by J. Harvey, of King's Lynn (*A*

---

[1] Compare Mr. Wright's excellent introduction to the play in the Clarendon
Press Series.

discoursive probleme concerning Prophecies, 1588) an allusion to eclipses in Oct. 1605. He adds, "these allusions can scarcely be doubted."

Again he refers some lines a little lower down to the treasons of the year 1605.

Mr. Wright thinks it highly probable that Shakespeare did not begin to write *Lear* till towards the end of the year 1605, and that his attention may have been directed to the story as a subject for tragedy by the revival of the older play above mentioned. [This must be contrasted with Mr. Malone's supposition quoted above.]

The Clarendon Press Editor, having reduced the period of composition to between the end of 1605 and Christmas 1606, tries, "conjecturing internally" to fix the precise season ; from the great storm in Act iii.; from the Fool's speech (ii. 4, 46, &c.) "Winter's not yet gone," &c. (though, he admits, this may have another meaning) ; " The bleak winds may sorely ruffle," &c. ; "'Tis a wild night," &c.; all which point to *winter.* But Lear's apostrophe is addressed to a violent summer tempest, so Kent describes it ; compare the colouring of Act iv.; "search every acre in the high-grown field," points to July (though we must not press the botany, because of the cuckoo-flower, and because of the samphire, which is gathered in May). "Perhaps" [Mr. Wright concludes, somewhat speculatively, it must be owned], "perhaps Shakespeare began *Lear* in the winter of 1605 and finished it in the summer of 1606 when the fields were still covered with the unharvested corn, and the great storm of March was still fresh in his recollection."

The following allusions may also be noticed :

iii. 2, 81—94, the Fool's prophecy should be compared with the Chaucer prophecy in Puttenham's *Arte of English Poesie,* 1589. It was probably inserted by the actor who played the clown's part ; for notice, besides the peculiar diction of the lines, the absurd remark at the end ; and compare *Hamlet,* iii., 2, 42, &c. (see p. 72).

ii. 3, 14, "*Bedlam beggars;*" 20, "*Poor Tom,*" compare Decker's *Bellman of London* (3 eds. in 1608), description of "*an Abraham man :*" "he swears he has been in Bedlam ; he calls himself by the name of 'Poor Tom,' and coming near any body cries out, 'Poor Tom is a-cold.'"

iii. 4, 125. Swithold = S. Withold. This saint is not known in legends ; but compare the old play of *King John,* 1591, where we find the line :

> "Sweet S. Withold, of thy lenitie, defend us from
> extremitie."

> "Hum, go to thy cold bed and warm thee."—(iii. 4, 58.)

This line is probably a parody on a line in Kyd's *Spanish Tragedy.* Compare *Taming of the Shrew,* Induction i. 10.

Doubtless there are other allusions to old plays in those wild utterances ; it would be an interesting point to find if any of these dramas had been revised at the theatres about this period.

The same may be said as to the songs, snatches of which are introduced into this play ; for instance, the song in i. 4, 191, 192 :

> "Then they for sudden joy did weep
> And I for sorrow sung."

occur in Heywood's play *The Rape of Lucrece,* published in 1608. With regard to another song in the same scene (i. 4, 340—344),

> "A fox, when one has caught her,
> And such a daughter,
> Should sure to the slaughter,
> If my cap would buy a *halter* :
> So the fool follows after,"

it may be remarked that Mr. A. J. Ellis says, "This vocalisation of *l* (see the word 'halter') was established shortly after 1600."

The " oath-test " (see pp. 105 and 116), is perhaps put out of court in this case by "the paganism of the play."

The classing of this tragedy with the group containing *Othello* and *Macbeth*, is discussed under the former of the plays just mentioned, and the proofs need not be repeated ; though one of them is so strikingly brought out here that an allusion must be made to it.   It was said that these plays " *end in confusion and sorrow ;* " now that this is more than a mere accident or chance, is proved in this case by the fact that in the old play, upon which this was founded, things end happily.   Why the change?   How can it be explained, except by attributing it to the peculiar frame of mind, in which the poet undoubtedly then was—a state of intense feeling and emotion?   Hence the intensity and the grandeur of *King Lear*, whether we consider the play as a whole or the characters individually !   " Where other tragedies," says Gervinus, " treat of separate passions, this one exhibits passion generally, so that it might be called *the tragedy* κατ' ἐξοχήν."   Shelley says it is "the most perfect specimen of the dramatic art existing in the world." Taking the characters, too, individually, not to mention Lear—the central figure—unsurpassed in any tragedy ever written ; think of the women—Cordelia, " the heart-lady," as Ruskin reads her name—and her sisters at the other poie of tragedy ; think of Edmund, compare him (as Augustus Hare bids us) with that other self-reflective villain Iago, and contrast him with Richard III. ; and think of the Fool, " he is no comic buffoon to make the groundlings laugh," no forced condescension of Shakespeare's genius to the taste of the audience.   Accordingly, the poet prepares for his intro-duction, which he never does with any of his common clowns or fools, by bringing him into living connection [1] with the pathos of the play.   He is as wonderful a creation as Caliban, " his wild bubblings and inspired idiocy articulate and gauge

---

[1] Compare Dr. Bucknill's remark, " Shakespeare's other fools are the grin-ning gurgoils of the structure, but the fool in *Lear* is a buttress of the tale."

the horrors of the scene " (Coleridge), while at the same time, it must be added, that with consummate art he is made to act as, if I may use the expression, a serio-comic safety-valve of the tragedy : lastly, mark, too, how the Fool *retires* when " the interest of madness has reached its height, and has to be gradually abated for the rest of the play " (Moberly).

MACBETH.

" The shameful murder of a guiltless king."—2 *Henry VI.*

There are various indications that the subject of this tragedy was gradually attracting public attention in England at the commencement of the seventeenth century. Passing by the various chronicles (Holinshed's, Buchanan's, &c.) we may note that as early as August 27th, 1596, there was an entry in the Stationer's Register of *A Ballad of Macdobeth.* Again Kemp's *Nine Days' Wonder*, 1600, refers to a *Story of Macdobeth, or Macsomewhat*, and advises the author to "leave writing these beastly ballets, make not good wenches prophetesses for little or no profit." The accession of James to the English throne in 1603 naturally directed attention to Scottish affairs, and suggested such subjects as that of this play ; we learn, for instance (both from Anthony Nixon's pamphlet, entitled *The Oxford Triumph*, 1605, and from a book called *Rex Platonicus; Narratio ab Isaaco Wake, Oxoniæ*, 1607) that when James visited Oxford in 1605, he was " addressed on entering the city by three students of St. John's College, who alternately accosted his Majesty, reciting some Latin verses, founded on the prediction of the weird sisters relative to Banquo and Macbeth ; " the piece was repeated in English to the queen and the young prince ; " the conceit thereof the king did very much applaude."

After this it is not surprising that the subject should be

dramatised for the King's Company ; whilst, it may be added, it is very unlikely that the subject would have been chosen in Oxford had the play previously appeared on the London stage ; where we cannot doubt that, when it did appear, it was received with much favour by the court, to which "the dynastic comfort," that it supplied, would doubtless be very welcome.   Indeed there is a tradition that James sent our author an autograph letter of thanks ; but the report is not worthy of any credit.

The question now presents itself, when did Shakespeare take the subject in hand ?   [Knight indeed thinks that Shakespeare visited Scotland with Laurence Fletcher and some of the Lord Chamberlain's Company ; but even Elze, who admits "the continental journey," will not allow the Scottish visit ; and 1599, of all years, was the least likely one for Shakespeare to leave London, where his *Falstaff* or his *Henry V.* was doubtless in continual request.]   The success, which had attended the piece produced at Oxford, would surely lead to an early preparation of a drama for the London boards, and Malone has, in a very able essay, produced various reasons for assigning our play to the next year (1606).   These reasons, and others confirmatory, will now be given :—

The allusion, in Act ii. Sc. 3, l. 5, to "the expectation of plenty" may refer to the abundance of corn in the autumn of 1606.   Malone points out that the price of wheat in the Windsor market in that year was lower than it was for thirteen years afterwards ; there was a marked difference between the value of it in 1606, and in either 1605 or 1607 ; the same remarks apply to the cheapness of barley and malt.

The expression, a few lines lower down in the same scene (9—13) : ["Faith, here's an equivocator, that could swear in both scales against either scale ; who committed treason enough for God's sake, yet could not equivocate to heaven : O, come in, equivocator"] : undoubtedly refers, as Malone has shown by extracts, &c. (*q. v.*), at considerable length to Garnet and the other Jesuits, whose trial and whose "equivocation" obtained so great a notoriety in the spring of 1606.

Messrs. Clark and Wright demur to these applications severally, but while we are of opinion that each may stand upon its own merits, we feel almost certain that, when taken together, and with other considerations already adduced or to be adduced, they are correct.

But, again, the next sentence ["Here's an English tailor come hither for stealing out of a French hose"] shows, as Warburton pointed out, that the hose were then very short and strait ; and a passage in Anthony Nixon's *Black Year*, 1606, proves that this mode of dress had been then adopted in England, and that "the taylors took *more than enough* for the new fashion's sake."

Malone reminds us, too, that the visit of the King of Denmark to his brother-in-law, in the autumn of this same year, was the occasion of great festivities ; and he conjectures that *Macbeth* may then first have been produced.

The celebrated lines, iv. 1, 120, 121 :—

> " And some I see
> That two-fold balls and treble sceptres carry,"

of course allude to the change of constitution after Oct. 24th, 1604 ; and surely so important an event cannot have lost its point before two years had passed. [We may here notice the skilful way in which Shakespeare omits Mary, Queen of Scots, in the vision of the Eight Kings, from which the above lines are taken ; he names *Kings* only, and, with Macbeth's remark " I'll see no more ! " passes from " the seventh " to " the eighth."] Another passage which was doubtless intended for the royal ear, is the somewhat forced insertion about "the King's Evil," in Act iv. Sc. 3, ll. 140—159. Chalmers points out in particular the lines :—

> " And *'tis spoken*
> To *the succeeding royalty* he leaves
> The healing benediction."

and he quotes a passage from Camden's *Remaines*, 1605, which mentions "that admirable *gift hereditary* to the anoynted princes of this realm in curing the King's Evil," and referring to "the learned discourse thereof *lately written*" (viz. Dr. Tooker's *Charisma*).

Again, Mr. Hunter, *New Illustrations of Shakespeare*, vol. ii. p. 153), commenting on i. 3, 108, &c., thinks " the ceremony of investiture should take place on the stage. . . . Now it happens that this ancient ceremony of investiture had been lately gone through by Sir D. Murray on his being created Lord Scone. The ceremony took place on April 7th, 1605, with great solemnity " [" what he [the Earl of Gowrie] hath lost, noble Macbeth [Murray] hath won " (see i. 1, 67). The account of the conspiracy of Lord Gowrie may have furnished Shakespeare with some hints for his tragedy. I have noticed in Somers' *Tracts*, Suppl. 1, an allusion to " a dagger " (p. 514) and to " wizards " &c. (p. 520). It may be here remarked, too, that Steevens thinks that in the account of the death of the Thane of Cawdor, Shakespeare may have had in view the behaviour of the Earl of Essex at his execution (1601) as related by Stowe, p. 793].

The points, already dwelt upon, limit the production of the play in one direction ; we have now to inquire what light is thrown upon the inquiry in subsequent years.

And first, it is to be noticed that William Warner, in the new edition of his *Albion's England*, in 1606, added an account of the *Historie of Makbeth*. Whether this addition was made previously or subsequently to the production of Shakespeare's play is uncertain, but either alternative favours the probability of the date here given to the tragedy.

But there can scarcely be any doubt, as Farmer long ago pointed out, that there is a reference to *Macbeth* in the following, among other passages, in a drama, entitled *The Puritan*, by W. S., 1607, which was acted by the Paul's children. " Instead of a jester we'll have a ghost in a white sheet, sit at the upper end of the table " (*Sir Godfrey Plus*, loq. iv. 1).

This seems, conclusively, to prove that an account, which Dr. Simon Forman gives of a performance of *Macbeth*, witnessed by him at the Globe on April 20th, 1610, cannot refer to the production of the drama as a *new* play, as the Clarendon editors think. It should be remembered, too, that the Doctor's MS. is confessedly a " book of plaies, and *notes thereof.*"

Again, in the same year (1607), " we meet with the following apparent imitation of Shakespeare in a tragedy called *Cæsar and Pompey,*[1] *or Cæsar's Revenge :*"—

" What think you, lords, that 'tis *ambition's spur*
That *pricketh* Cæsar to these high attempts ?"

Compare the well-known passage in Macbeth's soliloquy, i. 7, 25—28 :—

" I have no *spur*
To *prick* the sides of my intent, but only
Vaulting *ambition*, which o'erleaps itself
And falls on the other."

In 1608, Shakespeare probably brought out his *Antony and Cleopatra* (see p. 140), and Malone has pointed out that there are two passages in *Macbeth*, which show that Shakespeare was probably reading for his *Antony and Cleopatra* about the time when he composed the present tragedy [the production of which supplies a further motive for the interval between *Julius Cæsar* and the Roman play of which we are speaking (see p. 141)].

The passages referred to are the following :—

" The insane root that takes the reason prisoner."
(i. 3, 84.)

and " Under him, My genius is rebuked, as, it is said,
Mark Antony's was by Cæsar."—(iii. 1, 57.)

<hr/>

[1] This, Malone thinks, is the second edition. There is another, undated; if its date could be determined, we might be helped still further in our present inquiry; for the fact, that "in the running title it is called *The Tragedy of Julius Cæsar,*" perhaps the better to impose it on the public for the performance of Shakespeare, shows pretty clearly who was the borrower.

They are both founded upon words in Plutarch's *Life of Antony*. In 1609 appeared the 8th and 9th books of Samuel Daniel's *Civil Wars;* in the former of which occurs a passage which seems to be due to one in this tragedy :—

> " He draws a traverse 'twixt his grievances
> *Looks like the time ; his eye made not report*
> *Of what he felt within ;* nor was he less
> Than usually he was in every part ;
> *Wore a clean face upon a cloudy heart."*

Compare *Macbeth*, i. 5, 65—68, and iii. 2, 27—35.

The *Mask of Queens*, which appeared in the same year (1609), doubtless owes something to Shakespeare, though of course Ben Jonson does not acknowledge it in his notes.

Another allusion to Banquo's Ghost is found in Beaumont and Fletcher's *Knight of the Burning Pestle*, 1611, in Act v. Sc. 1 ; and our play seems to be remembered in the following lines from Webster's *Vittoria Corrombona*, 1612 :—

> " Here's a white hand !
> Can blood be so soon washed ? "

This comparison was made by Steevens.

Mr. Collier compares the famous line, ii. 2, 62 :—

> " The multitudinous seas incarnadine,"

with a passage in Chettle and Munday's *Death of Robert, Earl of Huntingdon*, 1598 :—

> " The multitude of seas dyed red with blood."

" This world I do renounce."—*King Lear.*

" Society is no comfort
To one not sociable."—*Cymbeline.*

The probable sources of this work had better first be mentioned : (1) in the life of Antonius, in North's *Plutarch*, there
is a rather long passage about Timon of Athens [this, Shakespeare would of course meet with in preparing for his *Antony
and Cleopatra*, 1608]; (2) the story is told at length in
Painter's *Palace of Pleasure* (i. 28) [this he had probably
seen when reading for *Romeo and Juliet*, and again for *All's
Well that Ends Well*]; (3) again, Lucian has a *Dialogue* on
Timon [Prof. Ward quotes Tschischwitz's opinion that several
points in our play, not common to the other sources mentioned, show that this must directly or indirectly have been
consulted ; but it must be noted that no English or French
translations of Lucian are known to have existed in Shakespeare's time]; (4) whether the subject had already been
dramatised I will now proceed to inquire [and I cannot help
remarking that this is a step which must always be taken in
such inquiries as this ; yet in Mr. Fleay's remarkable papers
upon *Timon* and *Pericles* such an inquiry is altogether
neglected].

Was there, then, an old play upon this subject ? The
following considerations seem to suggest that there was :
(1) Malone pointed out "a MS. comedy," or, perhaps it
would be better to say, an academical essay on Timon, which
should evidently be dated about 1600 ; it was edited by Mr.
Dyce for the (Old) Shakespeare Society in 1842 ; but it is
here referred to, not as having in any way come under the
notice of our author, for this is very improbable, but as
suggesting first, generally, the probability of an older play,

and secondly, specially (from certain common points), the
likelihood of it ; (2) the remark just made must be repeated
with regard to the points which are derived from Lucian ;
(3) certain references have been supposed to refer to the old
play (though, as Prof. Ward says, they may only refer to the
character[1]), e.g. one in Guilpin's *Skialetheia* (1598), and
another in *Jack Drum's Entertainment;* and (4) the internal
structure of our play itself has led many to suspect that here,
as in other cases, Shakespeare has been improving the work
of another (this view is stated, with various modifications, by
Knight, the Cambridge Editors, Spedding, Staunton, Delius,
and others) ; but (5) the inquiry would be settled if Mr.
Simpson's statement be correct, that "a *Timon* was, at the
date of the *Satiromastix*, in the possession of Shakespeare's
Company" (*N. S. S. Trans.*, 1874, p. 252) ; unfortunately I
do not know the passage on the strength of which this
assertion was made.

Assuming the existence of an older play [but, see below],
when did Shakespeare turn his attention to it? The hint
thrown out by Malone, that Shakespeare doubtless had his
attention called to the subject by the passage he met with in
reading[2] for *Antony and Cleopatra*, and that it is evidently
to be classed with *Macbeth* and the contemporary tragedies,
seems strongly to confirm the conclusion, at which Prof.
Ingram arrives by means of the "weak-ending" test, and
which he thus expresses : "The place of Timon is, without
doubt, before the opening of the last period, but not long
before it." Prof. Dowden, from æsthetic reasons, appears to
come to a similar result ; and, I may add, that the classical
allusion test strikingly confirms this opinion. We shall not

---

[1] It may be remarked, with Chalmers, that *Timon* is pretty frequently referred
to in works of that period ; for instance, in Dulcaster's *Positions*, 1581; in Lodge's
Incarnate Devils, where mention is made of " certain discontented, as Timon
and Apermantus," and in Shakespeare's own *Love's Labour's Lost*, iv. 3, 170,
where we read, "And *critic Timon* laughs at idle toys."

[2] If, in his reading for *Antony and Cleopatra*, Shakespeare stopped to dwell
upon the passage he had come across, we have another reason for the long
interval between the production of *Julius Cæsar* and *Antony and Cleopatra*.

therefore be far wrong, if *Timon* be placed in the year 1607.

But a question has been started, the answer to which may affect the chronology of the play : In what state did Shakespeare leave the play? and this question is, to a certain extent, independent of the points dwelt upon above; and must be replied to by those who, like Mr. Fleay and Herr Tschischwitz, think that Shakespeare originated the play, as well as by those, who, like the Cambridge editors, are of opinion that he was but an improver of an older drama. In considering this we may first notice some remarkable facts as to the pagination of the First Folio edition, in which *Timon of Athens* made its first appearance ; the Cambridge editors have the following remarks : "*Timon of Athens* occupies 21 pages, from 80 to 98 inclusive, 81 and 82 being numbered twice over. After 98 the next page is filled with the actors' names, and the following page is blank. The next page, the first of *Julius Cæsar*, is numbered 109, and instead of beginning, as it should, signature I I, the signature is K K. From this it may be inferred that for some reason the printing of *Julius Cæsar* was commenced before that of *Timon* was finished. It may be the MS. of *Timon* was imperfect, and that the printing was stayed till it could be completed by some playwright, engaged for the purpose. This would account for the manifest imperfections at the close of the play. But it is difficult to conceive how the printer came to miscalculate so widely the space required to be left."

Mr. Fleay has noticed further that "the play of *Troylus and Cressida,* which is not mentioned at all in the Index ('Catalogue') of the Folio, is paged 79 and 80 in its second and third pages, and was evidently intended at first to follow in its proper place as the pendant or comparison play to *Romeo and Juliet.* But as this play was originally called *The History of Troylus and Cressida* (so in the Quarto edition), and as there is really nothing tragical in the main bulk of it, it was doubted if it could be put with the

Tragedies, so the editors of the Folio compromised the matter by putting it between the Histories and the Tragedies and not putting it at all in the Catalogue, though they still retained its first title for it as *The Tragedie of Troylus and Cressida*. The space, then, of pp. 80—108, which would have *just* held the *Troylus and Cressida*, being left unfilled, it became necessary to fill it ; . . . . they therefore took the incomplete[1] *Timon*, put it into a playwright's hand, and told him to make it up to 30 pages" (*N. S. S. Trans.*, 1874, p. 137).

Ulrici is [also] " of opinion that the printing of *Julius Cæsar* was begun before that of *Timon* was finished, probably because the manuscript of *Timon* was imperfect, and the deficiencies could not be immediately supplied. Shakspere's manuscript was not forthcoming ; the play had to be made up from the scattered parts of the individual actors. These parts were marred by omissions, and by the introduction of passages not by Shakspere. Karl Elze adds the conjecture that only the parts of the principal actors[2] could be found. (The play seems not to have been popular, and perhaps it had not been acted for several years.) To complete the play the editors of the First Folio fell back, for minor parts, upon the old *Timon of Athens* (not much older perhaps than Shakspere's play), which may have been the work of George Wilkins.[3] Hence the incoherences and

[1] The entry in the *Stationers' Register* might have been thought to throw some light upon the assumption implied in the word "incomplete," and upon the general theory last discussed: but it does not seem to do so. For while the entry on November 8th, 1623, gives such plays as are entered in the same order as the Folio Catalogue, *e.g. Coriolanus, Timon, Julius Cæsar* (which would contradict the above theory), and while *Timon* is given without any note (which would negative the above assumption), yet the late date of the registration, and these very facts just stated about the order in the entry, and about the absence of comment on *Timon*, might tend to prove that the entry was made after the printing was entered upon (or finished). If it be objected that 1 *Henry VI.* is called " the Third Parte," that doubtless has reference to the Quartos of the First and Second Parts of *The Whole Contention*. Previous entries, even if unauthorised, were, I have elsewhere shown, always respected by the publishers who made the entry of November 8th, 1623.—(H.P.S.)

[2] It should be remembered that about half of the "principal actors" were dead when the First Folio came out (see Appendix, pp. 195—200).—(H.P.S.)

[3] Delius is of the same opinion, and he also thinks (with Mr. Fleay) that Wilkins had a share in the play of *Pericles.*—(H.P.S.)

inconsistences of the play as it exists at present." (See Karl
Elze's preface to *Timon* in Tieck's and Schlegel's translation
of *Shakespeare*, and Prof. Dowden's *Shakspere : His Mind
and Art*, p. 382.)

Mr. Fleay's reason for the gap in the pagination, which
the Cambridge editors pointed out, seems highly plausible ;
but I would suggest that the reason *Timon* was chosen for
the vacant space, was that none of the others would have
fitted (*Macbeth*[1] was too short, the others were too long), and
they were all pure Shakespeare, all pure gold ; but there was
Timon, an old play which Shakespeare had added to,[2] but which
he had left unfinished. This play, then, they therefore chose.

The date above assigned is now confirmed by the somewhat analogous case of the contemporary *Pericles ;* and as
it is probable Shakespeare may have prepared for Burbage the character of Pericles, which indeed we know he
sustained (see Collier), so is it likely that *Timon* was "over-
written with especial reference to Burbage's part." [The last
remark is by Dr. B. Nicholson, who adds a tolerably decisive
proof that *Timon* was an acted play. *N. S. S. Trans.*, 1874,
p. 252.]

One or two remarks must be added on this play [which
Dr. Johnson called "a domestic tragedy," and Schlegel
considered "a satire"].

Malone says it is possible that there are references in the
following passages to the great plague of 1609 :—

"I would send them back the plague, could I but catch it
    for them" (v. 2);

"Be as a planetary *plague*, when Jove
    Will o'er some *high-viced* city hang his poison
    I' the sick air" (iv. 3).

---

[1] The question of an adapter, &c. of *Macbeth* will be referred to under that
play, or we may avoid the point here by supposing that *Macbeth*, as well as
Julius Cæsar, was wholly or partially in print ; unless indeed Mr. Fleay sh· uld
say with Horace, "Utor permisso, caudæque pilos ut equinæ, paullatim vello,"
&c. !

[2] This does not agree with Mr. Fleay's opinion. but is not Shakespeare
more likely to have left unfinished a play that he was only touching up, than
one which he had originated himself ?

But it should be remarked that the word is rather a favourite one with Timon, and, as Mr. Malone himself points out, there were great plagues also in 1593 and in 1603.

Chalmers, again, as usual, sees in "the whole play" an "historical allusion to the state of men and things in London, during the year 1601, and the existence of Essex's rebellion."

Mr. Furnivall thinks "Lucullus imitates Justice Shallow" (*N. S. S. Trans.*, 1874, p. 245).

Tieck's conjecture, that the lines (iv. 3, 503—505)

> " I do proclaim
> One honest man—mistake me not—but one ;
> No more, I pray—and he's a *steward*,"

are intended as *flattery* for King James, is a most charming piece of Teutonic humour, which is enhanced by Ulrici's "laborious apology" for the supposed compliment.

PERICLES.

> " I think this lady
> To be my child."—*King Lear.*

We may first dismiss, with a few words, the arguments which have been brought forward to show that this work was an *early* composition entirely by Shakespeare ; Dryden, indeed, in his prologue to Davenant's *Circe*, says :—

> " Shakespeare's own muse his Pericles first bore,
> The Prince of Tyre was elder than the Moor."

But the statement was probably made carelessly, and it has nothing to support it. Ulrici, however, favours the view ; chiefly on the grounds that Shakespeare is unlikely at so late a date (as 1608, see Dyce and Delius) to have revised another man's work, and that, in his opinion, the supposed difference of style in the different parts of the play is not so striking as has been thought.[1] Very few, however, will be found to agree with this last remark, and the other point will be considered below.

We may next consider the evidence as to the existence of an older play. From Alleyn's *Memoirs* (edited by Collier) we find, among the theatrical paraphernalia, a mention of " spangled hose in *Pericles;* " but there is no evidence of the play itself, or, of course, of its connection with Shakespeare's company. In a poem, entitled *Pimlyco, or Runne-Red-Cap*, 1609, we have the following lines :—

> "Amazed I stood to see a crowd,
> Of civil throats stretched out so loud,
> As at a new play, all the rooms
> Did swarm with gentles mixed with grooms ;
> So that I truly thought all these
> Came to see *Shore* or *Pericles.*"

Malone dates *Jane Shore* as early as 1590, and, in spite of the mention of "a new play" in the above lines, the two dramas that are mentioned might merely be names from their popularity. Again, the sources of the play would suggest an early date (but see below) ; they are, Gower's *Confessio Amantis*, and a story by L. Twine, called *The Patterne of Painfull Adventures, &c., that befell unto Prince Apollonius*, &c., which was entered in 1576 (see below for the edition of 1607). Several passages, too, seem imitated from Sidney's *Arcadia* [*e.g.*, i. 1, 9, &c., i. 1, 62, &c., &c.] ; and from the same work the name Pericles (Pyrocles) was probably borrowed. With regard to the mention of the pirate Valdes (in iv. 2) Malone points out, that Don Pedro de Valdes, commander of the great galleon, was taken prisoner by Sir F. Drake, July 22nd, 1588. He was a prisoner in England when R. Greene wrote his *Spanish Masquerado* (1589). The epithet "pirate," probably inserted to please the people would be much more telling at an earlier date.

---

[1] " Mir erscheint auch die Ungleichheit der einzelnen Partien nicht so schroff," &c.—Ulrici's Introduction to Schlegel's and Tieck's *Translation of Shakespeare's Works*, p. 45, Note.

Delius makes a great point of the remark, on the title-page of the Quarto of 1609, about its being "the late and much admired play ;" but it might be said that equal stress should be laid upon the almost unexampled tautology on the same title-page, where we are told that it had been "*divers and sundry times acted.*"

Again, with regard to this description of the First Quarto [see it quoted *in extenso* below], it may be remarked that the "Pericles-part" seems to cleave off from the "Marina-part," and to be anterior to it ; it speaks of the adventures, &c. of Pericles, "*as also*" the adventures, &c. of Marina.

But still none of these points are very definite. We now turn to the evidence as to the connection of Shakespeare with the subject ; giving first of all the facts :—

1607. Twine's novel, mentioned above, was republished.

1608. May 20th, Edw. Blunt[1] entered at Stationers' Hall "a book called : *The Book of Pericles Prince of Tyre.*" [It may be noted that *Antony and Cleopatra* was entered at the same time.]

1608. Geo. Wilkins brought out a novel called "*The Painfull Adventures of Pericles, Prince of Tyre.* Being the True History of the Play, as it was lately presented by the worthy and ancient Poet, John Gower. Printed by T. P[avier] for Nat. Butter, 1608."

1609. A quarto appeared, the title-page of which had better be quoted : "The late, and much admired play, called *Pericles.* With the true Relation of the whole Historic, Adventures, and Fortunes, of the said Prince. As also, the no less strange and worthy accidents, in the Birth and Life of his Daughter Marina. As it hath been divers and sundry times acted by his Majesties Servants at the Globe on the Banck-side. By William Shakespeare. Imprinted for Henry Gosson, 1609."

Several Quartos followed ; Gosson bringing out another

---

[1] It will be remembered that this publisher had a share in the production of the First Folio, and that he re-entered *Antony and Cleopatra* on November 8th, 1623. *Whether* he transferred *Pericles* [to Gosson], or *why* he did so, is not known.

in the same year. Q_3 appeared in 1611 ; soon afterwards (but when is not known), Pavier obtained the copyright ; he brought out an edition in 1619, the title-page of which reads as follows :—

"*The late and much admired play, called Pericles, Prince of Tyre.* With the true Relation of the whole History, Adventures, and Fortunes, of the saide Prince. Written by W. Shakespeare. Printed for J. P. 1619." Yet, when the Folio of 1623 appeared, *Pericles* was not included [although there seems to have been no difficulty in arranging for the transferring or for the using the plays the rights of which were held by any others besides the four publishers who brought out that edition.]

The subsequent history of the play may be given. On 4 Aug. 1626, Pavier transferred " his rights in Shakespeare's plays" to Brewster and Birde. Birde brought out Q_5 in 1630, but in the same year (November 8th) he assigned *Pericles* and other plays to Ric. Cotes. [It is evident that most of the Pavier-plays are either wholly or in part spurious]. It is a strange fact that, although the firm of Cotes took part in the production of the 2nd Folio in 1632, *Pericles* was not included in that work ; and yet, three years later (1635), T. Cotes brought out a sixth quarto. When the 3rd Folio appeared in 1664, it included *Pericles*, as well as several plays attributed to Shakespeare, but undoubtedly spurious.

Considering these data then, what was Shakespeare's connection with the play ? and when did he write his part ?

It has been generally admitted that Shakespeare had some share in the work, and more particularly in the latter part of it ; this is stated, with more or less variation, by Rowe, Farmer, Percy, Steevens, Malone, Douce, Drake, and others ; the last-mentioned, noticing that " the interest accumulates as the story proceeds," thought that Shakespeare at first was joined with some other dramatist, but that after the second act, "he seems to have assumed almost the entire management of the remainder." Somewhat similarly Coleridge

was of opinion, that the great dramatist in preparing for use
some drama, warmed to his work as he got deeper into it ;
Hallam said the same.

But, lately, since attention has been drawn to Wilkins's
novel, the question has been narrowed. That writer almost
in so many words claims a great part of the play (the Gower
part for instance) as his own ; and "it is accordingly conjectured by Delius, that Wilkins had already composed the
play of *Pericles* with the aid of Twine's novel and of the
Confessio Amantis, when Shakespeare resolved to adapt it
for the use of the King's Players, who acted it in 1607 and
1608 under his, as the more attractive name" (Ward's *English
Dramatic Literature*, vol. i. p. 423). Mr. Collier even goes
so far as to suppose that there is a possibility of "recovering
a lost portion of the language of Shakespeare" from Wilkins's
novel ; but Mr. Fleay, in his very able paper (*N. S. S. Trans.*
1874, vol. i.), does not recognise more than a few sentences
of the great dramatist. Mr. Fleay, who thinks that the play
was written by Wilkins and Rowley, in conjunction with
Shakespeare (or rather with his work), dates the play 1607 ;
and is confirmed in his opinion by the fact that Act iii. Sc. 2
of *Pericles* is "distinctly imitated" in Act iv. Sc. 3 of
The Puritan, a play which appeared in 1607 (*Shakespeare
Manual*, p. 20).

It was, of course, written before the appearance of the
quarto in 1609, and perhaps almost equally certain before
the entry on May 20th, 1608 ; Mr. Fleay thinks it may have
preceded the republication of Twine's book ; but there is no
evidence to decide this ; and the date must be left 1607—8.

The theory that the play as connected with Shakespeare is
contemporary with *Antony and Cleopatra*, suggested as it is
by the simultaneous entry in the *Stationers' Register*, is
strikingly confirmed by the "weak-ending" test (see Prof.
Ingram, who places it in "the last period" of our plays) ;
while the classical allusion test and others class it with
Timon of Athens, &c.

ANTONY AND CLEOPATRA.

" The lover, all as frantic,
Sees Helen's beauty in a brow of Egypt."
A Midsummer Night's Dream.

Almost every commentator has agreed to date this play early (before May 20th) in the year 1608 ; Gervinus, however, and the provisional scheme of the New Shakspere Society, place it in 1607 ; while C. Knight, Verplanck, and W. W. Lloyd give it a later date.

The play does not seem to have been published before the First Folio appeared, though we learn from the *Stationers' Register* that Edward Blount (one of the publishers of that folio) had entered an *Antony and Cleopatra* on May 20th, 1608. This is generally assumed to be Shakespeare's play, which had probably been acted shortly before.

Chalmers supposes that the subject was "intimated" to Shakespeare by Daniel's tragedy, entitled *Cleopatra*, which was entered at Stationers' Hall on Oct. 19th, 1593 ; but he really owed nothing either to this, or to Lady Pembroke's translation of Garnier's *Antonie*, which appeared in 1595. The real source of this, as of the other Roman plays, is North's translation of Amyot's *Plutarch ;* which edition of that work he used is a point still *sub judice* (see p. 147). In Lodge's *The Devils Incarnate*, 1596, Chalmers points out the suggestive remark, that "Antony, dallying in delights with Cleopatra, gave Cæsar opportunitie of many victories."

The description of the Nile in Act ii. Sc. 7, may be taken from Holland's *Pliny*, or from John Pory's translation of Leo's *History of Africa*, 1600. Mr. Massey thinks that Cleopatra may be founded on Lady Rich, the lady of the dark eyes, whom he seeks to identify with the " black " lady of the *Sonnets ;* Prof. Ward approves the supposition. Lady Rich died in 1606.

Malone (*Appendix I.* p. 710) referring to *Antony and Cleopatra*, iv. 14, 2 :

> "Sometime we see a *cloud* that's *dragonish;*
> A vapour sometime like a bear or *lion;* &c."

compares Chapman's *Bussy d'Ambois*, 1607 :—

> "Like empty *clouds*,
> In which our faulty apprehension forge
> The forms of *dragons, lions*, elephants,
> When they hold no proportion."

Malone also pointed out a probable allusion to the spectacular attractions of this play in Ben Jonson's *Silent Woman* (iv. 4) where Morose says : "Nay, I would sit out a play that were nothing but *fights at sea*, drum, trumpet, and target."

External and internal evidence unite in proving that this play was produced subsequently to *Julius Cæsar*; it was formerly supposed that the dates of their production were separated only by an interval of a year, but modern research has antedated *Julius Cæsar* some half-a-dozen years ; Prof. Ingram and others support this conclusion (of a longer interval between the two plays) by metrical tests ; Prof. Dowden gives æsthetic reasons ; and I may add that the arrangement of the tragedies, as given in the First Folio, would suggest the same (see my remark on the position of *Coriolanus*, p. 150).

Craik, *English of Shakespeare*, p. 38, dwelling upon "the unemphatic final monosyllable" says : "there is no other single indication which can be compared with it as an element in determining the chronology of the Plays. It is therefore extremely difficult to believe that the three Roman Plays, *Julius Cæsar, Antony and Cleopatra*, and *Coriolanus* can all belong to the same period (Malone assigns them severally to the years 1607, 1608, and 1610), seeing that the second and third are among the plays in which verses having in the tenth place an unemphatic monosyllable of the kind in question are most frequent, while there are only ten instances of anything of the sort in the first."

Prof. Ingram in his paper "On Shakspere's use of light and weak endings" published in the *Transactions of the New Shakspere Society*, 1874, Part 2, pp. 450, 451, gives the following statistics :—

	No. of light endings.	No. of weak endings.
Julius Cæsar	10	0
Antony and Cleopatra .	71	28
Coriolanus	60	44

He adds : " The weak endings do not come in by slow degrees, but the poet seems to have thrown himself at once into this new structure of verse ; twenty-eight examples occurring in *Antony and Cleopatra*, whilst there are not more than two in any earlier play. Hence, the argument brought forward by Craik . . . . that *Julius Cæsar* and *Antony and Cleopatra* must be separated by a wide interval, because differing so much in this character of the verse, will have to be given up. They must, indeed, be so separated ; but not on this ground."

Before proceeding to an æsthetic consideration of this point, it may be remarked that the relative date here assumed is strikingly confirmed by "the rhyme-test" and by "the feminine-ending test" (see p. 174). Vatke, French, and Ward point out that, in working on *Plutarch*, Shakespeare's task was here a different one from that in *Julius Cæsar*. "The Brutus of Plutarch was a character ready made to his hands, but the Antony of history, of Plutarch himself, would have been no subject for poetry ;" Shakespeare's divergements from the biographer are characteristically poetic and artistic.

Prof. Dowden (*Shakspere: His Mind and Art*, pp. 178–180), most strikingly points out the difference between the poet's mental attitudes in the two plays referred to ; he also shows the mental link between *Antony and Cleopatra* and *Macbeth* on the one hand, and between *Antony and Cleopatra* and *Coriolanus* on the other ; he concludes : " Thus an ethical tendency connects these (last) two plays, which are also connected in point of time. While *Antony and Cleopatra*, although historically a continuation of *Julius Cæsar*, stands separated from it, both in the chronological order of Shakspere's plays, and in the logical order assigned by successive developments of the conscience, the intellect and the imagination of the dramatist."

The nearly contemporaneous production of *Macbeth* and *Antony and Cleopatra* is supported by the following connecting links, pointed out by Malone.

A passage in North's *Life of Antony* may have suggested the lines in *Macbeth* (i. 3, 84, 85) :—

> " Or have we eaten on the insane root
> That takes the reason prisoner ? "

Again compare *Macbeth* (iii. 1, 54—57.)

> " There is none but he
> Whose being I do *fear :* and, under him,
> My *Genius* is rebuked ; as it is said,
> *Mark Antony's* was by *Cæsar.*"

with *Antony and Cleopatra* (ii. 3, 19—22.)

> " O *Antony . . .*
> Thy demon, that's thy spirit which keeps thee, is
> Noble, courageous, high, unmatchable,
> Where *Cæsar's* is not ; but near him, thy *angel*
> Becomes a *fear*, as being o'erpowered."

[I would, parenthetically, confirm this result here sought to be established by remarking that, in the quotation from *Macbeth*, Octavius is styled " Cæsar " simply : this surely would not have been so, had not Shakespeare's mind at the time been " full of " the Antony-(Octavius) Cæsar story.]

This may lead to a few remarks upon the other classical allusions in the play. As Malone long ago remarked, Shakespeare in reading Plutarch's *Life of Antony* for this play, came across the story of "Timon," which he probably dramatised at about the same period (see p. 130). The same commentator also pointed out the allusion in *Cymbeline* to Cleopatra sailing on the river Cydnus as indicative of the chronological contiguity of those tragedies. I may add that while in the allusion in *Cymbeline* (ii. 4, 69—73) Shakespeare, so to speak, goes out of his way to introduce the story, so in that marvellous piece of scene-painting in *Antony and Cleopatra* (ii. 2, 191—223) the description is given in a manner that is almost chorus-like. Compare Prof. Dowden's remark (*Shakspere : His Mind and Art*, p. 121), ",the nearest approach perhaps to a chorus is to be found in the person of Enobarbus in *Antony and Cleopatra.*"

It is perhaps superfluous to remark, though it is interesting to note, that what may almost be called the only other allusion in our author to Cleopatra [viz., *As You Like It*, iii. 2, 152—156 :—

"Nature presently distilled
Helen's cheek, but not her heart,
Cleopatra's majesty,
Atalanta's better part,
Sad Lucretia's modesty."]

regards as her *spécialité* a side of her character, which (to Adolph Stahr's regret) Shakespeare has not so much regarded in the tragedy ; the allusion was evidently made some years before the queen had been psychologically studied.

The allusions to Ajax seem to me to indicate more extended knowledge and wider reading than those in several other plays (see p. 103, &c.) ; they are the following :—

"Oh ! he is more mad
Than Telamon for his shield."— (iv. 13, 1, 2).

The seven-fold shield of Ajax cannot keep
The battery from my heart."—(iv. 13, 38, 39).

The date assumed for this play, viz., 1608, nearly at the conclusion of his series of great tragedies, seems to be

supported by a general æsthetic consideration of the whole
drama ; Johnson, indeed, has censured it for want of discrimination of characters ; Drake has modified his praise
by remarking that "the subject is too complex and extended
to admit of a due degree of simplicity and wholeness, and
the mind is consequently hurried by a multiplicity of incidents, for whose introduction and succession we are not
sufficiently prepared ; " while Gervinus adds to this "inatten-
tion to dramatic clearness and unity," "other faults which
seem to disturb somewhat the pure enjoyment of this drama."
"The diction (he says) is very forced, often short and
obscure ; the crowd of matter creates a crowd of ideas, &c."
He then starts an ethical objection : "there is no great and
noble character among the personages ; no really elevating
feature in the actions of this drama, either in its politics or
its love affairs." The German Professor proceeds to account.
for this : "it would appear as if Shakespeare, about the time
between 1607 and 1610, had had, we will not say a period,
but intervals in which he wrote his poetry in a manner
altogether more careless, whether we consider it from an
æsthetic or from an ethical point of view. What might have
been the cause of this we can scarcely guess. It is possible
that his disgust for theatrical matters in general seized him
more strongly about this period ; it may be possible that the
traces of bodily exhaustion had already appeared in him,
and that this may have been the cause of his withdrawal and
the first intimation of his early death. Whether this be so,
or whatever may have been the cause of the careless treatment of some of the works of this period, the thing itself
seems incontestable."

Against this, however, may be placed the opinion of
Coleridge, who considered this play "as a powerful rival to
Lear and all the best dramas of our poet," and who saw in
it "a gigantic power in its ripest prime ; " the remarks of
Upton on the elevation of language used ; Mrs. Jameson's
analysis of Cleopatra's character ; and Dowden's statement

L

that the play is "written with intense and complete imaginative energy." It may be added that in no play is the adherence to the historical ground-work more striking, nor the divergence from it more artistic ; that the psychological development of the hero, the Antony of *Julius Cæsar*, the Antony of *Antony and Cleopatra*, should be carefully watched ; that the effective delineation of the character of Cleopatra, in that particular light in which Shakespeare chose to draw it, should be noted, till while we acknowledge with Milton [with whose Delila, by the by, Prof. Dowden contrasts our heroine]

> " That beauty is excelled by manly grace
> And wisdom which alone is truly fair ; "

we yet join in Enobarbus's enthusiastic and glowing description of the Egyptian queen, when he says that

> " Age cannot wither her, nor custom stale
> Her infinite variety."

Finally, let those, whose acute eyesight can detect flaws in the fair texture of this drama, be reminded that in this very play (Act iv. Sc. 8) Shakespeare exclaims :—

> " What girl ! though grey
> Do something mingle with our younger brown, yet ha' we
> A brain that nourishes our nerves, and can
> Get goal for goal of youth."

Can it be doubted that the remark has a tinge of personality in it ?

" This is the fruit of rashness ! "—Richard III.

No " entry " of this play, nor any edition of it, has been discovered prior to the year 1623 and the publication of the First Folio ; but the date of 1610 assigned to it by Malone, or that of 1609, in which Chalmers was followed by Drake, has been pretty generally received ; Delius dates it " before May, 1608 ; " I shall give reasons below for adopting the latest of these, viz., 1610.

As to its source, it is scarcely an exaggeration, says Archbishop Trench (*Four Lectures on Plutarch*), to say that the whole play is to be found in Plutarch ; the question, however, arises which edition of North's translation of *Amyot* did Shakespeare use ? Mr. Halliwell-Phillipps has thrown out a hint with regard to this ; he has noticed (see *New Shakspere Society's Transactions*, 1874, p. 376, &c.) in comparing the editions of 1579, 1595, 1603, and 1612, that in a passage in *Coriolanus* in the earlier numbers the word "unfortunately" is printed for "unfortunate ;" whilst the correct word is given in the 1612 edition, and in a corresponding sentence in Shakespeare's play. " There is therefore *primâ facie* evidence that Shakspere used the 1612 edition for his *Coriolanus*, if not for his other Roman plays....Coupling this fact with the other that Mr. Paton claims to have establisht, namely, that Shakspere's own copy of the 1612 edition of North's *Plutarch*, with his initials W. S., is now in the Greenock Library, we have a strong *primâ facie* case for the use of that edition by Shakspere in his *Coriolanus;* for, as Dyce well says, this play ' is proved by the style to have been one of the author's latest compositions.' " But to these considerations, it may be answered, first, that Shakespeare's " own instinct and ear " would doubtless lead him

to make the required alteration, and, secondly, that he must
have used an earlier edition for *Julius Cæsar* at any rate.

Malone pointed out, that some of the expressions used in
Menenius's speech in the first Act are taken from the same
tale as told of Adrian the Fourth by Camden in his *Remaines*, which appeared in 1605.

The same commentator at one time thought that the
expression in ii. 2, 104, 105 :—

> " In the brunt of seventeen battles since
> He *lurched* all swords *of the garland*,"

was sneered at by Ben Jonson, in his *Silent Woman* (1609)
Act v., last Scene, where, as Steevens had pointed out, we
read : " You have *lurched* your friends of the better half *of
the garland.*"   Malone, however, having met with the same
expression in a pamphlet written by T. Nashe, supposed it
to be a common phrase of the time.

Again, Malone's remark (on the passage in Volumnia's
speech, iii. 2, 79, 80 :—

> " Now humble as the *ripest mulberry*
> That will not hold the handling ")

is controverted by Chalmers, who refers the illustration not
to their first introduction into England at that period (for he
shows that they were well known in Elizabeth's time) but to
James's proclamation in 1609 in favour of the breeding of
silkworms.

Chalmers (*Suppl. Apol.*, pp. 435, 436) endeavours to prove
that the many references to famine and death in this play,
when compared with the deaths in England in 1608 and
1609, show " that the play was probably written in 1609,
while the pressure was yet felt."

Mr. Whitelaw (Rugby Edition of this play) says : " We
may suppose that in *Coriolanus*, Shakespeare intended a
twofold warning, to the pride of James, and to the gathering
resistance of the Commons.   The first of the Stuart kings

had lost no time in propounding his theory of kingship. From the first meeting of his first parliament to its dissolution *in this year* 1610, there were continual bickerings between King and Commons......In Feb. 1610, there was a Remonstrance against illegal impositions." But, as Prof. Dowden remarks, "it is matter of congratulation that Shakespeare approached history not through political theories, or philosophies, but through a wide and deep sympathy with human action, and human suffering."

The various metrical and other mental tests (see p. 174, &c.) suggest a late date ; and I would add that a verbal test, viz., the number of peculiar words and phrases employed, confirms this (compare *The Tempest*, &c.).

Prof. Ward (*English Dramatic Literature*, pp. 433, 434) says that "it will not be denied by any student of Shakspere that in this" play we have "a work of the poet's maturest period, even if the conclusion of H. Viehoff's plausible argument (Shakespeare's *Coriolan* in *Jahrbuch*, vol. iv., 1869) be considered daring, that no other of Shakspere's plays can be ranked above *Coriolanus*, and hardly any beside it, as to perfection in every point of artistic composition. Nor is it necessary to subscribe to Ulrici's view, as summarised by the same writer, according to which ' *Coriolanus* is the first play of a historic tetralogy, presenting the history of the' political growth of the Roman people in its most essential phases.'....In any case the style of the play belongs to Shakespeare's latest period."

In support of this last remark, I may add that we must also allow for considerable change and growth of mind before Shakespeare would choose such a story as this, and treat it in the way he has treated it ; that an interval should be allowed between, say, the emotional phases of Antony and the peculiar mental attitude of *Coriolanus ;* and so with regard to minor characters, for instance between the feeble and pompous garrulity of Polonius and the sarcastic wit and shrewd good sense of Menenius. Again, the fact that there is no entry of it on the Stationers' Register, coupled with the circumstance that after 1609 no entry (with the single exception of *Othello* in 1621) of any of Shakespeare's plays occurs, favours a date later than 1609 ; while I cannot but think, comparing the position of *The Tempest* (also late, see p. 158) in the arrangement of the comedies in the First Folio, with that of *Coriolanus* at the beginning of the tragedies, that this arrangement was due to the fact that each of these plays had been produced late in Shakespeare's writing days. These facts, and the peculiar diction alluded to above, lead me to date the drama at least as late as 1610.

CYMBELINE.

" A constant, loving, noble nature."—Othello.

Before any opinion is given as to the year in which this play was produced, it may be well to clear the ground by stating the sources from which either the general plot, or particular hints, may have been taken.

The story of Imogen was probably obtained from some translation of one of the novels in Boccaccio's *Decamerone ;* the tale is also told in *Westward for Smelts* (dated by Malone 1603, though no edition is known of an earlier date than 1620). The name, Imogen, is found in *Holinshed ;* but it is to be noted that Shakespeare seems at one time to have intended to use it in *Much Ado About Nothing*, where in the Folio Edition Act i, Sc. 1, opens with " Enter Leonato, Innogen (or Imogen) his wife, &c." Neither the name nor the character appears except in this stage-direction.

As Malone pointed out, the name Leonatus occurs in Sidney's *Arcadia*, and had evidently been observed by Shakespeare when writing his *Lear ;* now the story of *Cymbeline* in Holinshed's *Chronicles* lies near to that of *Lear* and not far from that of *Macbeth ;* again, the story of Hay, a husbandman, who with his two sons stayed his flying country-men in a lane, and turned the battle against the enemy, is found near the story of *Macbeth* in Holinshed's *Scottish Chronicles.* Malone therefore conjectured that the plays mentioned were produced nearly contemporaneously, and he placed them in the following order, *King Lear, Cymbeline, Macbeth.*

Again, because of the references to Cæsar's immeasureable ambition, and to Cleopatra's sailing on the Cydnus to meet Antony, Malone also thought it probable that about this time Shakespeare had been perusing the lives of Cæsar, Brutus, and Mark Antony.

Steevens noted the following parallel passages :—

> " I have bely'd a lady,
> The princess of this country ; *and the air of't*
> *Revengingly enfeebles me ; or could this carle,*
> *A very drudge of nature's, have subdued me*
> *In my profession ?* "—(*Cymbeline*, iv. 2, 2—6).

> " I hear the tread of people : I am hurt ;
> *The gods take part against me ; could this boor*
> *Have held me thus else ?* "—(*Philaster*, iv. 1.)

Other points of resemblance have been pointed out between the two plays ; it becomes, therefore, of importance to ascertain the date of Beaumont and Fletcher's work. It is alluded to in Davies' *Epigrams*, which are generally attri-buted to the year 1611 ; Malone dated Philaster in 1608—9, Dyce said 1608, but Mr. Fleay thinks it may be as late as 1610—1611.

Malone at first assigned *Cymbeline* to the year 1605 ;[1] but, afterwards from the last-mentioned comparison, and from " the great resemblance which the versification of this play bears to that of the *Winter's Tale* and *The Tempest*," he altered his opinion and dated it 1609. This date is very

---

[1] It may be stated, *en passant*, that Coleridge and Tieck strangely thought *Cymbeline* an "early youthful sketch."

probably nearer the truth ; and reasons will now be stated for assigning the play to the following year 1610.

Prof. Hertzberg has shown that almost all the verse-tests support this late date, or rather that of the following year ; he has employed the rhyme-test (which, however, he does not think should be relied upon), the feminine-ending test, the weak-ending test (both of which place it decisively among the latest plays), the Alexandrine, and verse irregularly constructed (including verses in which an anapæst is used instead of an iambus).

Mr. Fleay, however, is of opinion that the rhyme-test is a more valuable index than the feminine-ending test ; and he formerly came to the conclusion, by applying metrical tests, that *Cymbeline* "was begun in 1606, and completed between 1607 and 1608 ; and that Act iv. Sc. 2, was written separately as shown by the large proportion of rhymes and the correct pronunciation of Posthumus." But, lately, owing chiefly to the fact that *Philaster* may not have been produced so early as was formerly thought, he has somewhat altered his opinion, and he now assigns the main part of *Cymbeline* to the year 1610. And this date, it should be observed, is supported by the following external evidence : Dr. Simon Forman, as Mr. Collier pointed out, writing either in 1610 or 1611 (the exact date is not given), describes in some detail a performance of *Cymbeline* which he had witnessed ; and Richard Robinson who is known to have taken one of the (female) characters in this play, is also known to have joined the King's Company at this very time.

Mr. Furnivall (*N. S. S. Trans.*, 1874, vol. i., p. 18) says : " In general handling *Cymbeline* is more close to *The Winter's Tale* than any other play. Like that, it treats of the father's breaking of family ties[1] by his own injustice, and then rejoining them, and points (in my belief) to Shak-

---

[1] "Compare too Catharine's case in *Henry VIII.* of this time." (Note by Mr. Furnivall.) Mr. Furnivall might have increased the resemblance, by remarking that in the *Winter's Tale*, in *Cymbeline*, and in *Henry VIII.* the son and heir is dead.

spere's renewed family life at Stratford after he had left London, and to the contrast he must have felt between country and court."

In conclusion, the period, to which the play is here referred, is just the time at which we should have expected Shakespeare to have produced a play like this; for, notice the entire absence of a comic character (unless, indeed, with Schlegel, we count Cloten as such), and consider, with Drake (as against the absurd criticism of Dr. Johnson), "in spite of a slight weakness in the construction of the fable, the great poetic beauty,[1] the variety, the truth of character, the display of sentiment and emotion." Admire, too, the skilful development of poetical justice at the close, and rejoice that while Shakespeare felt it accordant with poetic justice to leave Desdemona, faithful and pure as she was, strangled by the hands of him who "loved not wisely but too well," and who was so soon to follow her, and while he thought it necessary to leave Cordelia, "whose voice was ever soft, gentle, and low," lying dead upon the arms of the father whose own life was just ebbing away, in this play, however, we may hear Posthumus exclaiming to the most pure, the most faithful, the most gentle and loving of all his marvellous creations—Imogen :—

> " Hang there like fruit, my soul,
> Till the tree die !"

---

[1] Compare the song in *Cymbeline* with some lines in one of the most exquisite of Shakespeare's Sonnets, the twenty-ninth: and note, by the by, how this particular Sonnet contains the very essence of that most marvellous poem of the present century, the *In Memoriam*.

"The pattern of all patience."—*King Lear.*

"A woman's story told at a winter's fire."—*Macbeth.*

There is no entry on the books of the Stationers' Company,[1] nor any quarto edition of this play, to help us in determining the date of its production ; this, however, may perhaps be fixed by the following considerations :—

And, first, that it was produced among the last of Shakespeare's works is rendered probable by its being placed last in order of the comedies as given in the First Folio, whilst, though it may seem somewhat paradoxical to say so, the position of *The Tempest*, first in the same list, perhaps suggests the nearly contemporaneous production of these two plays.

Malone found a memorandum in the *Office Book* of Sir Henry Herbert (vol. iii. p. 229) to this effect :—

"For the king's players. An old play called *Winter's Tale*, formerly allowed of by Sir George Bucke and likewyse by mee on Mr. Hemminges his worde that there was nothing prophane added or reformed, though the allowed booke was missing : and therefore I returned it without a fee, this 19th of August, 1623." Now the same investigator found that Sir G. Buck did not obtain complete[2] possession of his office of Master of the Revels till August, 1610, and he therefore conjectured "that the *Winter's Tale* was originally licensed by him in the latter part of that year or the beginning of

[1] The following entry, under date May 22, 1594, led Malone in his first edition to give an early date to this play. "Edw. White. A booke entituled *a Wynters nightes Pastime.*" It may be here mentioned that a suspected entry in "the Accounts of the Revels," &c. speaks of a performance of "a play called '*The Winter Nightes Tayle,*' on Nov. 5th," 1611.

[2] It should, however, be noticed that from 1607 Sir G. Buck had practically possession of the office, as the Stationers' Register distinctly and continually shows.

the next." And this date (1610—11) is confirmed by the since-discovered MS. of Dr. Forman, who tells us of a performance of this play at the Globe Theatre on May 15th, 1611 ; the Vertue MS. mention of the acting of it in 1613 also suggests that it was then comparatively recent.

Prof. Ward (*ut suprá*, p. 437) says : " It is possible that the pretty title was suggested to Shakspere by that of a *Winter's Night's Vision*, an addition to the *Mirror of Magistrates* published by Niccols in 1610, the year in which the *Winter's Tale* was perhaps written. But the term ' a winter's tale ' was familiarly used to express a wonderful story suitable to be told over the fire on winter nights ('So I am content to drive-away the time with an old wives' winter's tale ;' Peele's *Old Wives' Tale*)." [Compare also, it may be added, ii. 1, 23—25, " tell's a tale...a sad tale's best for winter ;" 3 *Henry VI.*, v., 5—25, " Let Æsop fable in a winter's night ;" *Macbeth*, iii., 5, 65, " A woman's story at a winter's fire ;" &c.]

There can be very little doubt that this comedy and *The Tempest* are nearly contemporary[1] in date (see p. 160) ; as to their relative order, however, Mr. Collier has made the following very acute conjecture : he noted that one of the points in which the *Wintre's Tale* differs from Greene's *Dorastus and Favonia*, or *Pandosto* [ed. 1588, 1607, &c.], upon which it is founded, is the manner in which Perdita is exposed in the deserts of Bohemia ; in the novel the child had been cast adrift in a sailless and rudderless boat ; he, therefore, accounted for the variation by supposing that Shakespeare purposely altered the manner of exposure in the *Winter's Tale*, because he had *already* used the other metho din *The Tempest.* It may here be noticed that a few years afterwards, in 1614, in the Induction to his *Bartholomew Fair*, Jonson ridiculed the two plays here mentioned : " If there be never a *servant-monster* in the fair

---

[1] Ulrici called *The Tempest* "the *companion* and the *complement* of this play."

(Caliban), who can help it, he says, nor a *nest of antiques ?*[1]
He is loth to make nature afraid in his plays, like those that
beget *Tales, Tempests,* and such like drolleries, &c. ;" and
Malone is inclined to think that Jonson "joined these plays
in the same censure,[2] in consequence of their having been
produced at no great distance of time from each other."

Turning to supposed contemporary allusions, we may first
mention as a charming instance of amateur meddling the
conjecture by Horatio Walpole (Lord Orford) that *A Winter's
Tale* was written as "an indirect apology for Anne Bullen,"
and therefore should be assigned to the reign of her daughter
Elizabeth ; and over against this we may set Sir William
Blackstone's reason for referring it to the reign of her
successor James I., viz., that the lines, i. 4, 357—361 :—

> " If I could find example
> Of thousands that had struck anointed kings
> And flourished after, I'ld not do't ; but since
> Nor brass nor stone nor parchment bears not one,
> Let villany itself forswear it,"

could not have been written in the time of her who deprived
Queen Mary of Scots of her life.   Chalmers proves the
inaccuracy of this inference, but we will not follow his
reasons, because the most appropriate suggestion for the
remark is surely the assassination of Henri Quatre in Paris
on the 14th of May, 1610, and the execution of the murderer
Ravaillac some few days after, amidst the execrations of the
populace.

Mr. Furnivall sees in this (and nearly every contemporary
play) an indication of Shakespeare's (supposed) reconcilia-

[1] Compare *Winter's Tale,* iv. 4, 331—351, and *The Dance of Twelve Satyrs.*
For the word "antique," note *Macbeth,* iv. 1, 130, "while you perform your
antic round."
[2] Drake demurs to the word "censure;" but in spite of this, in spite of
Jonson's own remarks a little further on in this Induction about the "politic
picklock of the scene, so solemnly ridiculous . . . that will pretend to affirm on
his own inspired ignorance what . . . is meant," &c. ; and in spite of Gifford, the
word "ridicule" has been used above, from a general view of the passage, and
from a remembrance of Ben Jonson's remark to Drummond of Hawthornden, some
half a dozen years afterwards. (See Append.x, on Shakespeare and Ben Jonson.)

tion with his wife and daughters ; he might have completed the parallel by remarking that the only *son and heir* in both cases *had been dead some "sixteen years"* (see Act iv. Sc. 1, l. 6 ; and Hamnet's death in 1596).

The date here assigned is supported by almost every internal test, metrical, æsthetic, and otherwise. The rhyme-test (if no account be taken of the chorus scene of Act iv.) places the play last in the list ; the weak-ending test, the feminine-ending test, and others give nearly similar results. From Ben Jonson's time to Samuel Johnson's, commentators have pointed to certain improbabilities in the play ; Gervinus indeed apologises for these by saying that Shakespeare found them in the novel, and seeing that "they could not be repaired by art, he therefore began upon his theme in quite an opposite direction ; he increased still more the marvellous, &c." But really no apology is needed by any save the hypercritical ; whoever feels what Mrs. Jameson so fully expresses about "the beautiful combination of the pastoral with the elegant" in Perdita, whoever watches the connection of tragedy and comedy by the peculiar expedient of the chorus[1] of Act iv., whoever enters into the beauty of the many grand passages which are scattered throughout this play, whoever catches the spirit of final calm and lasting peace which settles over the closing scene, will have no hesitation in classing this drama with the latest works of its great author.

[1] This chorus also professedly accounts for the neglect of the unities of *time* and *place* in this play. Jephson and Phillpotts, in their editions of *The Tempest*, both direct attention to this neglect, as compared with the observance in the contemporary plays, *The Tempest* and *Winter's Tale*, without dwelling upon the expedient which Shakespeare used to atone for it.

> " Though his bark cannot be lost,
>   Yet it shall be tempest-tost."—*Macbeth.*

> " In nature's infinite book of secrecy
>   A little I can read."—*Antony and Cleopatra.*

Considerable discussion has taken place as to the date
which should be assigned to this play ; in elaborate essays,
Hunter declared it was earlier than 1596, Elze fixed it in
1604, and Malone decided for 1610–11. The reasons which
the last-mentioned commentator advanced will here be
referred to, and confirmed by others ; while the arguments
of the former will, *en passant*, be discussed.

It may be first stated that there is very little external
evidence directly bearing upon the subject ; the drama itself
was not printed, nor was it entered upon the Stationers'
Register, till 1623 ; the entry on the *Revels' Record* of a
performance of it at Whitehall in 1611, has been declared a
forgery ; the Vertue MS., however, informs us that it was
acted by the King's Company before several members of the
royal family in the beginning of the year 1613.

It is a somewhat curious fact, that each of the essayists
mentioned above has endeavoured to fortify his position by
supposed sneers at our play in the works of Ben Jonson.
Mr. Hunter had no doubt about the intended allusions in
the following lines from the Induction to *Every Man in
His Humour*:—

> " Nor creaking throne comes down the boys to please :
>   Nor nimble squib is seen to make afeard
>   The gentlewomen ; no roll'd-bullet heard
>   To say, it thunders ; nor tempestuous drum
>   Rumbles, to tell you when the storm doth come ;...
>   You, that have so graced monsters, may like men."

Unfortunately, however, this Induction does not appear in the 1601 quarto, and there is no evidence to show that it was produced before the folio of 1616 ; so that the allusions to this play if they be admitted (and, it may be added, those to *Henry V.*, *Henry VI.*, *Winter's Tale*, &c., see Appendix, p. 207) do not help us much in fixing the date, while they certainly do not prove the early theory.

Again, Dr. Karl Elze quotes the following passage from the same author's *Volpone; or, the Fox*, 1605 :—

> *Lady Politic Would-be.*—" All our English writers,
> I mean such as are happy in the Italian,
> Will deign to steal out of this author, mainly :
> Almost as much as from Montagnié, &c."
>   [iii. 2 (Part I.)].

This, he thinks, refers to the celebrated passage in Act ii. Sc. 1 (which will be alluded to below), and to passages in *Hamlet* and other plays ; and he, therefore, concludes that *The Tempest* must have been written *after* the appearance of Florio's translation of *Montaigne* in 1603 and *before* the production of Jonson's *Fox* in 1605 ; that is to say, he assigns the play we are considering to the year 1604. He endeavours to support his date by certain allusions, which are imaginary, and by certain theories, which are untenable. This *Montaigne-theory* of the German Professor deserves no more attention than that started by the French critic, Charles, which will be glanced at a little later on.

On the other hand, the allusion in the Induction of Ben Jonson's *Bartholomew Fair* (1614) is both undoubted and helpful ; the passage is this :—

" If there be never a *servant-monster* in the fair, who can help it, he says, nor a *nest of antiques?* he is loth to make nature afraid in his *plays*, like those that beget *tales*, *tempests*, and such like drolleries."

When it is remembered that, in iii. 2—3, Caliban is styled a " *servant-monster*" and when the reference to *A Winter's*

Tale is noticed, there cannot be a doubt that we have here
a distinct allusion to *The Tempest*, and it may perhaps also
be inferred that the plays criticised were of comparatively
recent production.

While we are noting this contemporaneity of *The Tempest*
and *A Winter's Tale*, attention may be drawn to the acute
theory advanced by Mr. Collier to prove that the play we
are dealing with preceded the *Winter's Tale;* this has
been noticed in the section upon that drama. It may be
added however that Ulrici, from æsthetic reasons, thinks
The Tempest at once the companion and the complement
of the *Winter's Tale.*

Malone (2nd Appendix, p. 682) points out a striking
parallel between the services of Ariel in *The Tempest* (i. 2),
and of the Satyr in Fletcher's *Faithful Shepherdess* (v. 5) ;
but the date of the latter play is still *sub judice;* Malone
thought it was written before 1610.

We will now give a list of certain works which are supposed to have furnished Shakespeare with either hints,
expressions, names, or incidents for this play :—

(1) Malone and Douce drew attention to the account of
the shipwreck of the fleet (fitted out by the "Adventurers
and Company of Virginia" and patronised by the Lords
Southampton and Pembroke and other noblemen), especially
as given in (*a*) Silvester Jourdan's *Discovery of the Bermudas*
[cf. "still vexed Bermoothes," i. 2, 229] otherwise called the
Isle of Devils, dated Oct. 1610 (see also *Hakluyt*), and (β)
William Strachey's *True Repertory of the Wracke,* &c.,
reprinted in Purchas's *Pilgrimes* (1625), but doubtless first
produced (see Meissner) at about the same time as (γ) the
" *True Declaration of the Estate of the Colonie in Virginia,*
by the Councell," 1610. Malone has conclusively shown
that passages in *The Tempest* must be founded upon these
accounts of an expedition that excited the greatest interest
at that time.

(2) In Lord Sterling's tragedy of *Darius* [Edinburgh 1603,

London, 1604], there are, as Steevens pointed out, some lines
which were doubtless in Shakespeare's mind when he wrote
the celebrated passage iv. 1, 148, &c. ; they are :—

> "Let greatness of her glassy scepters vaunt,
>   Not scepters, no but reeds, soon bruised, soon broken,
> And this worldly pomp our wits enchant,
>   *All fades, and scarcely leaves behind a token.*
> These golden *palaces*, those *gorgeous* halls,
>   With furniture superfluously fair,
> Those stately courts, those *sky encountring walls*,
>   *Evanish all like vapours in the air."*—(iv. 2.)

(3) To another work published in 1603, Shakespeare was
undoubtedly indebted ; parts of Gonzalo's speeches, in ii. 1,
147—165, about "the commonwealth" where he would be
king, are taken *verbatim* from Florio's translation of Montaigne's *Essays* (1603), i. 30 ; the chapter from which these
words are taken is entitled " Of the Caniballes," and it has
been suggested that Shakespeare formed the name of his
" servant-monster" metathetically from the word Canibal.

(4) A few remarks may be made upon some other of the
names of *dramatis personæ ;* "Setebos" is perhaps due to
Eden's *Historye of Travaile in the West and East Indies ;* [1]
" Ariel" occurs, as Mr. Thoms notes, in Heywood's *Hierarchie of the Blessed Angels,* but it is evident (says Mr.
Wright, Clarendon Press Edition, p. xii.) that Shakespeare,
whatever may have been the source whence he borrowed it,
had his own etymology for the name, for in the list of the
Names of the Actors at the end of the play we find " Ariell,
an ayrie Spirit ;" doubtless, too, Shakespeare had a motive
in choosing the names, Prospero and Miranda, for the
principal characters in the piece [indeed (in spite of Mr.
Hales's observation : that "the riper Shakspere does not
like significant names ") Mr. Ruskin, in a striking and
characteristic passage (Works, Edition 1871, vol. ii. p. 102)
finds a "fundamental idea" in nearly every one of the

---

[1] To which also may be due the names Alonso, Ferdinand, &c.

M

heroine's names; *e.g.*, Portia (fortune-lady), Perdita (lost-lady), Cordelia (heart-lady), Desdemona (δυσδαιμονία), &c.]; the correct pronunciation of Stéphano (given as Stephāno in *The Merchant of Venice*), Shakespeare may have learnt when acting in Ben Jonson's *Every Man in His Humour;* lastly, the names Trinculo and Antonio occur in Tomkis's *Albumazar*, "acted for the first time in the Hall of Trinity College, Cambridge, March 9th, 1614—15, on the occasion of the visit of the king and Prince Charles; and this [the words are Mr. Wright's (*ut suprá*, p. xii.)] incidentally favours the supposition that *The Tempest* was then a comparatively recent play;" it should, however, be observed, that Malone says (Variorum Edition, vol. ii. p. 467), "*Albumazar* was printed in 1614, but is supposed by Dryden to have appeared some years before."

(5) A passage, v. i. 33, &c., may be due to Golding's *Ovid* (an edition of which appeared in 1603) : note that Heywood certainly borrowed from this in his *Brazen Age* (1613).

(6) Meissner thinks that Shakespeare copied the description of the Huns from Ammianus Marcellinus, as translated by Philemon Holland, in the year 1609. Jahrbuch, 1872.

(7) The same writer also argues that Prospero is an amplification of Cerimon in *Pericles* (1609); (see an article in the *Cornhill Magazine*, Oct. 1872).

(8) Mr. E. W. Gosse, in a letter to *The Academy*, Dec. 5th, 1874, compares [and Mr. Swinburne approves of the comparison] the following passage in Marlowe's *Hero and Leander*, published in 1598, with Ariel's song .—

> " Where all is *whist* and still,
> Save that the sea, playing on *yellow sand*,
> Sends forth a rattling murmur to the land."

(9) A ballad, entitled *The Enchanted Island*, bearing some resemblance to the subject of this play, was almost certainly posterior to it.

(10) Lastly, Tieck directed attention to the similarities,

both of incident and expression, between *The Tempest*, and Jacob Ayrer's *Die Schöne Sidea*. Whether they borrowed from a common original, or whether Shakespeare had (perhaps through the English actors who visited Nuremberg during the first decade of the seventeenth century) become acquainted with the German author, is a point yet to be decided.

Various opinions have been held as to the masque in Act iv. Sc. 1 ; the Cambridge editors and Mr. Fleay[1] consider it an insertion [but, it may be pointed out that lines 94--97, which refer to the main plot, seem to fit in so naturally that this supposition is improbable ; especially if we remember what Mr. Fleay has himself said (in his Canons for the use of Metrical Tests, *N. S. S. Trans.* 1874, vol. ii. p. 314), "in such cases as the Masque in *The Tempest*, &c., a different rhyming treatment was clearly adopted deliberately beforehand, in order to differentiate this part of the work from the rest"] ; Carrière thought it was an addition in 1613, at a performance in honour of the marriage of the Princess Elizabeth ; Holt suggested that it was "a compliment to the Earl of Essex on his being united in wedlock to the Lady Frances Howard in 1611 ; the Earl had been abroad ever since he was first contracted to her in 1607 ;" while Meissner is of opinion that the Masque was copied from the printed account of the show performed at the baptism of Prince Henry, son of James VI., in 1594 ; but he does not therefore adopt an early date, like Hunter, for he says, the death of the prince, in November, 1612, had revived the memory of the show !

Certain contemporary allusions, of more or less point,

---

[1] Mr. Fleay compares the vision in *Cymbeline*, Act v. Sc. 4, which he likewise thinks an insertion. But then again notice how naturally Posthumus alludes to it, in Act v. Sc. 5, ll. 424—433:

> " As I slept, methought
> Great Jupiter, upon his eagle backed
> Appeared to me," &c. ;

and remember that the rhyme, &c. was "clearly adopted deliberately beforehand."

have been noted, besides the shipwreck at the Bermudas, and the attempt to found a colony, referred to above ; about which we may further note that Malone has well remarked that " as the circumstance, from which this piece receives its name, is at an end in the very first scene, and as many other titles, equally proper, might have occurred to Shakespeare (such as 'The Enchanted Island,' 'The Banished Duke,' 'Ferdinand and Miranda,' &c.), some particular and recent event probably determined him to call it *The Tempest;*" that Chalmers thought the event alluded to was the great tempest which raged at the Christmas of 1612 ; and that, as regards the founding and ruling of colonies, Mr. Lloyd notices· "how many of the topics, brought up by colonies and colonization, are indicated and characterised in the play."

Mr. Hunter supported his theory of an early date by supposing that, iii. 3, 24—28,

"And I'll be sworn 'tis true : travellers ne'er did lie
    Though fools at home condemn 'em,"

and other passages (cf. for instance lines 43—49 in the same scene) were intended to ridicule Raleigh's pamphlet published in 1596. The allusions to "a strange fish" and "a dead Indian," as rarities, are not sufficiently definite or extra-ordinary to help in fixing the date ; nor does the allusion to "the red plague" (i. 2, 364; cf. *Coriolanus*, iv. 1—13, and *Troilus and Cressida*, ii. 1, 20) assist us much.

Of Klement's attempt to assign *The Tempest* to Elizabeth's reign, because he believed that her majesty was the model of *Sycorax*, we may exclaim

[*Seb.*] " No ; he doth but mistake the truth totally."
(ii. 1, 57.)

Lastly, it may be observed that the farewell of the epilogue has often been supposed to have a personal application to the poet himself, and to his retirement to Stratford and to family-life (even Elze admits this, but he endeavours to prove that this took place at an earlier date than is generally thought). Meissner is of opinion that "an autumnal mood" pervades the whole of the play; while Carrière looks upon *The Tempest* as the *very last* of Shakespeare's works, the poet could not (he says) possibly conclude his career with a dissonance like that in *Troilus and Cressida* or *Timon of Athens*, but must have harmoniously resolved the dissonance.

The date (1610—11) which may be adopted on the strength of some of these allusions, external and internal, and from a few of the æsthetic reasons mentioned, is supported by the evidence derived from a study of the versification and style ; Fleay, Hertzberg, and Ingram have shown, that the play (especially if its shortness be taken into account) must be placed very late in Shakespeare's literary career, by the application of the rhyme-test, the double-ending, the weak, and light-ending, and the speech-ending tests ; while the same conclusion is arrived at, if we mark the complete command over the extra-human materials upon which he worked, how " he exhausted worlds and then imagined new," [1] how "completely anything that might have been disagreeable to us in the magician is reconciled and shaded in the humanity and natural feelings of the father ;"[2] how artistically, too, " Shakespeare has avoided a prologue, by creating a *dramatic necessity* for the narration of the previous history of the characters,"[3] and how this speech itself is perhaps "the finest example of retrospective narration"[4] extant. Lastly, the very language itself tells of the same late date, which is shown too by the striking peculiarity of expression and of construction.

---

[1] Dr. Johnson.   [2] Coleridge.
[3] Philpotts, Rugby Edition.   [4] Coleridge.

" My father:
O that he were alive, and here beholding
His daughter's trial."—*Winter's Tale.*

The play was undoubtedly acted on June 29th, 1613 ; this
is proved by the following evidence (the record of which we
owe to destruction by fire of the Globe Theatre on that
day) :—

(1) Howes, in the continuation of Stowe's *Chronicles*,
says expressly that the play which was then exhibited, was
Shakespeare's *Henry VIII.*

(2) Sir Henry Wotton, in a letter dated July 6th, 1613,
says that the Globe was burnt during the performance "of
a new play, called *All is True*, representing some principal
pieces of the reign of Henry VIII., &c." [That the play
thus entitled is Shakespeare's is proved by consideration of
lines 9, 18, and 21 in the *Prologue;* by the burden of a
"sonnett upon the pittifull burneing of the Globe Play-
House in London," which is as follows :—

" Oh sorrow, pittifull sorrow, *and yet all this is true;*

(see Collier, *Annals of the Stage*) ; and by the details which
Wotton gives of the catching fire, as compared with a stage
direction in i. 4.]

(3) Thomas Larkin, in a letter dated "this last of June"
1613, says : "No longer since than yesterday, while Bour-
bage his companie were acting at the Globe the play of
Henry VIII., and their shooting of certayne chambers in
way of triumph, the fire catch'd, &c."

Though Gifford and others have disputed the fact, there
cannot be a doubt that the piece here referred to was Shakespeare's *Henry VIII.;* but the question arises, was it then

a *new* play? *Primâ facie*, it might seem that this question was settled in the affirmative by Sir Henry Wotton's distinct statement that it was "*a new play*," but Mr. Malone and others "strongly suspect that the only novelty attending this play, in the year 1613, was its title, decorations, and perhaps the prologue and epilogue," and the date of the production of the play has by these commentators been thrown back to the end of Queen Elizabeth's reign, or to the commencement of that of her successor. The evidence for a late date (not necessarily quite so late as 1613) seems, however, overwhelming, but the arguments on both sides will be here contrasted.

Early Date.	*Late Date.*
1. Wotton did not recognise the old *Henry VIII.* with its new title, &c. &c., or he may not have known it at all before.	1. Wotton calls it, in 1613, "a new play."
2. And, in 1613, many titles of Shakespeare's plays were changed.	2. Shakespeare (or the editor) may have given it a second title; cf. *Twelfth Night, or What You Will*, &c.; and see (*ut suprà*) prologue, burden of ballad, and stage direction.
3. "This play, with its apology for Henry, its glorification of Anne Boleyn, and its apotheosis of Elizabeth" (Elze), "its disgrace of Katharine" (Malone), &c. was surely written in Elizabeth's reign.	3. Henry's faults and peculiarities are given too; Anne Boleyn's story would have been left in silence; Elizabeth would not have endured being called an "aged princess," nor would she have allowed herself to be brought on the stage as an infant (Ward); call it Katharine's "triumph" not her "disgrace" (see Dr. Johnson). Therefore in James's reign.
4. The panegyric on James is an insertion. Notice, *e.g.* the abrupt "she" in v. 5, 57.	4. Read it through, it reads naturally enough, and Shakespeare in Elizabeth's time would not have "ventured upon splendid homage and a lofty piece of historical criticism" (Delius).
5. About the end of Elizabeth's reign there were several pieces on this or similar subjects produced; *e.g. Life and Death of Wolsey* (1599), and see Henslowe (1601 and 1602). They were either run in opposition to Shakespeare's, or suggested his.	5. This is no argument, in the absence of any evidence of the existence of Shakespeare's play.
6. The dying speech of Essex (1601) is worked up into that of Buckingham in this play (Massey).	6. Would this have been done in Elizabeth's reign?

Early Date.	*Late Date.*
7. When the panegyric on James was inserted, we may learn from the lines, v. 5, 51—53, ending "and make new nations," which doubtless refers to the colonization of Virginia in 1606-7 : or in 1612, when a lottery was granted especially for the establishment of English colonies in Virginia (Malone).	7. How much more natural it would be to refer the play itself to 1612.
8. Lorkin speaks of the performance, in 1613, of "THE play of *Henry VIII*" (Drake), as if it were well known.	8. This is not an unnatural way of speaking of a new play; and then Wotton says distinctly " a new play," and the prologue treats the play as a novelty (Gifford).
9. It may have served for a pageant at the coronation of Queen Anne (July 24th, 1603) (Collier); [and have been revived for the Princess Elizabeth and the Elector Palatine in 1613 (Malone);] or for Anne Boleyn's seventieth nuptial day, April 12th, 1603. (Elze, *vide infrâ*.)	9. It is more likely that it was produced for the Princess Elizabeth in 1613 (Spedding, Ulrici, Gervinus, Hertzberg.) [But the Elector left England early in the year, so how could Wotton call it "new" on June 30th? (Ward.) Malone's remark (Variorum Edition, 1821, ii. p. 396, Note 6), will not meet this.]
10. Rowley's *King Henry VIII.* (1605) [also called " When you see me, you know me"], and " Lord Cromwell, by W. S." (1602), and their republication in 1613, were perhaps brought out with a view to be confounded with Shakespeare's drama (Malone).	10. Quite so in 1613, but there is no proof of the other.
11. "Some strange Indian," &c. (v. 4, 34) [uncertain (Malone)].	11. In 1611 five Indians came to England three returned in 1614, one went on the Continent, the other died, and was exhibited, as a show. — (Chalmers).

Elze's elaborate essay, already referred to, may here again be noticed : he argues that " this play, with its apology for Henry VIII., its glorification of Anne Boleyn, and its apotheosis of Elizabeth, was not only written in Elizabeth's reign, but for some festive occasion ;" say for Anne's seventieth coronation day, June 1st, 1603, or for her seventieth nuptial day, April 12th, 1603 ; but the queen's death caused the play to be set aside, perhaps before it was finished. Perhaps, however, as Steevens suggested, the Stationers' Register, 12 Feb. 1604—5, "the enterlude of K. Henry 8th," shows that there was an intention of publishing Shakespeare's drama ; unless Rowley's *When You See Me You*

Shall Know Me (also called *The Famous Chronicle History of King Henry VIII.*) be the "enterlude" referred to. The Second Edition of Rowley's work,[1] in 1613, may have reminded the Globe company of Shakespeare's play, which was accordingly remodelled (by Fletcher) and acted. [See the German Shakespeare *Jahrbuch* for 1874.]

There is, however, scarcely anything to support Prof. Elze's guesses, and the internal evidence goes clean against it. Before turning to this evidence, the following recent suggestion by Mr. Fleay (Jan. 1876) may be noted :—

" Is it not a probable conjecture that Shakespeare originally wrote a complete play ; that part of the MS. was burnt in the Globe fire of 1613; that Fletcher was employed to re-write this part ; that in doing this he used such material as he recollected from his hearing of Shakespeare's play ? This would account for the superiority of his work here over that elsewhere." [*Shakespeare Manual*, p. 171.]

Roderick, in Edwards's *Canons of Criticism*, more than a hundred years ago, pointed out certain peculiarities in the metre of this play, viz., lines with a redundant syllable, recurring very frequently, and remarkable cæsuræ. Steevens attributed these to chance, or to haste, or to interpolations by Ben Jonson ; Malone, while he thought " Mr. Roderick's position hardly worth a contest," admitted the probability of a revision by another hand ; believing with Dr. Johnson and Farmer that Ben Jonson may have made "adycyons" to *Henry VIII.*, writing the prologue, &c. Mr. Tennyson, a long time ago, attributed parts of the play to Fletcher ; and Mr. Spedding and Mr. Hickson, by 1850, arrived at the

---

[1] Elze, in his edition of this play, supports the oft-mentioned explanation of the lines in the Prologue of Shakespeare's *Henry VIII.*, about a fellow in a long motley coat guarded with yellow," as applying to Summers, Henry VIII.'s jester, in Rowley's play, by seeing in the second title of the Globe play (*All is True*, cf. Prologue, *ut supra*) a cut at the foolery in *When You See Me*, &c. He explains the lines in the Epilogue,

" Others, to hear the city
Abused extremely, and to cry ' It's witty ! ' "

by parts of the Rowley play.

same result ; which has lately been confirmed by Messrs.
Fleay, Furnivall, and Ingram (see *N. S. S. Trans.*, 1874).
The metrical investigations have strikingly brought out the
fact that Shakespeare's part of the play is *late work ;* this is
proved by the flowing style, " the close-packing, the quick-
turn, the weak-ending, the run-on-line, &c." (see Mr. Furnivall, *Academy*, Jan. 29th, 1876, against Mr. Swinburne, in
the same journal, Jan. 22nd, 1876, and in *The Fortnightly ;*
but the modern poet is perhaps speaking of " a spiritual, not
a literal, chronology " when he claims an early date for
Henry VIII.) The late date has also been supported by
various æsthetic reasons, as, for example, Mr. Furnivall's
reconciliation theory (see Introduction, &c., pp. xli. xlii.)

With regard to the special date of Shakespeare's work,
there is nothing by which it can be decided, whether Shakespeare wrote an unfinished play a year or two earlier, or
whether he worked with Fletcher in 1613.

APPENDICES.

APPENDIX I.

CHRONOLOGICAL ORDER OF THE PLAYS ACCORDING TO

	STOKES.	MALONE	CHALMERS.	DRAKE.	GERVINUS.	DELIUS.	FLEAY.	NEW SHAKSP. SOC.
Titus Andronicus......	cir. 1530	—	—	—	—	1589	[1590]	1588?
1 Henry VI..............	cir. 1592	1589	1593	1592	—	b. 1592	[before 1592]	1590—1592 ?
2 & 3 Henry VI.........	cir. 1592	1591	1595	1592	1592	—	[before 1592] 1601	1594, 5 ?
Two Gentlemen of Verona	cir. 1591	1591	1595	1595	1591	b. 1591	1594	1590—1592
Comedy of Errors	1591	1592	1591	1591	cir. 1591	cir. 1591	1592	1589—1591
Romeo and Juliet	1591 [R]	1596	1592	1593	1591—5	cir. 1591	1596	1591—1593 ?
Love's Labour's Lost...	1591—2 [R]	1594	1592	1591		cir. 1591	1599	1588, 9
Richard III.	1593—4	1593	1595	1595	1597	cir. 1594	1595	1594
Taming of the Shrew..	before 1594 [R]	1596	1598	1594	—	cir. 1594	1602	1596, 7
Richard II.	1594	1593	1596	1596	—	cir. 1596	1593	1593, 4
John	1593—4	1596	1598	1598	1596	cir. 1596	1595	1595
Midsummer Night's Dream	1595	1594	1598	1593	1595	cir. 1595	1592	1590, 1
Merchant of Venice ...	1597—8	1594	1597	1597	1594	cir. 1595	1596	1596 ?
1 Henry IV.............	1597	1597	1596	1596	1597	1596—1599	1597	1596, 7
2 Henry IV.............	1598—9	1599	1597	1596	1598	1596—1599	1598	1597, 8
Troilus and Cressida ...	cir. 1599; cir. 1602	1602	1600	1601	1668, 9	cir. 1608	1594; 1595; 1607	1590—2; 1606,7

Merry Wives of Windsor	1598, 9 [R]	1601	1596	1601	1598—1602	1596—1599	1598; 1605	1598, 1599
As You Like It	1599	1599	1599	1600	1598—1600	cir. 1600	1600	1600
Much Ado	1599, 1600	1600	1599	1599	1600	1599	1599	1599, 1600
Hamlet	1599, 1600 [R]	1600	1597	1597	1602	1602	1601	1602, 3
Henry V.	1599	1593	1597	1599	1599	1599	1599	1599
Julius Cæsar	1599, 1600	1607	1607	1607	1601, 2	b. [Dec.] 1604	1600; [1613]	1601—1603
Twelfth Night	1601	1607	1613	1613	1600	b. [Feb.] 1602	1601	1601
Measure for Measure	1603, 4	1603	1604	1603	1603	b. [Dec.] 1604	1603	1603
All's Well	cir. 1592; cir. 1604	1606	1599	1598	1592; 1605, 6	1595—1599	1604	1589; 1601, 2
Othello	1604	1604	1614	1612	1600	b. [Nov.] 1604	1604	1604?
Lear	1605	1605	1605	1604	1605	1604—1605	1605	1605, 6
Macbeth	1606	1606	1606	1656	1605	1603—1610	1606	1605, 6
Timon of Athens	1607, 8	1610	1601	1602	1610	cir. 1608	1606	1607, 8
Pericles	1607, 8	—	—	1590	1590	cir. 1608	1607	1608
Antony and Cleopatra	1608	1608	1608	1608	1607	b. [May] 1608	1608	1606, 7
Coriolanus	1610	1610	1609	1609	1610	b. [May] 1608	1609	1607, 8?
Cymbeline	1610	1609	1606	1605	1609	1610—1611	1610	1610—1612
Tempest	1610, 1611	1611	1613	1611	1611	b. [Nov.] 1611	1607, 8; 1610	1610?
Winter's Tale	1610, 1611	1611	1601	1610	1611	1610—1611	1610	1611?
Two Noble Kinsmen	[1612]	—	—	—	—		1609; [1613]	1609—1612
Henry VIII	[1611?]1613	1603	1613	1602	—	1613	1611; [1613]	1613

The dates, as given by Malone, Chalmers, and Drake, are taken from Harness's Shakspeare (vol. i. p. 81); those assigned by Delius are borrowed from Mr. Fleay's Shakespeare (Manual, p. 130). The dates given in the first column are those assigned in this essay. ([R] means *revised*.)

APPENDIX II.

MR FLEAY'S METRICAL TABLE OF SHAKESPEARE'S PLAYS.

Play.	Total of Lines.	Prose.	Blank.	Rhymes, 5 Measures.	Rhymes, Short Lines.	Songs.	Double Endings.	Alternates.	Sonnets.	Doggerel.	1 Measure.	2 Measure.	3 Measure.	4 Measure.	6 Measure.
I.—PLAYS OF THE FIRST (RHYMING) PERIOD.															
Love's L. Lost...	2789	1086	579	1028	54	32	9	236	71	194	4	12	13	—	1
Midsum. N. D...	2251	441	878	731	138	63	29	158	—	—	—	5	3	—	—
Com. of Errors...	1770	240	1150	382	—	—	137	64	—	109	3	8	9	—	—
Rom. and Juliet.	3002	405	2111	486	—	—	118	62	28	—	10	20	16?	4	6
Richard II.	2644	—	2107	537	—	—	148	12	—	—	11	17	26	22?	33
II.—HISTORIES OF SECOND PERIOD.															
Richard III.	3599	?55	3374	170	—	—	570	—	—	—	20	39	13	23	16
King John.........	2553	—	2403	150	—	—	54	12	—	—	1	9	4	4	2
1 Henry IV.	3170	1464	1622	84	—	—	60	4	—	—	16	17	16	16	13
2 Henry IV.......	3437	1860	1417	74	7	15	203	[Pistol 64 l.]			3	13	7	—	6
Henry V..........	3320	1531	1678	101	2	8	291	[Pist. 157 l.]	14		2	13	10	4	23
Julius Cæsar.....	2440	165	2241	34	—	—	369	—	—	—	14	31	55	6	16
III.—COMEDIES OF SECOND PERIOD															
Two Gent. of V.	2060	409	1510	116	—	15	203	16	—	18	8	15	32	8	5
Mer. of Venice ...	2705	673	1896	93	34	9	297	4	—	4	8	16	22	2	14
Twelfth Night...	2684	1741	763	120	—	60	152	—	—	—	8	21	23	5	10
As You Like It...	2904	1681	925	71	130	97	211	10	—	2	3	10	33	1	5
Merry Wives.....	3018	2703	227	69	—	19	32	[Pistol 39 l.]		—	—	3	3	—	3
Much Ado.........	2823	2106	643	40	18	16	129	22	—	—	2	7	15	4	4
IV.—COMEDIES OF THIRD PERIOD.															
All's Well	2981	1453	1234	280	2	12	223	8	14	—	7	31	31	5	14
Measure for M..	2809	1134	1574	73	22	6	338	—	—	—	10	29	66	5	47

Play.	Total of Lines.	Prose.	Blank.	Rhymes 5 Measures.	Rhymes Short Lines.	Songs.	Double Endings.	Alternates.	Sonnets.	Doggerel.	1 Measure.	2 Measure.	3 Measure.	4 Measure.	6 Measure.
V.—TRAGEDIES OF THIRD PERIOD.															
Troylus & Cres...	3423	1186	2225	196	—	16	441	—	—	—	10	46	62	13	43
Macbeth..........	1993	158	1588	118	129	—	399	—	—	—	8	28	43	8	18
Hamlet	3924	1208	2490	81	—	60	508	[86 l. in play]			20	53	55	11	47
Othello	3324	541	2672	86	—	25	646	—	—	—	19	66	71	13	78
King Lear..........	3298	903	2238	74	—	83	567	—	—	—	18	34	116	22	56
VI.—PLAYS OF FOURTH PERIOD.															
Cymbeline..........	3448	638	2505	107	—	32	726	[84 l. in vision]			8	15	31	18	42
Coriolanus..........	3392	829	2521	42	—	—	708	—	—	—	3	33	76	19	42
Antony and C....	3964	255	2761	42	—	6	613	—	—	—	14	38	84	31	16
Tempest..........	2068	458	1458	2	—	96	476	[54 l. masq.]			2	16	47	5	11
Winter's Tale ...	2750	844	1825	—	—	57	639	[32 l. chor.]			8	14	19	13	16
VII.—PLAYS IN WHICH SHAKESPEARE WAS NOT SOLE AUTHOR.															
Taming of Shrew	2671	516	1971	169	15	—	260	—	—	49	4	18	22	23	5
Henry VIII.......	2754	?67	2613	16	—	12	1195	[46 l. in Prol. & Epilogue]			2	19	18	3	32
Two Noble Kins.	2734	179	2468	54	—	33	1079	—	—	—	9	19	46	17	5
Pericles	2386	418	1436	225	89	—	120	[222 l. Gower]			17	49	59	26	18
Timon of Athens	2358	596	1560	184	18	—	257	—	—	—	15	28	54	30	37
VIII.—FIRST SKETCHES IN EARLY QUARTOS.															
Rom. and Juliet.	2066	261	1451	354	—	—	92	28	—	—	7	26	30	21	92
Hamlet..........	2068	509	1462	54	43	—	209	[36 l. in play]			13	45	76	37	30
Merry Wives......	1395	1207	148	40	38[fairies]	19	—	—	—	—		1	—	5	4
Henry V.	1672	898	774	30	—	—	104	—	—	—	1	25	35	31	15
IX.—DOUBTFUL PLAYS.															
Titus Andronicus	2525	43	2338	144	—	—	154	—	—	—	4	8	9	9	12
1 Henry VI.......	2693	—	2379	314	—	—	140	—	—	—	5	5	4	7	12
2 Henry VI.......	3032	448	2562	122	—	—	255	—	—	—	8	25	15	21	12
3 Henry VI.......	2904	—	2749	155	—	—	346	—	—	—	13	11	14	11	7
Contention	1952	381	1571	44	—	—	54	—	—	—	—	14	16	32	44
True Tragedy. ...	2101	—	2035	66	—	—	148	—	—	—	14	21	29	38	34

APPENDIX III.

PROF. INGRAM'S TABLE OF THE NUMBER OF "WEAK" AND "LIGHT" ENDINGS IN SHAKESPEARE'S PLAYS.

[See *New Shakspere Society's Transactions*, 1874, vol. ii. pp. 440—464. This table will show conclusively the value of the "Weak-ending" test in discriminating between plays of the *third* and *fourth* period.]

	[No. of] Light Endings.	Weak Endings.	Verse Lines.
Love's Labour's Lost.......... ...	3	o	
Comedy of Errors	o	o	
Two Gentlemen of Verona ...	o	o	
Midsummer Night's Dream...	o	1	
Romeo and Juliet	6	1	
Richard II.	4	o	
Richard III.	4	o	
John	7	o	
Merchant of Venice	6	1	
1 Henry IV...........................	5	2	
2 Henry IV......	1	o	
Merry Wives of Windsor......	1	o	
Henry V.	2	o	
Much Ado.....	1	1	
As You Like It	2	o	
Twelfth Night...........	3	1	
All's Well	11	2	
Hamlet	8	o	
Measure for Measure.	7	o	
Julius Cæsar......................	10	o	
Othello	2	o	
Lear.	5	1	
Troilus and Cressida	6	o	
Macbeth..........................	21	2	
Timon.....	14	?	1112
Antony and Cleopatra	71	28	2803
Coriolanus..	60	44	2553
Pericles [Shakspeare Part]....	20	10	719
Tempest.,...........................	42	25	1460
Cymbeline...	78	52	2692
Winter's Tale	57	43	1825
Two Noble Kinsmen [non-Fletcher Part].................	50	34	1378
Henry VIII. [Shakspeare Pt.]	45	37	1146

SUPPOSED ALLUSIONS TO SHAKESPEARE'S PLAYS IN BEN JONSON'S WORKS.

	WORK OF BEN JONSON'S	DATE	PLACE.	ALLUSION.	PLAY OF SHAKESPEARE'S REFERRED TO.	BY WHOM POINTED OUT.
1	Every Man in, &c.	1598 (1616?)	Prologue	"To make a child now, &c."	Winter's Tale	Malone
2	,, ,, ,,	1598 (1616?)	,,	"York and Lancaster, &c."	Henry VI., &c.	,,
3	,, ,, ,,	,, ,,	,,	"Foot and a half words."	Richard III.	,,
4	,, ,, ,,	,, ,,	,,	"Chorus wafts you o'er, &c."	Henry V.	Hunter
5	,, ,, ,,	,, ,,	,,	"Creaking throne, &c."	Tempest	,,
6	,, ,, ,,	,, ,,	,,	"Tempestuous drum, &c."	Tempest	,,
7	,, ,, ,,	,, ,,	,,	"Graced monsters, &c."	Tempest	,,
8	,, ,, ,,	1598	iv. 1.	"Bagpipes, &c."	Merchant of Venice	Malone
9	,, ,, ,,	,,	—	[sadness]	cf. King John	Farmer
10	,, ,, ,,	,,	—	Stephano	M. of V. ; [Tempest]	—
11	Every Man out, &c.	1599	ii. 1.	"Stealing from Green, &c."	Henry VI.	Steevens
12	,, ,,	,,	iii. 1 [end].	"Crosswooing, &c."	Twelfth Night	Malone
13	,, ,,	,,	v. 2.	"Justice, silence"	Henry IV.	—
14	,, ,,	,,	v. 7 [end].	"Sir John Falstaff"	Henry IV. ; M. W. of W.	—
15	Cynthia's Revels.	1600	Induction	"One deformed"	Much Ado, &c.	R. Simpson.
16	,, ,,	,,	,,	"Old Books, &c."	—	Malone
17	,, ,,	,,	,,	"umbra, &c"	Hamlet, &c.	{N. British Reviewer.
18	,, ,,	,,	ii. 3	"A creature of the most, &c."	Julius Cæsar	Fleay
19	,, ,,	,,	Epilogue	{"Begging knee, &c." "Promise better"}	2 Henry IV. ; V. ; &c.	—
20	,, ,,	,,	,,	"If you like it, &c."	As You Like It	Tieck

APPENDIX IV.—*continued.*

SUPPOSED ALLUSIONS TO SHAKESPEARE'S PLAYS IN BEN JONSON'S WORKS.

	WORK OF BEN JONSON'S.	DATE.	PLACE.	ALLUSION.	PLAY OF SHAKESPEARE'S REFERRED TO.	BY WHOM POINTED OUT.
21	Poetaster.	1601	—	⁝	- Henry V.	—
22	Silent Woman.	1609	—	"Chorus behind the arras"	Henry V.	Malone
23	,, ,,	,,	iv. 4	"Fights at sea, &c."	Antony and Cleopatra	,,
24	,, ,,	,,	v. 2	"Jonson and t'other youth"	—	,,
25	,, ,,	,,	v. [end]	"Lurched o' the garland"	Coriolanus	Steevens
26	The Fox.	1605	iii. 2	"Steal from Montaignié"	Tempest, &c.	Elze
27	Mask of Queens.	1609	—	—	Macbeth	Davies
28	Oberon.	1610	—	—	Midsum. Night's Dream.	—
29	Lust's Dominion.	—	—	—	,, ,,	—
30	Alchemist.	1612	—	"Did'st thou hear a cry, &c."	Othello	Steevens
31	Bartholomew Fair.	1614	Induction	"Servant monster, &c."	Tempest	Malone
32	,, ,,	,,	,,	"Nest of antiquities, &c." "tales"	Winter's Tale	,,
33	,, ,,	,,	,,	"Watch, &c."	Much Ado, &c.	Ward
34	,, ,,	,,	,,	"Titus Andronicus"	Titus Andronicus (?)	—
35	,, ,,	,,	ii. 1	—	Julius Cæsar	Malone
36	Devil is an Ass.	1616	ii. 1	"Wrong . . . just cause"	Richard III., &c.	,,
37	Staple of News.	1625	Induction	"All the world's a play"	Julius Cæsar	,,
38	New Inn.	1629	i. 1	[Tradesmen's play]	As You Like It	Ward
39	Love's Welcome, &c.	1634	—	—	Midsum. Night's Dream.	,,
40	Sad Shepherd.	1637	—	—	Macbeth	Fleay

APPENDIX V.

THE REGISTRATION AND PUBLICATION OF SHAKESPEARE'S PLAYS.

[The following list is compiled from Steevens, Chalmers, Collier, Ashbee, and Fleay : the plays are arranged, for convenience of reference, in the order in which they stand in the First Folio.]

(1) THE TEMPEST.—This comedy was first entered on the Stationers' Register on November 8th, 1623 ; and appeared for the first time in the folio edition which followed that entry.

(2) TWO GENTLEMEN OF VERONA.—[The same may be said of this.]

(3) MERRY WIVES OF WINDSOR.—On January 18th 1601-2, we have the following entries :—

"John Busby]. An excellent and pleasant conceited Commedie of *Sir John Faulstof,* and the *Merry Wives of Windesor.*"

"Arth. Johnson]. By assign, from Mr. Busbye a B. An excellent and pleasant conceited comedie of *Sir John Faulstofe* and the *Mery Wyves of Windsor.*"

Shortly afterwards, 1602, a quarto edition (Q_1 imp.) appeared with a title corresponding to the entry ; "by William Shakespeare, as divers times acted by . . . my Lord Chamberlaine's Servants. Both before her Majestie and elsewhere. Printed by T[homas]. C[reede]. for Arthur Johnson, 1602." In 1619, Arthur Johnson published a second quarto (Q_2 of Q_1).

[These quartos were probably pirated ; but it may be here

N 2

noticed that at the entry, on November 8th, 1623, of those plays which were "not formerly entered to other men," unauthorised entries are not repeated ; and more than that, such rights, as such entries had acquired, were respected even after the First Folio came out ; cf. the Register, on August 4th, 1626, and November 8th, 1630.]

(4) MEASURE FOR MEASURE.—[See remark on the *Tempest*.]

(5) THE COMEDY OF ERRORS.—[The same.]

(6) MUCH ADO ABOUT NOTHING.—The absence of the date of the year in which the following entry was made can scarcely cause any doubt, when the subsequent entry is noticed, and when the publication in the same year (1600) of this play and of *Henry V.*, and in the next year (1601) of *Every Man in His Humour*, is considered. The caveat to the entry (which reads as below) should be noticed :—

27 May 1600.

To Mr. Roberts] My Lord Chamberlens mens plaies entred viz. *A Morall of Clothe breches and velvet hose :* 24 May, to him. *Allarum to London.*

4 August.

As you like it. a book. *Henry the ffifte.* a book. *Every Man in his Humor.* a book. The ⎫ To be staied. Comedie of *Much Adoo about Nothinge.* a book. ⎭

23 January 1603.

To Thomas Thorpe and Wm. Aspley] This to be their copy, &c. [Notice as proofs, that the entry was made in 1600, the mention of my Lord Chamberlens mens plaies, and *the absence of the year after* 24 *May*.]

The Register for the 23rd Aug. 1600, reads :—

"And. Wise Wm. Aspley] Two books, the one called *Muche Adoe about Nothinge* ; and the other [2 *Henry IV. vide infrà*] : wrytten by Mr. Shakespeare." In the same year these publishers brought out the only Quarto (†Q₁) entitled : " *Much Adoe about Nothing.* As it hath been sundrie times publikely acted by the Right Honourable the Lord

Chamberlaine his Servants.   Written by William Shakespeare.   Printed by V. J. [V. Simmes?] for Andrew Wise
and William Aspley, 1600."

When Andrew Wise assigned his copyrights to M. Lawe,
on 27 June 1603, Aspley retained *Much Ado* and 2 *Henry IV.*
and they did not again appear till the First Folio, of which
he was one of the publishers.

(7) LOVE'S LABOUR LOST.—The following is the title of
the only quarto known of (†Q₁) ; no entry of this has been
found :—

"A pleasant conceited Comedie called, *Love's Labours
Lost.* As it was presented before her Highness this last
Christmas.   Newly corrected and augmented by W. Shakespeare.   Imprinted by W. W[aterson]. for Cutberd Busby,
1598."

The Register for 22 January, 1606-7, has the following
note :—

"Mr. Linge]   By direction of a Court and with consent
of Mr. Busby under his hand wrytinge these iij copies, viz.
*Romeo and Juliett. Loves Labour Loste.   The Taminge of
a shrewe.*"

And, again, on 19 November 1607, there is another
assignment :—

"John Smytthick]   Under t'hands of the wardens, the
books following, which did belong to Nichūs Lynge.   6, a
booke called *Hamlett.   9, The Taminge of a Shrewe.*
10, *Romeo and Juliett.   11, Loves Labour Lost.*"   Lastly, it
is to be noticed that the owner of these copyrights (J.
Smethweeke) was one of the publishers of the First
Folio.

(8) MIDSUMMER NIGHT'S DREAM.—On 8 October 1600,
there is the entry :—

"Tho. Fysher]   A booke called *a Mydsomer Nights
Dreame.*"

In this year, too, we find a quarto (Q₁) issued by this
publisher : " *A Midsommer Nights Dreame.   As it hath been*

sundry times publickely acted, by the Right Honourable the
Lord Chamberlaine his Servants. Written by William
Shakespeare. Imprinted for Thomas Fisher, 1600."

But in the same year (1600) there appeared another quarto
(†Q₂), with the same title, but "printed by James Roberts."

Of this there is no entry, and yet the folio edition of
1623 seems to follow Roberts's edition. Unless Roberts
acted as printer for Fisher [which is perhaps supported by the
entry on 28 October 1600, see below], I cannot account for
this, except by supposing that the publishers of that folio,
being unable to obtain the co-operation of Fisher, turned to
Roberts, who was always ready to make money.

(9) THE MERCHANT OF VENICE.—On the 22nd July, 1598,
we find the following curious entry :—

"James Roberts] A booke of the *Marchaunt of Venyce,*
or otherwise called the *Jewe of Venyse.* Provided that yt
bee not printed by the said James Robertes or anye other
whatsoever, without lycence first had from the right honourable the Lord Chamberlen."

Again, on the 28th October, 1600, we read :—

"Tho. Haies] The booke of the *Merchant of Venyce.*"

In the same year appeared two quartos; one (†Q₂)
entitled :—

"The most excellent Historie of the *Merchant of Venice.*
With the extreme Crueltie of Shylocke, &c. As it hath
beene divers times acted by the Lord Chamberlaine his
Servants. Written by William Shakespeare. Printed by
J[ames] R[oberts] for Thomas Heyes, 1600;" the other,
(Q₁), has the same title, but does not refer to the company
of actors, while it finishes : "Written by W. Shakespeare.
Printed by J. Roberts."

There can be scarcely any doubt, when we remember the
proviso in the entry on 22 July, 1598, and when we consider
the omission in the title-page of Q₁, that Roberts brought
out this quarto surreptitiously (see general preface to F₁);
but the 1623 editors had no need in this case, as in that of *A*

Midsummer Night's Dream, to avail themselves of Roberts's copy, for they probably came to some arrangement with the Heyes firm. This conclusion seems to be justified by the fact that no edition was issued after the following entry, on 8 July, 1619 : " Lau. Hayes] a play called the *Marchaunt of Venice*." Though this publisher (L. Heyes) issued in 1637 a quarto of the play, the copyright of which he still held.

(10) AS YOU LIKE IT.—As was before remarked, this play was entered on Aug. 4th, [1600], with a memorandum that it was" to be staied " ; but as no edition of it had appeared, Messrs Blount and Jaggard, in their entry preparatory to the First Folio, felt justified in saying (8th November, 1623) that it was one of the plays which "are not formerly entered to other men."

(11) TAMING OF THE SHREW.—On May 2nd, 1594, an old play (to which this is related) was entered by Peter Shorte ; in the same year this was printed with the title "A pleasant conceited Historie, called the *Taming of a Shrew*, as it was sundry times acted by the Earl of Pembrook his servants."

Another quarto appeared in 1596.

The copyright of this old play had [in what year is not known] come into the hands of Cuthbert Busby before the 22nd January, 1606-7, on which day Busby assigned it, together with two undoubted plays of Shakespeare's, to Nicholas Ling ; who, the same year, brought out an edition of the (old) play, 1607 ; within a few months however he retired from business, and transferred this play, *The Taming of a Shrew*, together with the two plays mentioned above (viz. *Romeo and Juliet*, and *Love's Labour Lost*), as well as *Hamlet* (see p. 192), to John Smythick, Nov. 19th, 1607.

Smythick was one of the publishers of the First Folio, 1623, in which for the first time the play appeared in the form in which we now have it. Lastly, and this is one of the most remarkable facts in connection with the copyrights and rival plays of those times, when in 1631 Smythick produced the only quarto, which he brought out on this subject, it was reprinted, not from Ling's old version, but from the folio edition.

(12) ALL'S WELL THAT
ENDS WELL.
(13) TWELFTH NIGHT.
(14) WINTER'S TALE.

These three plays were not entered, nor printed, until 1623.

(15) KING JOHN.—The same may be said of this play as we now have it; but in 1611 there had appeared a quarto edition of a play of the same name which had appeared, in two parts, in 1591, and upon which Shakespeare had doubtless founded his drama. It is a remarkable fact, that in spite of the spuriousness of this quarto, and of the fraudulent intention of its publication (for it is described as "sundry times *lately acted* by the Queenes Majesties Players," and is even said to be "written by W. Sh."), it was yet not among the copies which Blount and Jaggard, on November 8th, 1623, said were "not formerly entered to other men." A third edition, published by Thomas Dewe in 1622, has the name of William Shakespeare inserted at length.

(16) RICHARD II.—Referring, as usual, to the Register, we find under date 29 August, 1597 :—

"Andrew Wise] The Tragedye of *Richard the Seconde*."

In the same year, Wise issued an anonymous quarto entitled :—

"The Tragedie of *King Richard the Second*. As it hath been publikely acted by the Right Honourable the Lord Chamberlaine his servants. Printed by Valentine Simmes, for Andrew Wise, 1597."

In the following year (1598) appeared Q_2; with the same title-page, and the author's name added—"William Shakespeare."

The Stationers' Register for 27 June, 1603, says :—

"Math. Lawe] in full courte iij enterludes or playes the ffirst is of *Richard the 3rd*. The second of *Richard ye 2d*. The third of *Henry the 4th*, the first parte all kings."

Q_3 came out in 1608, with the following title-page :—

"The Tragedie of *King Richard the Second*, with new Additions of the Parliament Sceane, and the deposing of King Richard. As it hath been lately acted by the Kinges Servantes at the Globe. By William Shakespeare. Printed by W. W[aterson]. for Mathew Law 1608."

In 1615, Mathew Lawe brought out a fourth quarto of *Richard II.*, which does not give the printer's name.

The copy of this play, as given in the First Folio (1623), is founded upon Lawe's quartos ; but his name does not appear among the names of the publishers of that volume. What arrangement he came to with the editors of that folio is not known, but I would suggest that some agreement was entered into with regard to this play and the first part of *Henry IV.*, for these plays were not again issued in quarto till 1632 (1 *Henry IV.*) and 1634 (*Richard II.*), after the publication of the Second Folio, in 1632 ; when Lawe's successor (if *Sheares* be such) felt himself at liberty to re-issue quartos.

(17) 1 HENRY IV.—The following entry occurs under date 25 February, 1597-8 :—

"Andrew Wisse] A booke intitled the Historye of *Henry iiiith*, with his battaile at Shrewsburye against Henry Hotspurre of the Northe with the conceipted Mirth of Sir John Falstaffe."

In the same year a quarto, with a title very similar to the entry, "was printed by P. S[hort]. for Andrew Wise, 1598 ;" and in the following year there appeared a second Quarto, printed by S. S[tafford]. for the same publisher, and "newly corrected by W. Shakespeare." On the 27th June, 1603, however, we find the following record on the Stationers' Books :—

"Math. Lawe] in full courte iij Enterludes or playes. The ffirst is of *Richard the 3rd*. The second of *Richard ye 2d*. The third of *Henry the 4*, the first pte all Kings."

Lawe brought four quarto editions :—

Q_3, 1604, printed by Valentine Simmes ; Q_4, 1608 (the same) ; Q_5, printed by W. W[aterson], 1613 ; and Q_6, 1622, printed by T. P[urfoot].

Matt. Lawe's name does not appear among the publishers of the First Folio, although two of his copyrights at least were used for that edition ; perhaps he sold them to the editors of that work. At any rate the copyright had changed hands in 1632, when the seventh quarto appeared. [I would suggest that Lawe granted permission for the printing of his plays in the 1623 folio ; but that when the 1632 folio came out, his successor (if *Sheares* were such) felt himself at liberty to bring out (as he did) quartos of three works (entered on June 27th, 1603).]

(18) 2. HENRY IV.—This was entered 23 August, 1600 :—

" And. Wise Wm. Aspley] Two books, the one called *Muche Adoe about Nothinge;* and the other The Second Part of the *History of Kinge Henry the iiiith;* with the Humors of Sir John Fallstaffe : wrytten by Mr. Shakespeare."

In the same year a quarto appeared entitled :—

" The Second Part of *Henrie the Fourth,* continuing to his Death, and Coronation of *Henry the Fift.* With the Humors of Sir John Falstaffe, and Swaggering Pistoll. As it hath been sundrie times publikely acted by the Right Honourable the Lord Chamberlaine his servants. Written by William Shakespeare. Printed by V. S[immes] for Andrew Wise and William Aspley, 1600." [Some copies vary slightly.]

When Andrew Wise assigned his copyrights to Mr. Lawe, on 27th June, 1603, Aspley retained *Much Ado* and 2 *Henry IV*, and they did not again appear till the First Folio, of which he was one of the publishers, *though strange to say* 2 *Henry IV* (F_1) *was not printed from the quarto edition.*

(19) HENRY V.—[This, of course, must not be confounded with the old play called *The Famous Victories of Henry the*

Fifth ; containing the honourable battle of Agincourt ; which
was entered by Tho. Creede on 14 May, 1594 ; and probably
published in the same year (says Collier, who adds that it
was acted prior to 1588) ; was certainly printed in 1598 ; was
transferred by Pavier to Bird, August 4th, 1626, being doubtless
one of the following : *The Historye of Hen. the fift*, and the
play of the same, &c.; and by Bird assigned to Cotes, November 8th, 1630, being then apparently known as *Agincourt.*]

Shakespeare's play was entered, on 4 August [1600], with
Much Ado About Nothing (q.v.) with an injunction "to be
staied ; " ten days later we have the following entry :—

"Thos. Pavyer] *The Historye of Henrye the Vth with the
battel of Agencourt.*"

[Whether this referred to Shakespeare's play does not
appear ; it will be seen below that Pavyer brought out the
Second Quarto ; but it should be noticed (*vide infrà*) that he
had the copyright of the old play too. Perhaps (*vide infrà*)
T. Creede and Pavyer amalgamated.]

Three quartos appeared in Shakespeare's lifetime, all
anonymous and all probably surreptitious :—

Q₁ "*The Chronicle Historye of Henrye the Fift*, with his
battell fought at Agincourt in France. Together with
Auntient Pistolle. As it hath been sundry times playd by
the Right Honorable the Lord Chamberlaine his Servants.
Printed by Thomas Creede for Tho. Millington and John
Busby, 1600."

[It should be noticed that Busby had a hand in the production of the surreptitious edition of *The Merry Wives of
Windsor* (q.v.).]

Q₂, same title, " printed by Thomas Creede for Thomas
Pavier, 1602."

[Note that Creede, in 1594, had entered the old play].

Q₃, same title, " printed for T. P[avier] 1608."

As has been remarked above, these quartos were all
mangled copies, and the First Folio probably used the
Theatre MS., although Pavier retained his copyright of both

the plays [*i.e.* the old play and the quarto edition] till in 1626 he transferred them to Bird ; who in 1630 assigned them to Cotes, the printer of the Second Folio.

(20) 1 HENRY VI.—This play is first unquestionably noticed in the entry, on 8 November, 1623, of those of Shakespeare's plays " as are not formerly entered to other men ; " it is then styled *The Thirde Parte of Henry the Sixt.*

(21) 2 HENRY VI. —The relation between this play and the firste parte of the *Contention of the Two Famous Houses of Lancaster and York,* &c., is discussed in the body of this work. The issue of the latter is here noted.

Tho. Millington entered it on March 12th, 1593, and issued it in 12mo. the next year (Tho. Creede being the printer) with the above title ; in 1600 he brought out another edition (printed by W. W[aterson]). [Continued below.]

(22) 3 HENRY VI.—The relation between this play and *The True Tragedie of Richard, Duke of Yorke,* &c., is discussed in the body of this work. We will here give the history of the latter.

Tho. Millington (*vide supra*) in 1595 issued a quarto with the following title : " *The True Tragedie of Richard Duke of Yorke, and the Death of good King Henry the Sixt, with the whole Contention between the two Houses Lancaster and Yorke,* as it was sundry times acted by the Right Honourable the Earle of Pembrooke his Servants. Printed at London by P. S[hort] for Thomas Millington, 1595."

[The two plays will now be treated together.]

In 1600, Millington brought out editions of each of these, with the same title as before, W. W[aterson] being the printer.

In 1602, April 19th, we have the following entry :—

" Tho. Pavier] by assignt. from Tho. Millington *salvo jure* cujuscumq. The 1st and 2nd pts. of *Henry the VI. ;* II. Books."

In 1619, Pavier issued " *The Whole Contention between the Two Famous Houses of Lancaster and Yorke ; with the*

Tragical Ends of the good Duke Humfrey, Richard Duke of Yorke and King Henrie the Sixt. Divided into two Parts : and newly corrected and enlarged. Written by William Shakespeare, Gent. Printed for T. P. P[avier]," no date, but the above is certain.

In 1626, August 4th, Pavier transferred his "rights in Shakespeare's plays or any of them" to Brewster and Birde ; and, in 1630 (November 8th), Birde assigned them to Richard Cotes ; among the plays thus transferred we have *Yorke and Lancaster.*

(23) RICHARD III.—Compare notes on *Richard II.* and 1 *Henry IV.;* like those plays *Richard III.* was entered by Wise (in 1597) and issued by him in quarto (Q_1 1593, "as it hath been lately acted by the Right Honourable the Lord Chamberlaine his Servants. Printed by Valentine Sims ; Q_2 1598, "by William Shakespeare." Thomas Creede, printer ; Q_3, 1602, the same) ; then, in 1603, it was transferred to Lawe, who, in 1605 issued Q_4, and in 1612 issued Q_5 ("as it hath been lately acted by the King's Majesties Servants. Newly augmented. By William Shakespeare "). Creede also printed this ; Q_6 came out in 1622, Thomas Perfoote being the printer.

It has before been remarked, that although Lawe's other copyrights (*Richard II.* and 1 *Henry IV.*) were used for the First Folio, that publisher's name is not mentioned in that edition. It is a remarkable fact [theories accounting for which have been advanced by the Cambridge Editors, Prof. Delius, and Messrs. Spedding and Matthew severally (see *N. S. S. Trans.,* 1876)] that the *Richard III.* quarto is not similarly followed ; and that Lawe in this case (*not in the others*) soon after issued another quarto (Q_7, 1629, printed by John Norton). Other quartos were afterwards issued.

(24) HENRY VIII. — Entered and printed, first, in 1623.

(25) TROILUS AND CRESSIDA. The following entries may be found in the Stationers' Register :—

" 1603. Feb. 3rd. Mr. Roberts] The booke of *Troilus and Cressida,* as yt is acted by my Lo. Chamberlen's men."

" 1609. Jan. 28th. Rich. Bonion and Hen. Whalleys] entered for their copie under the hands of Mr. Segar Deputy to Sir Geo. Bucke, and Mr. Warden Loynes : a booke called the *History of Troylus and Cressulla.*"

In 1609 appeared two quartos :—

Q₁ " *The Famous Historie of Troylus and Cresseid.* Excellently expressing the beginning of their Loves, with the conceited wooing of Pandarus, Prince of Lucia. Written by William Shakespeare. Imprinted by G. Eld, for R. Bonian and H. Whalley, 1609."

[This quarto contains a very remarkable preface, see p. 98.]

Q₂ [Same title as Q₁ but the word *famous* is omitted, while it is added that it is printed "as it was acted by the King's Majesties Servants at the Globe."] No other edition appeared till the folio of 1623 ; the position, pagination, and title of the play in this volume deserve notice (see p. 99.)

(26) CORIOLANUS.—First entered and printed in 1623.

(27) TITUS ANDRONICUS.—The following entry is dated 6 Feb. 1593 :—

"John Danter] A booke entitled a noble *Roman Historye of Tytus Andronicus.* Entered also unto him, by warrant from Mr. Woodcock, the ballad thereof."

In the following year (1594) according to Langbaine (1691) a quarto was issued, but no copy is extant.

In 1600, Q₁ appeared, entitled " *The Most Lamentable Romaine Tragedy of Titus Andronicus.* As it hath been sundry times playde by the Right Honourable the Earl of Pembrooke, the Earle of Darbie, the Earl of Sussex, and the Lord Chamberlaine their Servants. At London, printed by J. R[oberts] for Edward White, 1600."

On April 19th, 1602, we have the following entries [quoted in full, for a reason stated in note on page 2] :

" Tho. Pavier] by Assignt. from Tho. Millington *salvo*

jure cujuscumq. The 1st and 2d pts. of *Henry the VI.:* II. books."

"Tho. Pavier] *Titus and Andronicus*, entered by warrant under Mr. Seton's hand."

1611. In this year appeared "*The Most Lamentable Tragedie of Titus Andronicus*. As yt hath been sundry times plaide by the King's Majesties Servants. Printed for Edward White."

[Notice that Pavier's entry runs between White's two editions.]

In the folio edition, this play was printed according to White's quartos, which, by the by, had both been brought out *anonymously*.

1624, Dec. 14th, *for the second time* Mr. Pavier entered *Titus Andronicus*.

In 1626 Pavier transferred his "right in Shakespeare's plays" to Brewster and Birde ; and in 1630 Birde assigned the plays thus acquired and others to Richard Cotes. *Tytus and Andronicus* was included in these transfers.

(28) ROMEO AND JULIET.—Whether the following entry refers to this play is doubtful, Aug. 5th, 1596: "Edw. White] a new ballad of *Romeo and Juliett*."

Q$_1$ "An excellent conceited Trajedie of *Romeo and Juliet*, as it hath been often (with great applause) plaid publiquely, by the Right Honourable the Lord of Hunsdon his Servants. Printed by John Danter, 1597."

Q$_2$ "The most Excellent and lamentable Tragedie of *Romeo and Juliet*. Newly corrected, augmented, and amended. As it hath been sundry times publiquely acted, by the Right Honourable the Lord Chamberlaine his Servants. Printed by Thomas Creede, for Cuthbert Busbie, 1599."

In 1607, Busby transferred his rights to Ling, who in the same year assigned them to Smythick, who brought out two quartos ; Q$_3$ (anonymously, and without printer's name) and Q$_4$ (by William Shakespeare, also without printer's name.)

Smythick was one of the publishers of the First Folio ; it may be added that he retained his copyrights after that publication.

(29) TIMON OF ATHENS.
(30) JULIUS CÆSAR.
(31) MACBETH.
} First entered and printed in 1623.

(32) HAMLET.—The Stationers' Register for 26 July, 1602, has :—

"James Roberts] A booke, *The Revenge of Hamlett, Prince of Denmarke,* as yt was latelie acted by the Lord Chamberlayn his servantes."

[In 1603, Q₁ came out "as divers times acted by His Highness Servants in the citie of London : as also in the two universities of Cambridge and Oxford and elsewhere. By Wm. Shakespeare, 1603. N. L[ing] and J. Trundell.]

In 1604, Q₂ appeared : " *The Tragicall Historie of Hamlet, Prince of Denmarke.* By William Shakespeare. Newly imprinted and enlarged to almost as much againe as it was, according to the true and perfect coppie. Printed by J. R[oberts] for N. Landure [N. Ling and J. Trundell] 1604."

Q₃ [the same], 1605, printed by J. R[oberts] for N. L[ing] ; it is not known how Ling became possessed of this copyright (we know how he obtained his others), but on Nov. 19th, 1607, he transferred them all to Smythick, who brought out a quarto in the same year [says Malone] called " *The Tragedy of Hamlet Prince of Denmarke.* Newly imprinted and enlarged, according to the true and perfect copy lastly printed. Printed by W. T. for John Smithwicke." This is anonymous ; but Smithwicke brought out another edition in 1609 with Shakespeare's name.

Smithwicke was one of the publishers of the First Folio.

(33) LEAR.—The following elaborate entry is dated 26 November, 1607 :

" Na. Butter and Jo. Busby] Entered for their Copie under t'hands of Sir Geo. Burke, Kt. and the Wardens, a booke called, Mr. Willm. Shakespeare his *Historye of Kinge Lear*, as yt was played before the King's Majestic at Whitehall, upon St. Stephen's night at Christmas last, by his Majestie's Servants playing usually at the Globe on the Bankside."

In the next year (1608) Butter brought out a quarto with a corresponding title, or rather one or two editions with slight variations.

[The entries and issue of the old *King Leir* are referred to in body of work, p. 120.]

[Prof. Delius has a paper (*N. S. S. Trans.*, 1875–6) on the comparison of F_1 and the quartos.]

(34) OTHELLO.—1621, Oct. 6th, entry as follows :—

"Tho. Walkely] entered for his, to wit, under the handes of Sir George Buck and the wardens : *The Tragedy of Othello, the Moor of Venice.*"

The next year appeared a quarto :—

"*The Tragedy of Othello, the Moor of Venice.* As it hath beene diverse times acted at the Globe and at the Black-Friars, by his Majesties Servants. Written by William Shakespeare. Printed by N. O[kes] for Thomas Walkley, 1622."

This was not used in the First Folio which appeared next year, 1623 ; but it was reprinted in 1629, being printed by A. M., and published by R. Hawkins.

(35) ANTONY AND CLEOPATRA.—The Stationers' Register for 20th May, 1608, reads :—

"Edw. Blunt] Entered under t'hands of Sir Geo. Bucke, Kt., and Mr. Warden Seton, a book called : the booke of *Pericles, Prynce of Tyre.*"

"A book by the like authority called *Anthony and Cleopatra.*"

No edition, however, was published ; so, in 1623, Blunt, now one of the publishers of the folio, *re-entered* it, " as not formerly entered to other men."

(36) CYMBELINE.—Not entered nor printed till 1623.

O

(37) PERICLES.—Entered, as above (*Antony and Cleopatra*) by Blunt in 1608.

Blunt's conduct with regard to the two books he then entered is inexplicable.

The next year appeared Q_1, with the following title-page :—

" The late, and much-admired play, called *Pericles, Prince of Tyre*. With the true relation of the whole Historie, Adventures, and Fortunes of the said Prince. As also, the no less strange and worthy Accidents, in the Birth and Life of his Daughter Marina. As it hath been divers and sundry times acted by his Majesties Servants at the Globe on the Banck-side. By William Shakespeare. Imprinted for Henry Gosson, 1609."

[How Gosson got the copyright does not appear.] Several quartos followed, Gosson bringing out another the same year ; Q_3 appeared in 1611, printed by S. S[tafford]. The copyright had passed in 1619 [but *how* or *when* we know not] into the hands of Pavier, who in that year brought out a quarto (Q_4) entitled :—

" The late, and much admired Play, called *Pericles, Prince of Tyre*. With the true Relation of the whole History, Adventures, and Fortunes, of the saide Prince. Written by W. Shakespeare. Printed for T. P[avier], 1619." It was not included in F_1 (1623). Pavier transferred *Pericles* and other (spurious) Shakespeare plays to Brewster and Birde in 1626 ; Birde brought out Q_5 (printed by J. N[orton]) in 1630, and the same year assigned his rights to Ric. Cotes. It is a strange fact, that although the Cotes firm were concerned in the bringing out of F_2 (1632), *Pericles* was not included in that folio ; and yet, three years later (1635), T. Cotes brought out a sixth quarto. When the Third Folio appeared in 1664, it included *Pericles*.

APPENDIX VI.

THE ACTORS IN SHAKESPEARE'S PLAYS.

THE following notes are compiled from Malone, Collier, Halliwell, and Fleay; in several cases they either confirm results already known, or suggest hints as to the dates of Shakespeare's plays :—

ARMIN, ROBERT.—Acted in *Much Ado About Nothing;* is mentioned in the 1603 list; died 1611.

BENFIELD, ROBERT.—Acted in *The Tempest;* he probably left the Revels' Children for the King's Company about the time of Shakespeare's death.

BRYAN, GEORGE.—Acted in *Henry VI.,* Parts 1 and 2; died in 1598.

BURBAGE, RICHARD.—This great impersonator of Richard, Hamlet, and other of Shakespeare's most marvellous characters, died in 1619.

CONDELL, HENRY.—Acted in *The Tempest;* one of the editors of the First Folio, 1623.

COOKE, ALEXANDER.— Acted in *Midsummer Night's Dream;* he probably acted as Puck, or as one of the female characters, for, though he was playing with the King's Company in 1603 (*Sejanus*), he was certainly acting with the Revels' Children in 1609 (*The Silent Woman*); he died in 1614.

COWLEY, RICHARD.—Acted in *Much Ado About Nothing,* taking the character of Verges. It has been fantastically conjectured that he also sustained the part of the clown (Lavache, v. 2, 1) in *All's Well That Ends Well.*

CROSSE, SAMUEL.—Acted in *The Comedy of Errors,* though his name is not included in the list of principal actors prefixed to the First Folio ; he is supposed to have died in the year 1600.

ECCLESTONE, WILLIAM.—Acted in *All's Well That Ends Well;* like Cooke, he played for the Revels' Company after he had joined the King's.

FIELD, NATHAN.—Acted in *Othello;* this celebrated young actor probably joined the King's Company about the time of Shakespeare's death.

GABRIEL, ——.—Acted in 3 *Henry VI.*, where the name is left (in i. 2, 46) in the First Folio, instead of "a messenger." If this be Gabriel Spencer, we know that he was killed in a duel by Ben Jonson, in 1598. The name does not occur in the First Folio list.

GILBURNE, SAMUEL.—Acted in *All's Well That Ends Well*, as we are informed by Mr. Halliwell-Phillipps ; he died in 1597.

GOODALL, T.—Acted in 1 *Henry VI.;* but the date of his death is not known.

GOUGHE, ROBERT.—Acted in *All's Well That Ends Well;* he belonged to what was afterwards called the Queen's Company in Elizabeth's time, though he did not die till just towards the close of the reign of her successor.

HARVEY, ——.—Acted in 1 *Henry IV.*, taking the part of Bardolph ; nothing further is known of him.

HEMINGE, JOHN.—Acted in 1 *Henry IV.;* this actor (also called Hemmings, &c.) was one of the editors of the First Folio. ·

HUMFREY, ——.—Acted in 3 *Henry VI.*, where he appeared as "a keeper"; according to Mr. Fleay, he died in 1592.

Some have supposed that an actor, named Humphrey Jeffes, is meant ; he was, however, a member of the Admiral's, or Prince's, Company.

KEMP, WILLIAM.—Acted in *Much Ado About Nothing*, as Dogberry ; in *Romeo and Juliet*, as Peter ; and perhaps in 2 *Henry IV.*, as Justice Shallow. In June, 1592, we learn from Henslowe's Diary, he was with Alleyn, acting at "the Rose" on the Bankside, and perhaps at "the theatre" in Shoreditch (cf. *A Knacke to Knowe a Knave*, published in 1594); in 1594, he was acting with Lord Strange's men, that is to say, with the Company afterwards called the Chamberlain's, or King's; in 1598, he was again (or still) with the Chamberlain's Company, taking part in *Every Man in His Humour;* soon after this, he appeared in *Much Ado About Nothing* and in *Romeo and Juliet;* he did not act in *Every Man Out of His Humour* in 1599, and it has been conjectured that about this time he left the Chamberlain's Company; perhaps when Alleyn and Henslowe built "the Fortune" in Golden Lane, Cripplegate, in the year 1600, they may have induced Kemp to leave "the Globe" and "the Blackfriars" for their own theatre; perhaps he was engaged upon his celebrated *Dance to Norwich;* perhaps (though, if this ever took place, it was probably somewhat later), he was performing a similar feat upon the Continent. *Hamlet* was produced at this period with its remarks upon the acting of clowns; if these refer, as is extremely probable, to Kemp, we have therein as well a chronological hint as to one of the most interesting of Shakespearian facts. Kemp, we learn from Henslowe's Diary, was with the Earl of Nottingham's Company during at least parts (viz., March, August, and September) of the year 1602. [According to Mr. Collier (*Memoirs of Actors*), a complaint was made, in May, 1605, against "Kempe, Armyn, &c., plaiers at the Blacke Fryers."] This celebrated comedian died in the year 1608.

The above facts have been chiefly gathered from Mr. Collier's *Memoirs of Actors*, certain statements being altered owing to recent investigations, and some facts not found in that work being added.

LOWIN, JOHN.—Acted in *Merry Wives of Windsor;* it has also been supposed that he took part in *All's Well That Ends Well*, but this idea is founded upon the improbable conjecture that the name of the clown in that play (Lavache,

v. 2, 1) has some connection with this actor ; he survived Shakespeare many years.

OSTLER, WILLIAM.—Acted in *King John;* according to Collier (*Memoirs of Actors*, p. 210), he left the Chapel Children in 1604 to join the Chamberlain's Men. The date of his death is not known.

PALLANT, RICHARD (or ROBERT).—Acted in 1 *Henry VI.;* he afterwards left the Lord Chamberlain's Company, for we find him with the Queen's Company in 1609.

PHILLIPS, AUGUSTINE.— Acted in *The Two Gentlemen of Verona;* he died in 1605, and it is interesting to note that he remembered Shakespeare in his will.

POPE, THOMAS.—Acted in *Love's Labour's Lost;* died in 1603.

RICE, JOHN.—Acted in *The Tempest;* he does not appear to have joined the Company till quite late in Shakespeare's life.

ROBINSON, RICHARD.—Acted in *Cymbeline;* the remark made about Rice refers to Robinson too, for we first hear of him as acting in the play of *Catiline;* which was produced in 1611.

ROSSIL, ——.—Acted in 1 *Henry IV.*, taking the part of Peto ; nothing further is known of him.

SHAKESPEARE, WILLIAM.—Kurz (*Jahrbuch*, 1871) conjectures, from the often-quoted expression in Greene's *Groatsworth of Wit* (1592), that Shakespeare played, as the Duke of York, in the Second and Third Parts of *Henry VI.* Chettle, *Kind Hart's Dreme*, 1595, says : "Myselfe have seene his demeanour no less civill than he exclent in the qualitie he professes." He acted in *Every Man in His Humour* in 1598 ; his name occurs in the warrant issued on May 17; 1603, by James I. to "our servants, Laurence Fletcher, William Shakespeare, Richard Burbage, &c., to use and exercise the arte and faculty of playing comedies, &c." We know, too, that in the same year (1603) he acted in *Sejanus*. In *The Scourge of Folly*, published in 1607 by

John Davies of Hereford, "our English Terence, Mr. Will. Shakespeare," is addressed as follows :—

" Some say—good Will—which I in sport do sing,
    Had'st thou not *plaied some kingly parts* in sport,
Thou had'st bin a companion for a king,
    And beene a king among the meaner sort."

A tradition, founded upon a statement by his brother, attributes to him the part of Adam in *As You Like It;* and it also obtains, that he appeared as the Ghost in *Hamlet.* There is no mention of him as an actor after 1603.

SHANCKE, JOHN.—Acted in *The Twelfth Night;* this actor is included in the list given in the First Folio ; he appears, however, in the year 1603 at any rate, to have belonged to the Admiral's Company. He survived till 1650.

SINKLO, ——.—Acted in 3 *Henry VI.*, in 2 *Henry IV.*, and in *The Taming of the Shrew;* these interesting points peep out through the careless printing of the First Folio ; but Sinklo's name is not in the list prefixed to that edition, nor do we know anything more of him beyond the fact that he played in *The Seven Deadly Sins*, and that he appears in *The Malcontent*, 1604.

SLY, WILLIAM.—Acted in *Hamlet;* this is suggested from the fact that he appears in *The Malcontent*, 1604, quoting a line from Osrick in *Hamlet.* He died (according to Collier) in 1608 (according to Fleay in 1612).

TAWYER, ——.—Acted in *Midsummer Night's Dream;* this we learn from a stage-direction in the First Folio (Act v. Sc. 1), "Tawyer with a trumpet ;" we do not know anything more of him.

TAYLOR, JOSEPH.—Acted in *Hamlet,* and in *Othello* as Iago ; he was with the Prince Charles's Company in 1610, and does not appear to have joined the King's till about the death of Shakespeare ; and we cannot think that he would have taken the part of Hamlet during the life of Burbage.

TOOLEY, NICHOLAS.—Acted in *The Taming of the Shrew;* we do not know much of this actor, who died in 1623.

UNDERWOOD, JOHN.—Acted in *Othello;* he had belonged to the Chapel Children; it is not known exactly when he joined the King's Company, but we find him playing in *The Alchemist* in 1610. He died in 1624.

WILSON, JOHN.—We learn from the First Folio that "Jack Wilson" sang as Balthasar in *Much Ado About Nothing* (Act ii. Sc. 3); this statement is not in the quarto, 1600. [A person named Wilson belonged to the Admiral's Company in the year 1600.] John Wilson, who was a musician of some eminence (see Dr. Rimbault's *Essay*), was born in 1585, and died in 1624.

20'

INDEX.

INDEX.

Hall, 8, 45
Hallam, Mr., 53, 63, 66, 81, 139
Hallamas Day, 116
Halliwell-Phillips, Mr., *passim*
Halpin, Mr., 23, 50, 51
Hamlet, 3, 6, 39, 62, 66, 85, 89, 112, 121, 159
Hamnet Shakespeare, 40, 157
Hampton Court, 16
• Hans Towns, 17
Hare, Augustus, 32, 81, 105 118, 123
Harefield, 115
Harness, Mr., 173
Harness Essay, 1874, 10
. *Harness Essay*, 1877, Introd.
Harrington, Sir J., 27, 34, 64, 76
Harry Hotspur, 54, 55, 56, 111
Harsnet, Dr., 95, 118
Harvey, Gabriel, 26, 50, 73, 196
Harvey, historian, 119
Harvey, astrologer, 120
Haughton, 35
Have with you to Saffron Walden, 29
Hawkins, 13, 23
Hay, 150
Hazlitt, 39, 77
Hebler, 66
Hector, 100, 101
Helen, 139, 144
Hell, News from, 19
Heminge, John, 7, 154, 196
Henriade, 80
Henry III. of France, 17
Henry IV. of France, 17, 18, 41, 49, 65, 156
Henry IV. Part I, 7, 44, 45, 54, 110
Henry IV. Part 2, 36, 57, 83, 91
Henry V., 3, 7, 9, 72, 74, 82, 89, 91, 111, 125, 159
Henry V., old play, 54, 57, 84
Henry VI., Part 1, 3, 4, 8, 29, 33, 45, 101, 159
Henry VI., Part 2, 3, 10, 101, 111

Henry VI., Part 3, 10, 36, 88, 109, 111, 155
Henry VIII., 43, 87, 111, 152, 166
Henslowe, 2, 3, 4, 5, 9, 61, 67, 68, 84, 87, 167
Herbert, Sir Henry, 154
Hercules, 72
Hero and Leander, 13, 76, 162
Hertzberg, Prof., 15, 19, 37, 110, 152, 165, 168
Heywood, 39, 45, 122, 161, 162
Hickson, Mr., 33, 169
Hierarchie of Blessed Angels, 161
Hieronimo, 1
Hippolyta, 52, 53
Hippolyta, Julius and, 12
Historical MSS., 25
Historie of Gargantua, 80
Histrio-Mastix, 99, 104
Hoby, 111
Holinshed, 8, 40, 45, 54, 84, 119, 150
Holland, Philemon, 115, 162
Holofernes, 26, 28
Holt, 163
Homer, Chapman's, 105
Honour, Book on, 23, 79
Horn, 66
Howard, Lady Frances, 163
Howard, Lord, 90
Howes, 166
Hubert, 42
Humfrey, 196
Hunsdon, Lord (his company), 20
Hunter, Mr., 94, 95, 110, 127, 158, 163
Hyren, the Fair Greek, 60

Iago, 32, 118
Illustrations, Douce's, 73
Illustrations, Hunter's, 95
Il Pecorone, 63
Imogen, 150, 153
Ina, King of Wessex, 119
Inductions, 1, 4, 68, 155

P

THE END.

LONDON : R. CLAY, SONS, AND TAYLOR, BREAD STREET HILL, E. C.

www.ingramcontent.com/pod-product-compliance
Lightning Source LLC
Chambersburg PA
CBHW030315270326
41926CB00010B/1370